PENGUIN BOOKS

ALASTAIR COOK

THE AUTOBIOGRAPHY

ABOUT THE AUTHORS

Alastair Nathan Cook was born in Gloucester in December 1984. He is considered to be England's greatest cricket player of our time, playing more Tests, scoring more runs – over 10,000 – and scoring more centuries than any other England cricketer in history. He now plays for Essex County Cricket Club and lives with his wife and three children.

Michael Calvin, collaborator on Alastair Cook's autobiography, was named Sports Writer of the Year for his despatches as a crew member in a round-the-world yacht race and has twice been named Sports Reporter of the Year.

ALASTAIR COOK

THE AUTOBIOGRAPHY

with Michael Calvin

PENGUIN BOOKS

PENGUIN BOOKS

UK | USA | Canada | Ireland | Australia
India | New Zealand | South Africa

Penguin Books is part of the Penguin Random House group of companies
whose addresses can be found at global.penguinrandomhouse.com

First published by Michael Joseph 2019
Published in Penguin Books 2020
001

See page 357 for picture credits

Set in 10.93/13.44pt Garamond MT Std
Typeset by Jouve (UK), Milton Keynes
Printed and bound in Great Britain by Clays Ltd, Elcograf S.p.A.

A CIP catalogue record for this book is available from the British Library

ISBN: 978–0–241–40144–6

www.greenpenguin.co.uk

For Elsie, Isobel and Jack

Contents

1. Digging to the Well

'I'm sorry, lads. I can't believe I just got out like that.'

Joe Root, waiting on the glass-fronted balcony of the dressing room at the Oval, smiled, slapped me lightly on the back and told me to 'shut up'. He probably had a point, since the old ground hummed with excitement and commentators were suggesting I was some sort of national treasure, but batting is a serious business.

Joe followed me through a second doorway into an inner changing area, where I took twelve paces to my double peg close to the far right-hand corner. Life went on; the rhythm of professional sport is set by personal priorities, and Jos Buttler, surprised by the sudden fall of wickets, bustled in to complete his preparatory rituals.

After a brief flurry of congratulation, I was left to myself. I sat there for three or four minutes with my pads still on, savouring the silence and sifting through my senses. I looked around, through the organized chaos of discarded kit, lotions and potions. I was in a special, sacred place, where harsh truths are occasionally shared, yet balanced by the intimacy of individuals involved in something bigger than themselves.

The dressing room is a sanctuary, safe from the second guessing of social media and the exaggerated attention of the outside world. It is unique, precious. Each team is different, a collection of distinctive personalities, but this is the only place in which it can truly be itself. I loved that feeling of solidarity, freedom and friendship; that's why, as captain, I encouraged players to linger over a beer at the end of play.

Disappointment, even one as strictly relative as being dismissed carelessly for 147 in my final Test innings, has certain formalities. I've never been a bat-thrower, a blame-shifter or excuse-seeker. I prefer quick and quiet rationalization; my instinctive apology might have been a bit cloth-eared, but losing two wickets, especially those of well-set batsmen, to successive deliveries is a cardinal sin.

In time, it will be a killer pub-quiz question: name the Indian Test debutant who dismissed two England captains in two balls. Hanuma Vihari is an occasional right-handed off-spinner, a dispenser of what old pros refer to as 'filth'. There's no disrespect implied, intended or taken in that, by the way. It is merely our form of industrial language.

Rooty had holed out to midwicket for 125. In a world of fine margins, my mind wasn't locked in to the next ball. It was dragged down and I got a little greedy. Instead of making the slightly easier shot, in front of square, I acted on the momentary mental image of a thin gap between two fielders behind the wicket.

I wasn't consciously thinking of the boundary that would have taken me past 150, but I lacked that critical edge of concentration. I smiled and sagged forward, leaning on my bat momentarily, because I couldn't believe I had edged it to the wicketkeeper. All that was left was that final walk to the pavilion, bat aloft and brain whirring.

I noticed the dressing-room TV was replaying those scenes as I sat there, decompressing. The screen showed Alice, my wife, cradling our daughter Elsie and telling her 'there's Daddy'. I didn't cry, despite the temptation; the closest I came to doing so was during that amazing extended ovation for my second-innings century. There wasn't an ounce of me that wanted to carry on. I was done.

The only time in my career I wept uncontrollably was in the dressing room at the MCG during the Boxing Day Ashes Test in 2017. I was 104 not out at the close of play on the second day, on my way to carrying my bat for 244, and couldn't stop myself. I was as puzzled as anyone; on reflection, it was a moment of release after sustained private questioning of my mood and motives.

Retirement is not a snap decision, because representing your country is the greatest of an athlete's privileges. It rattles around the brain for months, sometimes years, and ambushes you when you least expect it to. For me the process began at Edgbaston in August 2017, during the first Test against the West Indies, when Rooty joined me at the crease. We were 39–2 and facing an all too familiar obligation to build a score.

I might have looked calm and dispassionate to the casual spectator, but I felt an enormous weight of expectation, an insidious surge of pressure. That inner voice, a cold, caustic commentator on my faults and weaknesses, piled in on cue: 'Here we go again,' it said. 'Why are you putting yourself through this mental torture? You've got nothing else to prove.'

I went on to score 243. Joe made 136 and we won by an innings inside three days. But a pebble had been dislodged; an internal conversation with an inevitable conclusion was underway. This wasn't about anything as selfish as personal achievement; it was a private progression of truth and reconciliation. I had to be true to myself, and my teammates.

A player dealing with personal turmoil needs a coach who

empathizes with his dilemma. Mark Ramprakash, England's batting coach, was the first person I turned to, as we walked back from a net session before our second warm-up match of that winter's Ashes tour, a day–nighter against a Cricket Australia XI at the Adelaide Oval.

Ramps was, by common consent, the most technically accomplished batsman of his generation. He was a driven character, an accumulator of 114 centuries, who retired with a first-class average of 53.14 a couple of months before his forty-third birthday. He fought against the dying of the light but understood where I was coming from.

'I don't know why I'm doing this any more,' I confessed. 'How many times do I have to dig to the well before there is nothing left?' That's a horrible phrase, a reflection of declining hope and increasing desperation. I was only thirty-two, theoretically years away from unarrestable decline, yet mental decay had set in.

Physically, I was fine, the fittest I had ever been. The ECB had looked after me exceptionally well, streamlining my schedule so that I had the occasional respite of a couple of months at home. A governing body of any sport has a corporate dimension, but behind the scenes it has good people on whom we rely as players.

Our families are hugely grateful to Medha Laud, whose liaison work has taken cricket out of the Dark Ages, the pre-Duncan Fletcher era in which tours were planned without thought for a player's personal life. This inevitably added to the strain on relationships, and caused quiet resentment. Medha is thoughtful, efficient and empathetic; her MBE for services to cricket was widely celebrated.

Another long-term member of the support team, Phil

Neale, makes sure everything runs smoothly. He has been the England team's operations manager since 1999, and utilizes a huge range of experience, as the last of the old-time footballer-cricketers. He played 358 matches for Lincoln City and 354 first-class games for Worcestershire, where he was captain for ten years before moving into coaching. He is as likely to be found helping slip practice as organizing our bags.

The old grind of airport–hotel–ground–hotel–airport had been minimized by modern performance planning, but eventually in a sport like ours, resilience wears thin. I was going through the motions of stretching, lying on the outfield in Christchurch midway through the second Test during the subsequent series in New Zealand in March 2018 when I unburdened myself to Chris Silverwood, England's bowling coach. We were at ease in each other's company, having just shared Essex's title win in the County Championship.

I had scored twenty-three runs in my four Test innings in a losing series and was thinking beyond a match we were destined to draw. 'I'm done with it,' I told him. He didn't seem desperately surprised, but urged caution: 'Look, whatever you do don't say anything. Obviously, you've had a tough tour and a tough winter. Just get through the next two days, then go home and see how you feel.'

I had begun to dread net sessions. I had always found them hard work throughout my England career and disliked their imperfections. Everyone oversteps the mark, bowling from seventeen or eighteen yards, no matter how stringent the bowling coach. They'd argue it was irrelevant, since they didn't bowl no-balls when it mattered, but it was a constant source of irritation.

There is a time for experimentation in the nets, but I hated the embarrassment of getting out. I never wanted to give my wicket away, whatever the circumstances. When I allowed myself to be more proactive, I would try new things away from prying eyes, in a private session with our batting coach, Graham Gooch. Seeing people showboat, trying to sweep flashily or hit every ball over the top, used to get to me.

Nets can be subtly confrontational. I can't lie – I used to love it when I got Jimmy Anderson or Stuart Broad. I knew Jimmy would be bowling at 75 per cent, which is bloody hard work but manageable, and Broady wouldn't be trying to prove himself too often. Emerging bowlers such as Chris Woakes or Mark Wood would seek to make a personal statement in every session.

As captain, I understood and applauded that, but as a batsman, seeking rhythm in England in early summer, where nets are not as flat as they are on the subcontinent, the challenge became claustrophobic. I'd maintain my performance level, operating at about 98 per cent of my capacity over three twenty-minute sessions, often against lads I'd never seen before, but it became wearing.

I consulted with Mark Bawden, England's team psychologist, about how I could deal better with the dilemma. We spoke about having a very clear focus, a specific task to work through before a particular match, but eventually the dials just went round and round without registering. I made a conscious effort to sustain my intensity, but it became more of a chore.

Once instinct tells you the end is near, lethargy seeps into the system like slurry in a watercourse. Most people can't detect the difference, but long-term teammates have a sixth sense for mood swings. I'd played with Broady for eleven years; one throwaway line after a net session early in that final series against India told me he knew, deep down, what I was fighting.

'Jeez, you've finished already?' he said with arched eyebrows. I'd just done an hour's batting and catching, but he'd seen something. I might not have hit as many balls as usual; I could have been unconsciously hasty in heading back to the pavilion. Whatever it was, he hit the mark, because, as he told me when I eventually confirmed my retirement, 'We're pretty similar, aren't we?'

Game recognizes game at the highest levels of international sport. Jimmy had just bowled at 75 per cent for an hour. He never missed a length, and it looked as if it had taken nothing out of him. I knew that his ankle, shoulder and elbow hurt, but it looked so easy. Broady, standing beside me, murmured, 'If I did that, I'd be all over the place.'

He had to charge in, in every net session, to reach the standards he expected of himself. He knew that if he tried to be self-contained, in Jimmy's fashion, he would bowl poorly, and be difficult to deal with while he worked through the frustration. I can say that as a friend, because we have so much in common. We've made the most of any ability we've been given, but it has taken a lot of effort to do so.

I'd lost that edge. I played out certain scenarios in my mind – obviously finishing with a home Ashes series in 2019 would have been ideal – but getting out for 13 and 0, to a couple of good deliveries, in the first Test against India at Edgbaston that summer of 2018 proved to be a persuasive reality check. My mind was finally made up during the third Test at Trent Bridge.

This wasn't submission to the self-doubt that inevitably creeps in during a run of low scores; it was the liberation of sudden clarity that there was only one solution to the problem. I arrived back at the team hotel on the third evening of the match, when I was 9 not out overnight, fully intending to tell Alice I was in my last series. She was heavily pregnant with our son Jack, and to wind down, with the girls asleep next door, we watched the *Inbetweeners* movie in bed.

I fall asleep to the TV series on tour all the time. It has a comforting familiarity; I know all the words, and I'm usually out like a light before the introductory music ends. I've only watched the movie occasionally; that night we laughed out loud at the adolescent antics. I knew I had to tell her, but it seemed wrong to darken the mood.

Instead, I ignored the ICC anti-corruption code (belated apologies, chaps) and didn't hand my phone in when I reported to the ground the next morning. I texted Alice: 'Are you OK? I've got to tell you this. The end of this series is going to be my last game for England.' I saw the two blue ticks on WhatsApp, which signalled that she had read it, and felt a sudden nervousness as the word 'typing' appeared on screen.

I was thinking, 'Please don't fight it,' and praying for her acceptance. She had been a constant source of strength when I'd struggled with the complexities of captaincy, and the isolation of life on a difficult tour. We'd had a couple of long telephone conversations from Australia that winter, and she was attuned to my tentative cries for help. It seemed to take for ever for her to reply, but when she did so, she needed only two words.

'I know . . .'

Relief accompanied the realization that my inner struggle must have been blatantly obvious. Alice is, after all, the person who knows me better than anyone. I found a quiet anteroom in the changing area and made a call: 'I just can't keep going,' I told her. 'I've lost what makes me different from everyone else and I want to go out with my head held high.'

Weight lifted, I ran rapidly through my priorities. I told Jimmy first, as we sat on the balcony watching the day's play. I had my sunglasses on as usual, pulled my cap down low and indulged my habit of chewing the collar of my sweatshirt. 'I'm really sorry I'm doing this to you now,' I said, behind a casually cupped hand, 'but I'm packing it in.' His face was a picture. 'I can't believe it,' he said. 'Are you sure? I'm sad – sad but shocked.'

Rooty was next on the list. I arranged to play nine holes with him on the golf course adjoining the Ageas Bowl in Southampton, before training began in earnest on the following Tuesday. I suspected, correctly, he had sussed out what was going on, but wanted to tell him face to face. I told Broady on the outfield the next morning; the secret was safe with all three.

Was there any need for the cloak-and-dagger stuff? Probably not, though I didn't want to be a distraction. Trevor Bayliss, the England coach, told me that, for the first time, the selectors were discussing my position. 'That's absolutely understandable,' I acknowledged. 'I haven't delivered a good stat this summer and have had a couple of big scores with not much in between for twelve months, but you don't have to worry. The next game will be my last, if I'm picked.'

He looked at me inscrutably: 'Oh, right. Thought that might happen . . .'

Trevor and Rooty led a happy dressing-room debrief immediately after we clinched the series by winning that Test, before handing over to me. I was a few beers in at that time, to quell the nerves, because I didn't know how I was going to react to telling the rest of the lads. I didn't go full Oscar acceptance speech, but my voice caught a couple of times.

The scene encapsulated what I will miss in the years to come. The deep satisfaction of the group, sharing the exclusivity of the moment. Job done, juices flowing, tension eased. 'This might be a sad day for some people or a happy day for others,' I announced, 'but I just want to let you know that my next Test, if picked, will be my last. I've run out of steam and this has been a great way to finish.'

Sportsmen take the piss at every opportunity, of course, so I didn't get away scot free. I had wanted to come across as thoughtful, despite the obvious intensity of emotion I felt, so ended with a light-hearted apology for dampening the mood. Moeen Ali, who has a dry sense of humour and a quick wit, shot back: 'Well, you just have, haven't you?' Not his best line, perhaps, but enough to crack everyone up.

Somehow, I managed to condense twelve years of international cricket, and a lifetime of support, into a 395-word retirement statement, released from Lord's at noon the following day. I tried to capture my pride, my sense of purpose and the pragmatism of the player who knows it is time to go. I expressed my gratitude to my mentor, Goochy, and to the Barmy Army, but above all to my family. They are the constant in a cricketer's life, the foundation on which so much can be built.

The response was humbling, uniformly warm and

respectful. I don't care what anyone says, when you are reading nice things about yourself for two or three days straight it creates a weird sense of detachment; it's almost an out-of-body experience. It felt like I was reading my obituary – one of my friends even texted me, asking, 'Are you dead?'

I played golf with Jimmy at Woburn before we reported to the Oval for the final Test. He grabbed a photo of me sitting in an armchair in the clubhouse, reading a newspaper article with the headline: 'Cook the Modern Legend Calls It a Day'. Inevitably, the image was posted on his Instagram account with the comment: 'The thing I love most about Cookie is that he has absolutely no ego.'

Ed Smith, the England national selector, had called during the round to check I was still in the right frame of mind to play in the last Test. I hope he excuses the white lie I told at the time, to cover up the reality that I was struggling with the fear of letting people down. The build-up was surreal, since everything, from the last net to the valedictory press conference, had an element of finality.

People were kind, considerate, and unwittingly challenging. 'Just go out and enjoy it,' they told me. 'It doesn't matter how many runs you get.' Well, sorry, but it did. Cricket is one of the only sports where you are primarily defined by your statistics. Runs are your currency, and the thought of ending with a pair in my last Test made me more nervous than at any time in the previous 160.

I was driven back to the standards I set myself, the fear of failure that spurred me to perform constantly under pressure. That desperation to do well, dealing with anxiety created by the expectations of people you will probably never meet, takes its toll mentally. Did that process involve a degree of self-worth? I honestly don't know, but I needed to live up to the numbers.

I had to dig deep, work bloody hard for every single run I scored down the years. Ambition is double-edged. I remembered being in a lift at Edgbaston with Michael Vaughan early in my career, when he told me I could score 10,000 Test runs. That very quietly became a huge goal of mine. When I fulfilled it, a tiny light went out.

Looking back, that was because I realized it would never get easier, and I needed additional motivation. I spent the next six months or so searching for what, deep down, I knew would be an artificial target. I thought about seeking forty Test hundreds, and ended with thirty-three, but I never found what I was looking for, a goal that consumed me. The fact I can live comfortably with that tells me there wasn't too much substance to the quest.

Unusually, I slept well the night before the final Test began. I didn't need to use the trick I developed on the road with Graeme Swann, where alarms would be set for 2 a.m., so we could go straight back to sleep in the knowledge we had another four hours before the pressure ratcheted up again. Barking mad, against the logic of sports science, but effective, without preventing the anxiety dreams which assail many batsmen.

In the classic cricket dream I'm waiting to bat. I know I will be timed out if I can't get my kit on, and I'm thrashing around, trying to find my pads. I have two other recurring dreams; in the first I go for an easy three, but I'm run out by half a pitch because it is as if my legs are trapped in treacle. In the second I'm playing indoors while everyone else is playing outdoors; instead of getting a boundary when I find the gap, the ball rebounds off the wall to the bowler, who runs me out.

I've always been an early bird, so leaving the team hotel near Tower Bridge at 8 a.m. felt like a lie in. For the first time, a group of us, including Jimmy, Keaton Jennings and James Foster, the former England wicketkeeper who has been a long-term teammate at Essex, decided to travel by Tube; one stop on the District line, five more on the Northern line and we were there. A few commuters did a double take, and we took a photograph for posterity, but it was hassle free.

At 10.15 we began warming up, which can be incredibly dull. I have such respect for athletes who are enslaved by conditioning coaches, doing plyometrics day in, day out. There's no need for such regimentation in international cricket, because players know their own roles and listen to their bodies. We slip into individual routines once the toss is conducted, half an hour before play.

The highlight of the morning was a light-hearted fifteen-minute game of football on the outfield. I'm not that great, but at least I don't have Ben Stokes's delusions of grandeur; he thinks he's David de Gea when he'd struggle to get a game in goal for the Dog 'n' Duck. I know people worry about unnecessary injury, but it takes my mind off what's to come.

Some openers secretly relish losing the toss and fielding, since it postpones the pressure, but I was keen to get on with it. I have a set routine: change into whites, insert box, put on right thigh guard, and then inner thigh guard. The process ends with me strapping on my right pad, and then my left. I like the same sense of order at the crease, where I scar the ground by dragging my studs on the line of my guard after every delivery.

You are taught as an eleven-year-old to give yourself sufficient time to adjust to the light before you bat. I did so by rehearsing my stance, and playing the occasional imaginary shot on the glass-fronted balcony. It felt like I was an attraction in a human zoo; I couldn't help but notice the cameras and phones being trained in my direction from a scrum of spectators at the bottom of the Bedser Stand.

I didn't have a tear in my eye as I walked on to the outfield, in deference to the legend of Don Bradman's final Test, at the Oval, when a 0 took his average below 100. I was too busy concentrating on not tripping up, because spikes are tricky on those stairs. The noise surprised me, and grew in intensity as I strode, self-consciously, through the guard of honour.

I entered the game at seventeen, determined to carve my name on it, though playing for England was an Everest-like image, peeking through the clouds in the distance. Yet there I was, shaking the hand of Virat Kohli, Indian captain and national hero, and feeling real warmth and a rare sense of affinity from a capacity crowd. Nervous? Of course. The only antidote was an immersion in familiar virtues.

I'm not big on slogans, but over the years, I determined to be the best version of me that I could be. No gimmicks, no fashion statements, no borrowed habits. I took my usual guard, two, or middle and leg. Then a reminder of the basics: one of the tricks to opening the batting for England is to play the next ball as if the last one never happened.

Watch. The. Ball.

No one really enjoys an innings, especially in the early stages, because it is so fraught with danger. This was double jeopardy, because failure, on this first morning, wasn't purely personal. It would have disappointed so many people. The relief when I got off the mark to the seventh ball I faced, with a push for three, was immediate and intense.

Posterity will record that was the shot that took me to 1,000 Test runs at the Oval. My attention was seized by the flock of pigeons, pecking away at the outfield. They serve no useful purpose, other than to interfere with the grind of concentration and accumulation. A top footballer like Harry Kane can have a poor opening twenty minutes and still have time to excel. If I do the same, I'm back in the pavilion, more often than not.

Moeen Ali had told me, earlier in the week, that it was written that I would get a hundred. He was one innings out, yet I began to believe him when I was dropped in the gully soon after lunch, when I had made 37. Mystic Mo's certainty about my destiny grew with our partnership; his confidence made me smile when I brought my 50 up.

Athletes are taught to prioritize process over outcome, but once I passed 60 the prospect of a century became real. 'Shit, I might be able to do this,' I thought. Mistake. I dragged the ball on, an inside edge into the middle stump from a decent-length delivery that didn't bounce as much as I expected, and was dismissed for 71.

The gift horse had bolted. I was annoyed but made a conscious effort to register and respond to the applause, because it could have been the last walk back with an innings of substance behind me. The chances of successive half-centuries weren't great. Once we had dismissed India for 292, and I had ten minutes to prepare for my 291st, and final, Test innings, I tried to take it all in. Time passed surprisingly slowly. When I emerged on the balcony, I noticed everyone in the crowd had turned to face me.

Forty minutes' play remained before tea when I walked to the crease. I didn't want this to be the last day I batted for England, since a large group of family and friends were coming to watch me the following morning. I knew they'd be following my progress on TV, or on their phones. No pressure, Chef. I had a simple mental mantra: 'Don't make this the last ball.' It is amazing what you can train your brain to do.

Batting is so instinctive, and you have so little time to react, that movements become automatic. Thoughts might flash through your mind – 'Get forward', 'Don't play a cover shot', '*Do* play a cover shot', 'Don't pull this one, leave it' – but I tended to rely on trigger words or phrases to aid my concentration. On this endless afternoon, I followed principles I had discussed with Bawds years before.

Commit and watch the ball.

The aim was to be able to take my pads off in the dressing room, knowing that I had followed that instruction, whether I had scored 0 or 100. For a while, I needed only to look at the back of my bat for a reminder of my priority. It carried the name of a sponsor, Clydesdale Bank. 'C' and 'B'. Commit to the Ball.

In terms of temperament I wasn't that different from the young lad who flew halfway round the world to make his Test debut against India in Nagpur in 2006, but my technique had improved. I was a better driver of the ball, left it with greater accuracy, was more confident off my legs and more capable of hitting the short ball for four. I was able to get my weight back into the ball, and my hands were a lot closer together.

We all have our hallmarks. I make two taps of the bat as I prepare to face. The bat is raised to thigh height, and then raised again. Keep the head still, the knees flexible, shoulders slightly open. Move back and across the crease, to help play off the back foot. Then it's down to the other guy, with the ball in his hand. He's pretty good at what he does.

I played and missed at four deliveries from Mohammed Shami, moral defeats that didn't matter when he gave me the chance to straight drive for four. I held the follow-through, and walked forward, like a golfer reading the line of a putt into the hole. I made eye contact with the bowler, and we both smiled. The game within the game was underway.

I'd looked in all sorts of trouble, needed luck to survive, but that cameo proved the next delivery is all that matters. I suppose it also confirmed I could deal with the hullaballoo, isolate outside influences and focus on the ball coming towards me. I wasn't in the zone golfers talk about, where events occur in slow motion and the crowd is a multichromatic blur, but I was at ease with myself.

I was 46 not out overnight, grateful that Rooty had taken most of the strike in a nervy last fifteen minutes. He wanted two from the final ball of the day, but I strolled a single. There was no way I wanted to be first up the following morning, because I didn't want to get out to the first delivery of the day on this, of all occasions. That nigh Ian Elliott, my former partner at Maldon, passed on important news from Statto, the club's resident numbers man. I needed four more runs to secure an average of 45, and thirty to beat Kumar Sangakkara on the all-time lists.

I reached that second milestone with a crudded single. 'I didn't know that,' I mentioned to Rooty, when the screens announced the news. 'You're a fucking liar,' he laughed, reading my smile. I knew the century was on; when it arrived, at 12.43 on Monday, 10 September 2018, it was a mixture of high drama and low comedy.

I took an easy single to deep gully on 96, thought, 'That's one closer,' and then saw Jasprit Bumrah launch the return, harder than he'd ever thrown it. 'Run, run, run,' screamed Rooty. I followed the ball out of the corner of my eye as it sped towards Cheteshwar Pujara who, thankfully, isn't the quickest fielder on the deep point boundary.

I started laughing when I realized he was never going to get it. The ball ended in the groundsman's hut, a suitably surreal footnote to a moment that meant so much. It would have been nice to get there with a poetic flourish, or a favourite shot, but to be brutally honest I'll take it. Mo might just have been right. It was written.

The ovation was amazing, rolling around the place like thunder. It just kept on going. Rooty hugged me hard and didn't need to say a word. I raised my bat towards the boys behind the glass on the dressing-room balcony and saw movement that, on closer inspection of TV replays two days later, involved Jimmy pogoing up and down like a five-year-old.

Thank God I didn't cry. I came close, exhaled deeply and regularly, tried and failed to keep things in the present tense. I went back down the wicket, urged Joe to 'watch the ball', but the words had little immediate meaning. They couldn't reflect the purity of my happiness. I found myself looking at the crowd and thinking, 'Boy, they must be having a good time.'

I knew Mum would be somewhere, in tears. I thought of Alice's sacrifices, in putting her life on hold for my cricket, and hoped the girls would remember the moment. Jack, our son, was due to be born the following day, but hung around for a couple of weeks before making an appearance.

By that time I had learned that Gemma Broad, Stuart's sister, had sat for half an hour in a B&Q car park, listening to the radio in anticipation of me reaching a century she was determined not to miss. When I did so she leapt up and screamed; suddenly self-conscious, she looked at the adjoining car, where the driver was also in tears.

Sport has that effect on people. Strangers share your life without you knowing. It is an emotional, communal experience. I probably walked off too quickly when I was out that afternoon, since Jonny Bairstow had to scamper after me to offer his congratulations, but I felt I'd gone out on the right note.

2. Boy to Man

Suddenly, I was alone. My parents said their farewells, turned, and were gone. My companions, as I sat on my bed in the dormitory at the St Paul's Cathedral choir school, were a brown teddy bear and a soft rubber cube, which I would gnaw when I was nervous, and throw at the wall when I needed catching practice.

I was aged eight. I felt awkward, confused, horrible. When I started to cry someone asked me whether I was homesick. 'No, I'm not sick of home,' I replied, with childish logic. 'I want to go home.' I would never want my children to experience that feeling, but there is absolutely no doubt the experience made me the cricketer I became.

It was pretty brutal. Even on that first evening, when I longed for the certainties of life in the Essex village of Wickham Bishops, we were expected to buckle down to choir practice. There was no gentle transition to this other world, just immediate immersion in the disciplines of our new craft. We were expected to learn quickly about the power of concentration and performing under pressure.

Choir practice, with vocal techniques and sight-reading, began at 7.45 a.m., before a normal six-and-a-half-hour academic day started at 9 a.m. We would practise for forty-five minutes until 5 p.m., when we would participate in the hour-long Evensong service. Supper provided half an hour's respite and preceded ninety minutes of academic homework and music practice. Lights were out at 9 p.m.

Our playground was a walled concrete rectangle measuring no more than five metres by ten, though it seemed much bigger. I longed for Thursday afternoons, when cathedral services were replaced by football or cricket in Regent's Park. We resumed Evensong on Friday and had a long morning rehearsal on Saturday before a four-hour window to meet our parents. We sang in three services on Sunday, including Choral Matins and Sung Eucharist.

There are parallels here with professional cricket. The choir school, founded with the cathedral in 604 and instituted in its modern form in 1123, when eight boys in need of alms were taken in and educated, has the same reverence for history and tradition. You are expected to be a team player, to commit to a common creed of dedication and self-discipline. The world is often watching.

It is always interesting to search for the man by studying photographs of the boy. I'm on duty, conscious of the camera, during a promotional shot in the cathedral alongside Dame Kiri Te Kanawa. I'm second from the left in the front row, dressed in a black surplice with a red sash and white ruff. Two hands on the lit candle, just in case.

That's one representation of me. The other emerges in classroom shots, where my grey shirt is untucked and my tie has ridden above the collar. Let's just say my blazer has growing room. Another picture has me, eyes on the ball, executing what looks suspiciously like a slog sweep on the way to scoring 110 out of a total of 127 for the choir's cricket team.

When that was taken, I was a novice in a world of international tours, performances in front of royalty, Proms and recording sessions. I relished the freedom of holidays and developed enduring resilience, but as I grew older, began to question the sheltered nature of life. Playing representative cricket for London Schools was a release, though cathedral staff were none too happy when it led to an invitation to an England training camp over Easter.

Music was similar to cricket in that we were judged collectively, but vulnerable to individual error. St Paul's is a hard place to sing, because it has an eight-second echo in the dome, and if one of the thirty choristers makes a fractional misjudgement it can all fall apart. The choir master, and the professionals with whom we were surrounded, would not have been amused.

I wasn't fazed by the more important concerts, or the pomp and ceremony of certain services. I was the workhorse, the guy who rarely took solos, never got ill and sang consistently to an acceptable standard, all good preparation for professional sport, where coaches love the player they can rely on, rock solid without being exceptional.

Management specialists love to talk about success leaving clues, and it is certainly true that talent has a traceable timeline. Mum remembers me pestering her with a soft ball when I was not much older than two. She'd break off from the washing-up and throw it at me across the kitchen, with the promise I'd get a biscuit if I caught it at the furthest point in the room.

It was only later that I realized she would throw it that little bit harder when the treat was due. I wasn't deterred. I would sit on the floor of my bedroom, with my head resting against the side of the mattress, throwing and catching the ball off the ceiling, walls and furniture. I was unconsciously developing hand–eye co-ordination.

We rehashed countless snooker World Championships in the kitchen, on a table measuring two feet by four feet, propped up by stools. Before I went up to St Paul's the family would play tennis or badminton in the village hall three times a week. A combination of nature and nurture was involved across disciplines.

Musically, my parents were talented. They used to sing in the church choir at Wickham Bishops, and I had learned to read music by the time I was six. My paternal grandad was a very, very good violinist and would make instruments for my brothers. I specialized in the clarinet and saxophone but couldn't consistently play by ear.

That's an incredible skill; even now, the only piano piece I can play without a music score in front of me is the intro to 'Crazy Little Thing Called Love', by Queen. I'm a diligent learner, though. If I were to practise daily for a week, I could probably get the whole song off pat. As for my angelic singing, it went south when my voice broke at the age of sixteen. It's difficult to retrain.

There is an ethereal quality to the best choirs, a natural ease and beauty. I'm not sure you can say the same about my batting, though I do consider myself a natural batsman in that I am largely self-taught. In the choir I read the notes; at the crease I watch the ball. I have scored runs at every level because I have an ability to play every ball on its merits, no matter how daunting the occasion. I've never felt overawed, and, as strange as it sounds, can almost sight-read the bowler.

Dad opened the batting for Great Totham and partnered Joe Root's father-in-law when he played for a time in Gloucester. He bowled right-handed but batted and played golf left-handed. My grandad tried to teach me to play golf as a right-hander, but as soon as I was alone, I would twirl the club around and play left-handed. Ironically, in everything else I am strongly right-handed.

I would watch left-handed batsmen such as Mark Butcher and Graham Thorpe on TV, then go out into the garden and try to copy them. That's probably where I developed the instinctive trigger movement of going back and across my crease. I never realized I did the double backlift until I was about fifteen. It was an unconscious action; when I tried to take it out of my game for a couple of months I was terrible.

Don Bradman famously hit a golf ball with a stump for hours in his back yard. My classroom, in a cricket sense, was the eleven-yard pitch in the back garden. We taped up tennis balls or used slightly softer practice balls with a seam, known as Incrediballs. Adrian, as the eldest brother, demanded to bowl. Laurence as the youngest, kept wicket. I batted and was highly competitive; Adrian, naturally, tried to knock my head off.

He was quick for his age, and because the pitch was so short, he would never let me play a drive. If I did so, and hit the greenhouse at extra cover, we'd all get in trouble. The ball would come through to me at hip height; that's why and how I learned to play my trademark shots, the cut, the pull and the clip. I was small, and lacked power, but my technique was good.

Occasionally I pretended I was Brian Lara – as a bowler I tried to mimic Darren Gough, Angus Fraser or Gladstone 'no neck' Small – but when Adrian raced in from the patio the challenge was realistic because it was so personal. This was brother against brother, him versus me. I love the individual battle in cricket, within the team context.

It is a game that allows you to share experiences and memories but doesn't always shine the best light on your personality. I've always been stubborn. My grandad once asked me to get my stumps from the garden when it was raining. I refused point blank, even though I was told off for challenging his authority. I argued that since they were mine I could do what I wanted with them.

I definitely had a temper on me, and hated failure. One day Dad came home with a video camera. Naturally enough, we were his cinematic guinea pigs. I went into bat, pads and helmet on, did the Robin Smith crouch and the exaggerated knee jiggling, and Adrian got me out first ball. That was it. Tears everywhere.

Dad found my meltdown hilarious, and filmed me sitting behind a tree, screaming. I'm not entirely sure I'm over it to this day. At least I was forced to bowl, against my will. In retrospect that was a valuable test of character. You don't often see the bigger picture when you're ten, and aware of people saying you have real talent.

I played for the Under-11s at eight, scored 50 for the Maldon thirds when I was eleven. I was too young to regard failure to score runs as an educational experience; perspective comes later, when you realize there will be days when you dominate the bowler, and days when he dominates you. The important thing was that I played a lot of cricket because I wanted to, rather than being made to.

My technique had to be natural, since we rarely had formal coaching. I never saw myself bat until I was thirteen, when I realized the local paper, which had prematurely praised me as the new David Gower, might have gone a little over the top. I lacked his fluency and languor. At best, I was crablike but effective.

I was aware of a climate of expectation, but it didn't become oppressive because it wasn't generated by my parents. They cared, of course, but they never pushed me. They seemed to trust the self-reliance I had acquired as a boarder. It wasn't quite sink or swim, but they didn't exactly rush for a lifebelt if I got into deep water.

My own perspective of parenthood tells me such measured detachment must be healthy. On the schools circuit there have been more naturally gifted players emerge and break records, only to regress in senior cricket, where they seemed worn down by the responsibility of meeting parental demands. If my son Jack wants to play cricket in the future that's fine, but I will never force the game on him or renew my competitive instincts through him.

All you can do is allow a young player to be himself. There is a danger, across sport, of academy players becoming homogenized. They are treated like a protected species, nurtured in three-day England training camps at the age of thirteen. Talent becomes a barrier to a normal life; a promising cricketer may not be allowed to play a variety of sports because of the danger of being injured in, say, schools rugby.

They specialize too early, and consequently lack the balance of someone who develops other skills in other sports, such as athleticism or physical resilience. They are shielded from everyday life. A boy who knows only cricket has a problem, because he hasn't been given the environment to become a well-rounded human being. There is more to life than being a slave to the MCC coaching manual.

I left St Paul's at the age of thirteen, having won a music scholarship to Bedford School. Andy Pick, Richard Bates and Derek Randall coached me at Bedford, but rarely analysed my technique with the intention of making fundamental changes. A development session with Essex led to the observation that I needed to make my eyes level on addressing the ball, but I didn't really have too much technical input until I was eighteen.

My attitude was a far more powerful formative influence. I was fifteen when Jeremy Farrell, the master in charge of cricket at Bedford, challenged me to become fitter and stronger by joining preschool swimming sessions with the staff. He felt I was too weak to consistently hit the ball square.

Though I could just about tolerate swimming if I wore goggles, I honestly loathed it. The first morning I turned up at the pool Jeremy Farrell and Barry Burgess, the rugby master, ordered me to swim for twenty minutes. I could barely do twenty-five metres, yet my competitive streak kicked in. Within three months I was quicker than my cricket teacher. It took me six months to overhaul the rugby master, but ultimately, I was flying past the pair of them.

I was obsessively single-minded. I swam twice a week and went out running with the boarding-house dog before breakfast. Derek Randall, a World Cup finalist as a player and a world-class eccentric, got up early to work with me on the bowling machine. The 7.45 a.m. alarm call on down days was a luxury because of the principles which had been unconsciously instilled in me at choir school, where I had to be up by seven each morning and have the time-management skills to juggle twenty-four hours' music a week around normal academic work.

Although I was studying music at Bedford, the St Paul's choir master had read me well. His final report concluded that he expected to hear more from me as a cricketer than a singer in the years to come. I enjoyed my musicality, and particularly loved singing Handel's 'Zadok the Priest', which has been rearranged as the Champions League anthem, but knew I lacked the passion to be the best in that field.

Sport was my priority, my best chance of carving out a career. Although that led to occasional friction, I was fortunate that Andrew Morris, the school's director of music, was an MCC member and an ardent cricket fan. I played in the school jazz band and sang in the choir but began to define myself by the conventions of a professional athlete.

It wasn't quite a binary, win-or-lose lifestyle, but, philosophically, my apprenticeship had begun. I was storing realities for future reference. Batting gives you nowhere to hide. You either score runs or you don't. Your actions have consequences. You must learn to live with everything that goes with that. It involves balancing satisfying moments of success with setbacks that demand urgent self-questioning.

I'd had a distinctive upbringing. The hard graft of five years in choir school meant that I lost my innocence prematurely, but also ensured that I cherished slithers of spare time. It taught me the truth of that trite assertion that, if you want something done, ask a busy man. I would eventually sacrifice teenage rites of passage such as chaotic lads' holidays to Ayia Napa or Magaluf, but I don't think I missed out on much.

My close friendships at home in Essex were usually developed in school holidays, through cricket. One in particular has provided painful perspective. I knew David Randall through the Maldon club. We opened the batting together from the age of eleven and were named in the same England development squads. Since Ravi Bopara batted at three with us for Essex, the poor guys down the order rarely needed to strap on their pads; we were dominant.

We knew David as Arkle. He scored more runs than me and Ravi but, as is often the way, he never pursued professional cricket, preferring to go to university. His death, from bowel cancer at the age of twenty-seven, hit hard, because it reminded us of the limits of mortality. It united the Maldon cricket club, and inspired the local community. The work done by the charitable foundation established in his name, in helping those with life-limiting illness, remains close to my heart.

Though our paths diverged professionally, we had remained close personally. I found boarding at Bedford a release after the slightly claustrophobic environment of the choir school, and though I was small and relatively immature physically, I was determined to make an immediate impact in first-team cricket.

Not so quickly, young sir. Jeremy Farrell took me aside before the first game of the season and explained he had instead picked a sixth-former named James De Groot, who ironically, I now see regularly in his role as MCC's Head of Catering. I was told to go out and score runs for the Under-14s; I did so, making 80-odd not out as we chased down 140 against Haileybury, but my name still wasn't on the board announcing the team to play MCC the following Tuesday.

I was drifting in double physics, gazing out of the window on to the playing field, where the first team was warming up, when Mr Farrell interrupted the lesson. MCC were one short, and he wondered whether I fancied filling in. I didn't give him time to reconsider. It normally took seven minutes to walk to my boarding house; I reckon I did it there and back in six.

More lessons for later: in sport the biggest opportunities have a habit of presenting themselves when you least expect them. Be ready for anything. Make the moment matter. The MCC captain said I'd be batting at three; I'd barely got my pads on before I was walking to the wicket. Someone blurted out 'send him back to primary school' and I was greeted with a couple of bouncers.

Cricket, like other sports, is a state of mind. I could sense the tide turning in my favour as my score increased and the fielding team became more subdued. I reached my century with a shot that is daunting even for a senior pro, running down the wicket to clip the ball over midwicket, against the turn of an off-spinner. The match petered out into a draw, with the school eight wickets down in reply, but I felt like a winner as Mr Farrell shook my hand.

I was an honorary adult for the day and allowed to enjoy the rituals of men's cricket. I sat in the away changing room, drinking beer and listening to the stories become more improbable, before they drifted off. I returned to the boarding house around 9 p.m., gabbled my story to my parents and woke the next morning as a new man.

Suddenly, I was a name around school. I was still a little kid, but by the following Saturday my name was on the first-team message board. I read it several times, to make sure it was real. Word was getting round that I was a half decent player, and when I played for Essex seconds at Dunstable at the age of fifteen there was a whisper that Nottinghamshire, a county with strong links to the Bedford coaches, were after me.

I don't consider myself insecure for recognizing my fear of failure. Doubt has always been there, but manageable. Motivation for the extra batting sessions, or the early morning runs, varies; for some it is the prospect of adulation, basking in the crowd's warmth as they walk off, bat up, helmet removed to reveal a reddened face and sweat-streaked hair.

There's nothing wrong with that sort of egotism. It's earned and legitimate. Sometimes the exuberance of the celebration is a sign of relief, an acknowledgement of the inner struggle. Everyone loves a pat on the back, but I was simply driven to do it all again the next day. Success counts for nothing if it is not repeatable.

I knew the big score would be irrelevant if I failed the next four times I was at the crease. That's what kept me back, as the last man hitting balls. That's what made me train harder than anyone in my generation. I had to have an edge in personal fitness, because the regimes now employed by the likes of Ben Stokes, Jos Buttler and Jonny Bairstow – proper athletes – were giving the game a different dimension.

My breakthrough moment as a young pro was discovering the meaning of mental toughness. It involved dealing with the Gimp, the bloke on my shoulder who loved to beat me up in moments of difficulty. The day I learned to live with him, and not become too down on myself, was a massive turning point in terms of my career's longevity.

This is not the it-was-better-in-my-day rumination of an old pro, but I watch some young county cricketers train today and wonder whether they appreciate the privilege of the life-changing opportunity they have been given. Why wouldn't you do more than the standard session, between nine and lunchtime? Why wouldn't you do that little bit more than the next man?

God-given talent offers no insurance. Will you fulfil your potential if you've half an eye on that afternoon on the golf course, or the session on the sofa, playing *FIFA* with your mates? Cricket has rewarded me with everything I have. There are no short cuts. I was lucky that I knew the value of hard work from an early age. I love it when I see younger players taking the same approach.

Maybe their programmes are too precise, too considered. My generation worked more on instinct and had greater self-awareness. I'm imperfect: I'm not the quickest and probably didn't do enough preparatory work with the strength-and-conditioning coach. But would more speed have made me a better player? I don't think so. I concentrated on long-distance running, to enhance my endurance.

Maybe the modern teenage boy needs a little bit more freedom to be himself, to think for himself, but there are obvious sporting examples they can follow. The common denominator, linking Owen Farrell to David Beckham, Rory McIlroy to Graham Gooch, across the generations, is that they were there, working, when everyone else had gone home. That's why they are, or were, the best.

I've worked sixteen-hour days on the family farm in Bedfordshire, doing the job until it is done. There's not that much difference, in terms of mindset, from reporting to pre-breakfast sessions with Goochy when I was taken on by Essex. I lapped up every word he said. The end, the reward of my first professional contract, paying £667 monthly after tax, justified the means.

I hadn't yet learned to drive during my first year as a pro – not that I could have afforded a car – and Mum and Dad weren't prepared to be taxi drivers, so that meant catching a bus at 6.43 a.m. and a connecting train to Chelmsford at 7.15. Provided public transport didn't let me down, I'd be at the ground for eight. I'd grab breakfast, spend two hours in the gym, at least two hours batting, and then do the reverse commute.

I was knackered. I'd sleep for two hours in mid-afternoon, have an early dinner and then go back to bed. With hindsight, I was adjusting to the demands of professional sport. The transition from emerging player, scorer of seventeen centuries, two double-hundreds and 4,396 runs at an average of 87.90, to first team wannabe was stark.

A county second team is a team in name only, a melting pot of players with different career trajectories and variable levels of motivation. It can be a shared adventure – there was an obvious affinity with Will Jefferson, James Foster and Ravi Bopara, because we were on similar pathways – but it is essentially a selfish experience. Everything is seen through the prism of your own progression.

I was fortunate in sharing a dressing room with Barry Hyam, a senior pro with a rare generosity of spirit. A second-team stalwart, who played sixty-one first-class games in nine years from 1993, he was a huge source of encouragement and advice. It is no surprise he has developed into a thoughtful and innovative coach, who now runs the Essex second team and Academy.

He was released as a player at the end of the 2003 season, by which time I'd been given three first-team games on relatively flat pitches. I made 84 in a win over Surrey, contributed two more half-centuries to average 47.80, but learned most from the example of two players from diverse backgrounds and abilities.

I watched Waqar Younis become a different player when he sensed victory, shifting up several gears to bowl fast reverse swing, take five wickets and mop up the win. I studied Andy Flower from the other end at the Oval, when he made 201, and listened to him distil common sense and experience. He was thirty-five, in the final game of a relegation season, and his application was absolute.

I was growing up, on and off the pitch. I moved away from home and learned on the job. During one defeat by Hampshire, I'd got out to a massive hack against James Bruce, the right-arm fast-medium bowler who would retire prematurely in 2007 to take up a job in the City of London.

My error was compounded by the fact that it was the final ball of Bruce's spell. I should have stayed around to see him off. I was headstrong, an aspiring, adolescent pro, who thought he knew best. I was right in the first-team mix, desperate to make my way. This was my living, and I was beginning to realize that avoidable mistakes had consequences.

The boy had become a man, with rough edges and many more miles to travel.

3. The Survival Gene

Rats scurried along bare concrete walls. Cockroaches congregated in corridors, where we did press-ups and sit-ups to compensate for the lack of a gym. They told us the hotel in Dhaka was structurally sound, though it was half-built and anything above the fifth floor was open to the elements. The beds were damp, and the electrical system made playing *Tiger Woods PGA Tour* on the Xbox a lottery.

Welcome to international cricket, and my first experience of captaining an England team, in the Under-19 World Cup in Bangladesh in 2004. Despite the privations, it was an invaluable four-week crash course in team building and personal resilience. Those sessions, working down from twenty press-ups to two, and back up again, did no one any harm.

When we moved to Chittagong, our hotel was the one in which the senior side refused to stay later that year. We thought it was a palace. We should have done better than lose to the West Indies in the semi-final but cracked under the pressure and were bowled out for 155. It demonstrated how much I had to learn, about both group dynamics and individual obligations. We were so far from being the finished product.

Though I had captained Bedford School, there seemed more chance of making a day trip to Narnia than captaining my country. Samit Patel was our original skipper, but he failed a fitness test and Andy Pick, who coached the squad in conjunction with John Abrahams after taking over from Paul Farbrace, made a brave call in asking me to take over. He wanted to deliver a life lesson to Samit, that talent is only part of the equation.

Samit has huge natural ability, and I had enough faith in him as a spinner to bowl him at the death in our five-run group win over Pakistan, the eventual winners of the tournament. He came through, taking the final wicket of Zulqarnain Haider when the game was on the line. He had to deal with similar doubts about his work ethic throughout his senior international career and insists he has never missed a game for county or country through injury, but that's not actually the argument, is it?

Being in peak physical condition might have been negotiable in a previous era, but in the modern game it is a fundamental symbol of commitment. No one likes fitness sessions. There's nothing exciting about going to the gym, doing the horrible, unglorified bits. There's nothing nice about hurting yourself during those long-distance runs that never seem to end.

The Aussies call it 'ticker'. Have you got the heart to withstand tough periods, when your character is under scrutiny? Can you get through by sheer force of will? You can't replicate a critical game situation in practice, but that old cliché about the tough getting going when the going gets tough has more than a hint of truth. Guys who are genuinely successful tend to be the ones who put themselves through the sessions no one sees.

I prefer to train early in the morning. My routine at home is to get up at half past five, do some gym work and then run around the lanes between six and seven. It's a quiet time of the day, an absorbing and strangely intimate process. I am proving myself to myself, if you like. I could so easily lie in, do the work mid-morning, but there is something about being out there on my own, not really wanting to be there. Knowing you are ready to do the hard stuff adds to your self-confidence.

I'm not comparing myself to a Martin Johnson, who led England's World Cup-winning rugby team by the power of his example, but I suppose they picked me as an inexperienced captain of the Under-19s for the same reasons they asked me to lead the full team. People probably respected the way I went about things. There were no great secrets to my approach.

I worked hard, put myself on the line by opening the batting. I topped the fitness tests. I wanted others to have the same drive, and people seemed to listen to what I said. Tactically, I was too conservative in Bangladesh. I probably wasn't sufficiently assertive with the team, but that is not altogether surprising, given my youth.

I was integrated into senior dressing rooms from the age of fifteen, when I was taken under the wing of Ian Elliot and Robbie Barber, who opened the batting for Maldon. The average age of the team was late twenties; I sat there, listening almost in awe to their piss-taking and their unlikely shagging stories. The cricket was extremely competitive and they were brilliant, sharp-witted sledgers.

I'd barely gone through puberty and was small, so I was an obvious target, especially for the overseas pros we would come up against in the East Anglian Premier League. They were generally good cricketers, mostly South African or Australian, but their insults weren't terribly inventive. 'What the fuck are you doing here?' they'd ask. 'I'm going to kill you.'

I wasn't intimidated by the verbals and could handle the short stuff when it inevitably arrived. By the time I was eighteen I was able to dominate the opposition at club level. Typically, I wanted to end one game, at Mildenhall in Suffolk, early so that I could go out that evening with Alice, whom I had just met.

We were chasing 170, and I drove a South African bowler to distraction by tearing into him from the outset. Clearly peeved that a kid was showing him no respect, his default mechanism was to bowl shorter and shorter, and try to bounce me out. I scored 80-odd in no time, and the course of true love was smoothed.

It was a great learning experience. There was a brief trend for county academies to play in men's leagues. I didn't agree with the basic premise, that there would be continuity in the challenge. A promising player can become too insulated in youth cricket. There's a sense of dependence when support staff provide the throwdowns, and coaches are taking notes.

By playing for your club, rather than representing your county academy, you're dealing with the real world, playing teams of different ages from different backgrounds. You are playing alongside a forty-year-old with three kids who has no inclination to mollycoddle you. You organize throwdowns with your mates. You embrace the mentality of a clubman, share such rituals as the Thursday-night barbeque around the pavilion.

Playing for an academy doesn't mean you've made it. The county badge on your helmet gives you no privileges. It doesn't hurt to raise your head above the parapet. In some public schoolboys there's a distance, a slight sense of entitlement, that needs to get knocked out of them. I had the privilege of a private education because of scholarships that recognized my talent, but there was no silver spoon in our family's cutlery drawer.

Some of the lads in the Essex Colts teams were more worldly, and maybe spent a little more time in front of the mirror than I was used to. I was fortunate to grow up in a first-team dressing room in which the standards were set by the likes of Ronnie Irani and Darren Gough. They were hard, but fair, in setting definable limits.

You knew what you could, and could not, get away with. Anyone who took a liberty quickly regretted it. Ronnie was a nuts-and-bolts captain, a cricketer who made the most of himself, as an England all-rounder before chronic knee problems forced him to filter his determination through a revised role as a specialist batsman.

He would look out for younger players, like Ravi Bopara and me, if the opposition tried to bully us, and was at ease with strong characters, though he didn't exactly see eye to eye with Nasser Hussain, who gave me a three-week master-class at the end of his career. I opened with him in his final match for Essex, scoring 51 as he marked his farewell with a trademark second-innings century.

'You're going to take my job,' he told me. Kind, slightly startling words, but his example had as great an impact. Here was a former England captain who had played in ninety-six Tests, giving his all when others would have coasted into retirement. I watched, entranced, as he worried away at his batting grip and twiddled nervously. He was seeking answers, searching for secrets until the end. It was the first manifest-ation of the survival gene that characterizes successful sportsmen. He cared all right.

The sense of wonder, when I first stepped into that Essex dressing room with Ravi, at the age of fifteen during the school holidays, has never really left me. I'd be given a few token throwdowns at the end of nets, go through the fielding drills with the seniors, and then be allowed to sit in on the team meeting. I was being introduced gently to the trade.

Any airs or graces were fair game. I slaughtered James Foster for walking past me without a word when I went to see him play for the first team at Colchester, but knew he was in his own little world, and we were forming lifelong bonds. The democracy of cricket unites people who, outside the game, might have little in common.

I consider Ben Stokes one of my better mates. He's from a completely different background to me, and from the other end of the country, but we text and speak often. He's a great guy, despite the well-documented controversies, and will, I'm sure, respond positively to the fame generated by his contribution to the World Cup win. Conversations about cricket are the glue in our relationship; his commitment to the England team is total.

Friends outside the game who have gone the traditional route, through public school, university and the City, have probably missed out on that type of connection. I see them as much as I can, but it is inevitable that contrasting lifestyles make that difficult. As I began to make my way in the game my horizons were narrower, because I was concentrating on the stepping stones of professional sport.

As an emerging pro I wanted the perks of the trade, the personalized car-parking space and the sponsored car with my name signwritten on the driver's door. Needless to say, I got neither. They took parking privileges away as a result of one of those fathomless health-and-safety orders. The personalized sponsored car, which first seized my imagination when I saw Peter Such drive past me, went out of fashion.

Not a bad thing, all told, because, in hindsight, they looked ridiculous. I settled for a locker, given to county players, but it took time to wean myself off my dodgy car habit. The stick I received for one aberration of taste and decency, a bright orange Ford Focus, was unrelenting and entirely deserved.

The dressing room began to school me with its brutal humour. Even to this day I'm known as Woggle, because of my slightly wonky left eye. It can lead to some horrendous still photographs when I'm concentrating on my batting, since I appear cross-eyed. I get hammered left, right and centre, from senior players and kids alike. You must be big enough to take it, if you want to give it out.

Cricket tends to attract a broader base of personalities than, say, rowing, where a successful eight tends to come from a similar demographic and is more interconnected. A cricket team can overcome individual errors but if one oarsman catches a crab during a race it's all over. As an established Test batsman, I could survive a short run of very low scores and still win a series through the efforts of others.

That helps to create a distinctive tolerance within the dressing room. It is an enlightening environment, because you unconsciously, or even consciously, reveal aspects of your character within it. What makes it so special is that teammates see everything of you, and share your struggle, without the outside world knowing anything of it.

England teammates had a 360-degree view of my career. They saw me as a bloke at rock bottom and fearing for his future in 2010, as a fighter scoring 766 in an Ashes series in

Australia the following winter, and as the authority figure going through the fires of captaincy and controversy in 2014. It is an individual trial, but a collective experience.

Together, you experience the highs of winning and the dreadful lows of losing a tight game. You are strapped into the same emotional roller coaster and can relate to one another. I'm drawn to the exclusivity of the process. No one else is allowed into the inner sanctum, where you must be true to yourself and those around you.

With trust comes understanding. Steven Davies and I go back to that Under-19 World Cup, yet I was unaware of his deepest secret until a telephone call from Andrew Strauss and Andy Flower before the 2010–11 Ashes tour. Steve, selected as understudy to Matt Prior, wanted us to know of his homosexuality and, as a group, we pledged to keep it in-house until he wished to make an announcement.

I found his air of liberation, when he came out in February 2011, deeply affecting. The barriers were down on that tour, when he felt free to share the isolation he had felt previously. He had been in the T20 group for two years and would retreat to his hotel room rather than go out with the lads. The frustration of being too inhibited to be himself was profound.

He spoke of being sick with nerves in our pre-tour get-together at Lord's, where, like the rest of the group, I made a point of offering my support. He was Steve, the cricketer. Nothing more, nothing less. Professional sport is a pressure chamber at the best of times and for him to carve an international career when enduring such internal turmoil is a convincing summary of character.

Acceptance was instant, universal and enduring, once he

made his announcement. That's as it should be. Straussy and Andy deserved a great deal of credit for their approach, which combined empathy with practicality. On a professional level, they saw it as an issue to be dealt with and filed away for future reference, when required. On a personal level, they related to the humanity of Steve's dilemma.

We all need a helping hand, in various ways. Mine, in a cricketing sense, came consistently from Graham Gooch. His 333 against India in July 1990, a ten-and-a-half-hour marathon that would be voted as the greatest innings seen at Lord's, was my first conscious sporting memory. I was five at the time, bewildered when TV coverage of the Test was interrupted by horseracing.

I queued for his autograph as a child and grew up quickly because of his patronage. He was hugely influential, supporting me financially in grade cricket in Perth during a gap year, where the wickets were slow and low, and I didn't even appear to merit the traditional verbal abuse from Aussie bowlers.

Sometimes, in sport, the circle of life accelerates. Goochy saw something in me, drove me hard, but looked after my wider welfare. Like my mum, he urged me to go to university instead of prematurely committing myself to full-time cricket. His rationale was based on bitter knowledge; he had seen too many young players released in their early twenties with nothing to fall back upon.

He didn't want me to make a common mistake. I resisted, in part due to the beliefs and disciplines he had instilled in me from the outset. I worked hard with him, ritually and regularly. I would chop wood at his house with Swampy, my housemate and fellow hopeful Mark Pettini, before training sessions designed to test us physically and mentally.

He would send us on long early morning runs and pedal beside us, offering admonishment and encouragement. He would bombard us with bouncers for half an hour in the nets before tiredness thankfully took a toll. Sessions on the outfield at Essex were demanding: ten shuttle runs, face four balls, and then do another six shuttles. He would make us run backwards at speed and stand over us as we sweated through a series of burpees and press-ups.

He was a distinctive cross between an army PTI and a solicitous housemaster. Once the work was complete, he wanted us to clear our minds, relax and release. I was eager for knowledge, and he warned against self-reproach when I disappointed myself. It was a significant message, delivered simply and illustrated by personal experience.

He confided that his method of finding mental equilibrium on losing his wicket was to sit with his pads still on. He would have a cup of tea and answer his mail. This was before the internet and smart phones, the days when pen and paper weren't museum pieces. That triggered my imagination; how could he be so phlegmatic? What was behind his acceptance of fate?

Yet it carried over into his tutelage. He wouldn't scream at me if I got out to a poor shot; a look of piercing sadness was usually enough. He knew I knew what I'd done: why raise the temperature if you, as a coach, have faith that your pupil will respond? His most persuasive method of motivation was the quiet but telling one-liner.

For example, a big turning point for me was an early four-day second-team game against Warwickshire, with shortened boundaries. I was in decent nick, and 97 not out at lunch, with Swampy also unbeaten in an opening partnership of

160. Goochy, who had made a point of postponing his first-team duties for our match, sat us down, and said, 'Get yourself back in, don't give it away, and you've got a really big score.'

You're probably ahead of me here, but, sure enough, I had an airy drive at the second ball of the afternoon session, nicked it and was out. I was expecting a massive bollocking that never arrived, and had to watch, stewing in my own juices, as Swampy got 200. When he was dismissed, Goochy tapped me on the leg, whispered, 'He's just got your runs there,' and walked off.

Enough said.

Graham was old school. Hit the boundary, take a single off the next ball, and get off strike. You've got five in two balls. It's your partner's turn to take the strain. Simple enough advice to absorb, you'd think, but young players are prone to brain fades and rushes of blood. They unerringly take the wrong option. Though he didn't show it, it must have driven him mad.

I was sitting next to him, as twelfth man, during a T20 quarter-final at Leicester. Graham Napier, our pinch hitter, was batting at three. When he hit his second ball for six Goochy murmured, 'Great shot, great shot. Now get a single. You've done your job, Napes. Don't do anything stupid.' Needless to say, he got out to a huge slog at the next delivery.

Goochy looked in a world of pain. 'Wanker!' he exclaimed, in that reedy voice, which seemed to echo across the wilderness. I was desperate to laugh, because the emotion expressed in that single word was hilarious, but had enough common sense to keep schtum. When your coach is suffering for his art, and your foolishness, silence is a shield.

It's a jarring expression, but you need someone to live the journey with you. A little luck doesn't come amiss. I was fortunate that Goochy was brought in by Andy Flower as England's batting coach, initially as a consultant in 2009, so that the relationship we had established at county level could be strengthened and sustained. Trust and respect were mutual. He was prepared to put the hours into me.

International sport can play out frantically, because of the exposure it commands. My mentor continued to deal in quiet certainties. Some days you get out, some days you don't. Take the long-term view. When I got a low score, he would seek to reassure rather than accuse. 'We'll work hard tomorrow,' he'd say. 'Don't look back.'

There were other, better, technical coaches, but no one could rival his understanding of the mechanics of building an innings, the subtleties of game management. Sport is cyclical; he was passing on the formative lessons he'd learned under Ken Barrington and developed in partnership with Geoffrey Boycott.

He used to talk about 'The Knowledge'. This encompassed the power of concentration, the importance of building a firm base before becoming too expansive. He taught me to study the weather as well as the wicket, and to make sure I was mentally secure in what I was seeking to achieve.

His priority was to make me play positively. He liked it when I was ambitious, looking to score runs rather than merely survive. His logic was, as usual, easy to follow: if you seek the initiative, you are transferring the pressure to the bowler. Don't give him the respite of shuffling about, soaking up thirty or forty balls for the odd run.

Work hard. Earn the right to play. Trust in your talent and

preparation. Groove your movements. Pick up the line. Hit the ball back where it came from. Send the message to the bowler that you know what you are doing. One dog-stick drill summarized the simplicity of the process: I had to do one of three things, drive the ball, leave the ball or execute a forward defensive shot.

Perhaps he had worked out that I was uncomfortable with lavish praise. When I did well, scoring a century or putting into practice something on which we had worked, he knew all I needed was a nod, the odd word. When we made technical changes, I usually made the first move after a lot of contemplation.

It is a dangerous period – you have only to look at the number of golfers whose fortunes have nosedived after making a fundamental swing change. Habits are deeply ingrained and resistant to anything more than gentle evolution over time. In my case, I looked a lot taller at the crease, more natural, when I was with the Under-19s.

The catalyst for change was an average of 28, across two Ashes series. These are the definitive examinations of temperament and technique. I was averaging between 45 and 50 against other nations but falling short against the best team in the world, in the most exposed environment the international game offers.

I rejigged things, revising my technique entirely so that I could hit the ball straighter. It was initially successful, since I had an immediate run of three Test centuries, but I eventually became too rigid. My game had self-imposed restrictions, and it set me up to fail. Goochy's principles were sound: they had to be reasserted.

Batting is a manifestation of the mind. There were times,

on the Ashes tour of 2010–11 and in India in 2012, when I wasn't exactly in the zone, that Zen-like state snooker players speak of, when everything slows down and doubts are dispelled, but I just found the rhythm. I wasn't seeing the ball better or quicker, but I had a sense of flow. When I got to the crease it just happened for me, without the battle.

A particular session in Adelaide before the second Test in December 2010 is imprinted on my memory. It was one of those occasions when Flower consciously put us under pressure in the nets. This was the antithesis of cosy, confidence-building training. He told the coaches to discomfort us by flinging the ball aggressively, trying to find the edge or shatter the stumps. If you got in the way of one, tough. It was a reassertion of the old principle of training hard to play easy.

Goochy was hurling the ball down with the dog-stick, the pet training aid which had come into fashion as a perverse aid to practice around 2007. It was a flat wicket, so it wasn't too tough in terms of an examination of technique, but he was trying to knock my head off, or hurry me into a mistake. Confrontation makes the adrenaline flow.

I left anything that wasn't hitting the stumps. I was driving, cutting, clipping, pulling anything that was slightly wide or short. I was surprised by the intensity of the feeling of being at ease. I wasn't forcing myself to score the runs or find the shot. If it wasn't there to drive, it remained undriven. Everything just happened. After forty minutes or so, when I was error free, Goochy came down to me and said, 'You're in good nick. Make it count.'

Some golfers become almost mystical when they talk about that unconscious excellence. I never allow myself to ignore the danger of getting out, but that effortlessness is seductive to any professional sportsman. I don't experience things in slow motion, like others. If anything, time goes too quickly for me. Occasionally, though, the game becomes metronomic.

The best personal example of that was in Abu Dhabi, playing Pakistan in October 2015. I batted for 836 minutes, after being in the field for two days, in temperatures that rose to 40 degrees. A weird physiological anomaly, known as anhidrosis, means I don't sweat, but the air was very hot and still. Conditions were simply unpleasant.

Somehow, I entered another dimension. It was surreal, a 528-ball vigil in a near-deserted stadium. I got to my hundred relatively quickly, but after that was as regular as clockwork, scoring thirty runs a session, until I got out, gently top-edging off-spinner Shoaib Malik to short fine leg for 263 just before the close on the fourth day.

It couldn't be that straightforward, of course. Replays confirmed it was a no-ball. It was a strange sensation: the body, in the end, succumbed to understandable fatigue but the mind remained rock solid. If I am being honest, I surprised myself. I usually refresh myself after every ball by walking towards square leg to clear the mind, but this felt different.

Mental strength, to use widely applied shorthand to the virtues of sustained self-containment, fascinates across sport. It is a very hard thing to define, but its functionality underpinned a mutually educational visit by the Essex team to Saracens, a rugby club that prides itself on the development of an innovative, performance culture.

These visits are sometimes superficial. The only thing we really took from a similar visit to Ipswich Town FC was an appreciation of how hard the pros kick the ball. Football, I suppose, exists in its own bubble. I'm generalizing a little, but the players weren't that interested in impressing a bunch of cricketers or sharing insight.

The rugby guys were different. We warmed up with them, playing four-goal football with two balls. It required sharpness, peripheral vision and rapid decision-making, and was hugely enjoyable. We played a bit of touch rugby, shared a fitness session and watched their skill-specific training. They had fun but knew when to work.

They then invited us into their team meeting, where we swapped ideas and examined common experiences. Theirs is a harsh, physically demanding sport, but the best need mental discipline to cope with the relentlessness of the challenge. Their survival gene is also deeply ingrained; they know careers are getting shorter and more intense.

Like it or not, sport at the highest level is not a friendly environment. During my twelve years with England I began to get a sense of who would thrive and who would fall away relatively quickly. It wouldn't be fair to name him, but one guy, a younger player who had excelled in county cricket, came to me soon after his call-up. 'This is very intense, isn't it?' he said. 'I didn't expect that.' I knew he was lost. That's what it is. Hard. Pitiless. Unforgiving.

The weeding out process begins early. That fifteen-strong England Under-19 squad, judged in hindsight, was probably above par, since seven of us, Samit Patel, Ravi Bopara, Steven Davies, Luke Wright, Tim Bresnan, Liam Plunkett and I, progressed to play senior international cricket.

James Hildreth, who has scored in excess of 16,000 first-class runs for Somerset, can count himself unlucky not to have been given an opportunity in England's middle order.

James is one of the finest county players of my generation. We go way back; his father used to pick me up from Newport Pagnell services on the M1 and ferry us to and from our training sessions at Loughborough University. We were roommates and partners on *Tiger Woods* golf, during the Under-19 World Cup in Bangladesh in 2004. His one taste of the big time was an appearance as substitute fielder in the 2005 Ashes series, when he caught Ricky Ponting off Matthew Hoggard in the first Test at Lord's.

The fate of others reflects the uncertainty, misfortune and disappointment of professional sport. David Stiff, a fast bowler who took 4–7 against Uganda in one of the group games in Bangladesh, was courted by a dozen counties when he opted to leave Yorkshire. He played twenty first-class matches for Kent, Leicestershire and Somerset, who released him after the 2010 season.

Wicketkeeper-batsman Tom New settled for the role of long-term understudy to Paul Nixon at Leicestershire until 2011. Mark Turner, a medium-fast right-arm bowler, played for three counties over nine years until 2014. Leg-spinner Mark Lawson moved into developmental coaching. Dan Broadbent, a left-handed batsman, didn't make a first-class appearance. Adam Harrison was forced to retire in 2007 due to a persistent ankle injury.

It is sobering to see a career, the destiny of someone's dream, summed up in a single sentence. But that is the way of things. Judgement is harsh, often final. Coaches and chief executives wonder what you have done for them lately. Sometimes we all forget we are in a people business. We are dealing with sensitive individuals whose feelings are occasionally compromised by their faults, or their familiarity.

One of my enduring regrets is the way I handled my role in the decision to part company with Graham Gooch as England's batting coach after the Ashes whitewash in Australia in 2014. We were dealing with a legend of the game, a good man. Without his dedication and selflessness, I would never have become the player I did.

The logic, that we needed to wipe the slate clean after the departure of Andy Flower and the bitterness of Kevin Pietersen's exit, was cold but understandable. The thought processes involved were pretty straightforward. It was an easy decision. When you get blown away so badly, someone has to take the rap.

Goochy was so close to Andy that I didn't think we could move forward with the same messages being delivered. We needed a fresh start, the momentum of new personnel. I should have refused when Peter Moores, the new head coach, asked me to communicate our decision. We were, after all, rationalizing his support staff. I had no influence in Peter's appointment, but a cricket captain's job description includes the passing on of bad news.

Not only should I probably not have been given the responsibility of doing so in this instance, but also the manner in which I did so was wrong. I should have just climbed into the car and informed him face-to-face. I owed him that. I rang him three times to arrange a meeting, but we kept missing one another, and eventually I told him over the phone. He knew what was coming. 'Just tell me,' he said. It was distant and impersonal, unworthy.

This was different from our mutually agreed decision to scale back my personal coaching sessions with him. Goochy had implanted that idea in my brain by asking whether, after ten years working closely together, I needed to listen to another voice. I went to work with Gary Palmer, whose input was purely technical, in the way a swing coach informs a golfer.

But, with England, I blame myself. Faced with the same decision today, I would have done it differently. There was an understandable distance between us for a couple of years, but Goochy is not one to hold grudges and our relationship has repaired. Scars heal, but we should never forget the pain we can inflict, knowingly or unknowingly.

People like him deserve better.

4. Collateral Damage

We need 561 runs to win the first Test at the Gabba, with more than two days to play. Deep down, I know the game has long gone. But I go through my mental checklist, promise myself I will sell my wicket dearly. I will not let them grind me down. Then, just as I am about to walk out into the cauldron, I see something so personal, so painful and so profound that I'm shaken to the core.

Jonathan Trott, due to bat at number three, is putting his pads on across the dressing room. He has welled up until he is unable to stem the flood of tears. In any other environment I would retrace my steps and attempt to console a friend in distress. This is not the moment, nor the place, for instinctive compassion. Millions are waiting, unaware and ultimately uncaring.

There is a job to be done. This may appear heartless, when taken out of context, but I'm on autopilot. 'Sort that out, just sort it out,' I tell Andy Flower, our head coach. 'I've got to go out and bat. I don't care if he doesn't bat. You make that decision.' With that I go out with Michael Carberry, who is making his Ashes debut. I owe it to him to normalize abnormality.

Eighteen minutes later he is bowled by Ryan Harris, from the fourteenth ball he has faced: 560 runs to win, with nine wickets left. I look back and see Trotty walking towards me. It is only later that I will truly appreciate the poignancy of the moment, the moral courage it took for him to attempt an innings that bordered on self-sacrifice.

He played compulsively, with a terrible desperation, attempting his trademark clipped shot at almost every delivery. He somehow made all nine runs in our fifteen-ball partnership before he directed a Mitchell Johnson bouncer to Nathan Lyon at deepish backward square leg. The gloom was deepening, literally and metaphorically.

It must have been horrendous for him. It is unthinkable that a game you love so much represents such a threat that you don't want to expose yourself to the battle. I know the analogy may grate in such sensitive circumstances, but that is what Test cricket is, a battle. For someone of his talent to shy away from the challenge he had confronted so well, so often, asked questions of us all.

We all balance competitive intensity and personal welfare. We all understand the parameters of professionalism. We all admit to ourselves that we occasionally exceed sensible levels of commitment. We all knew, instinctively, that Trotty was in a bad way. For that trip, at least, there was no way back. We lost by 381 runs on the fourth day, an ominous defeat. In retrospect the tour started to fall apart before it had barely begun.

Some people, who should have known better, said things that should have remained unsaid. Though, to his credit, he subsequently apologized for describing Trotty's second-innings dismissal as 'pretty poor and weak', the Aussie opener, David Warner, was utterly out of order in suggesting he typified a team playing with 'scared eyes'. He was rightly taken to task by Flower for such disparaging nonsense.

Andy told us in the dressing room that Trotty was flying home. His emotional response underlined the gravity of the situation. Here was a tough coach, an honourable man, who had demanded everything from the group for four or five years. The hard-edged persona he had adopted softened to reveal a sensitive soul who cared deeply for the well-being of the players under his control.

He spoke passionately, emotively and tenderly about events, and the nature of what we do. Trotty was not there and left without a formal farewell. The media were told it was due to a 'stress-related illness'. A captain in such a terrible situation is torn between his responsibility to the group and his duty of care to the individual. The squad is the rock, the stricken player is in a hard place.

I was obliged to sift through the wreckage of that Test match, in November 2013, for clues or slithers of encouragement. Australia weren't infallible; we had them at 132–6 in the first innings, before Johnson and Brad Haddin put on 114. Would Johnson, who took nine wickets in the match, be able to keep blowing us away? Would Harris revert to type and struggle to sustain himself physically over a series?

As it turned out, the answers were yes, and no.

Something clicked for Johnson only two overs into the series, when he opted to bowl around the wicket, to a spread field. A sensational bowler who went through massive peaks and troughs, he suddenly found he could take wickets with his bad balls. Confidence surged; by the end, he was in complete control. Harris would be forced to retire in 2015 through a knee injury, but these were the days of his life.

The part of my brain that deals in logic, analytical thought and reasoning was occupied by the fragile, overarching goals of the tour. The other part, more creative, and focused on such things as imagination, intuition, insight and holistic thought, was devoted to Trotty's plight. In short, could I have done any more to help?

It is something I wrestle with to this day. My mind keeps returning to a session with the bowling machine during the warm-up period in Sydney. It is one of my major regrets that I never stopped it. Trotty seemed to be intent on purging himself. He turned the machine up to top speed and was being hit all over the body. It was alarming, unprecedented in my experience for its wilful destructiveness.

I didn't have the confidence or ability to do my job as a leader. I knew he was struggling mentally, and confiding in Mark Saxby, the masseur with whom he had a strong relationship, but I failed to appreciate the extent of the problem. In the later years of my captaincy I would have been more forceful and proactive, and demanded to be allowed into the inner circle.

Trotty has subsequently admitted to me that he regrets not sharing his issues, because he didn't want to burden me. That's where self-containment, encouraged and almost demanded by international sport, works against the individual. He later wrote of having his male dignity stripped away by his perceived inability to deal with the short ball.

There is a tightrope strung between leaving someone alone and trusting them to do things their way, and wrapping them in cotton wool. This, remember, was a senior player who had been part of three Ashes-winning teams. He had scored one helluva lot of runs over forty-seven Tests. Without being specific about Trotty, you can't mollycoddle anyone in Test cricket.

I get on really well with the bloke. I love him to bits. I didn't spot the warning signs early enough. I should have knocked on his door and talked through everything in as much detail as he could stand. Instead, I relied on those passing, inconsequential conversations that make up so much of the day.

'You all right, Trotty?'

'Yeah, yeah, good. Just battling a few things.'

He always battled things. That's what made him so good, his OCD, his single-minded pursuit of brilliance. Obsessed by the minutiae of the game, he would measure his pads to the millimetre. He was visibly driven to put in a performance for himself, his parents, his team. His determination and desire were as ferocious as his demons. His autobiography, *Unguarded*, which revealed relentless self-imposed pressure to please his mum and dad, makes sobering reading.

I prefer to remember our classic unbeaten partnership of 329 in Brisbane, three years earlier. Andrew Strauss had made 110 in our opening stand of 188. Trotty and I were similar in terms of the deliberation of our approach, but he was meticulous beyond reason. He loved the cadence of our batting until we declared just before tea on the final day.

We were 517–1. That was one hell of an achievement. The locals had voted with their feet, so the Gabba was colonized by the Barmy Army. One of the tabloid boys got a bit over-excited, compared it to England's World Cup win in 1966, and suggested that Trotty and I 'didn't just occupy the crease – they built holiday homes on it'. Even Graham Gooch wandered out to take a photograph of the scoreboard for posterity.

Strauss 110. Trott 135. Cook 235. England 517. Magic numbers.

Like most of us, Trotty learned on the job. He rarely

drank, unless it was in celebration at the end of a series, when he gave it a little nudge. He realized, very quickly, very early in his career, that his lifestyle had to be tailored to his ambitions as an elite professional.

There is a sharp dividing line between the pressure you put on yourself to excel and the pressure you put on yourself to be a good husband, father and teammate. Is there something about cricket, the long hours and extended absence from home, that makes suppressing things that bit more damaging? Probably.

Cricket is such a time-consuming game. Retirement, for many players, is challenging because the game leaves a void. We are unaccustomed to having a lot of downtime. It is not like a rugby or football player, who trains between two games a week. Our respite tends to come during matches, when the opposition is in the field, but even then, the variables of form preoccupy the mind.

I'm not qualified to talk about the intricacies of depression, or provide a clinical analysis of the condition, but any sport forces you into a negative space quite a lot of the time, because you invariably fail. Athletes in all disciplines have been more forthcoming about the strain in recent years; cricket has become more open in the decade or so since Marcus Trescothick laid himself bare.

In no particular order, Andrew Flintoff, Monty Panesar, Sarah Taylor, Graeme Fowler, Michael Yardy, Steve Davies, Graham Thorpe, Steve Harmison, Tim Ambrose and Iain O'Brien have all spoken about mental-health issues. In itself that's unsurprising, since research has suggested that, on average, around 15 per cent of elite athletes suffer similarly.

High achievers, high stakes, high pressure.

I wouldn't want to dwell on individuals, because that is personal territory and involves specialist knowledge. My issues were not of that magnitude, though when I was really struggling for runs, and dealing with the fallout from the Kevin Pietersen affair, I was not in a good place. I rarely argue with Alice, since we are not that type of couple, but I was taking out some of the pressure on her.

I felt alone, exposed. In that state of mind, it is easy to forget that strain also affects those closest to you. The ECB organize a box for players' families, and offer a crèche, but the elephant in the room is individual form. There is always someone whose partner is under pressure. Conversely, there is also someone whose loved one is absolutely flying, relishing life, scoring runs or taking wickets. The extremes of concern and joy make things complicated when they are expressed in close proximity.

It doesn't matter, in a way, that the wheel tends to turn. No one is a media darling for ever. Anyone who cannot contribute consistently is liable to fade away. Our families live our cricket, and deal with the consequences, without direct influence on the outcome. That's difficult when, understandably enough, they identify with your dreams, and are desperate for you to do well.

They offer comfort in the toughest of times. I reached my lowest point in the second Test against Sri Lanka in June 2014. We had a first-innings lead of 108, and my captaincy was fiercely criticized when we allowed Angelo Mathews, their captain, to accumulate 160 when the game was in the balance.

Angelo is a gutsy cricketer, with an ability to play a special innings. We were conscious of his potential to hurt us, and attempted to frustrate him when he was joined, with seven wickets down for 277, by Rangana Herath. Reasoning that the tail-ender was unlikely to score the runs required to set us a testing target, I spread the field for the first four or five balls every over, inviting the skipper to expose him.

The tactical strategy worked, to a degree, because Angelo nicked off a huge drive, which dropped an inch short of second slip. My mistake was in persisting too long with it; Herath made 48 before he was run out by Joe Root, and the Sri Lankans set us 350 to win.

I was first out, for 16, in that evening session on the fourth day. At the close we were five down, with only 57 on the board. Dear old Shane Warne was playing to the gallery by suggesting my leadership was 'horrific' and the worst he had ever seen. It was more of the same, sniping and toxicity, with an obvious subplot.

Thank goodness my family were with me that night. Alice had been following the scores, and drove up to Yorkshire that afternoon because she sensed I needed support. I was as close as I had ever been to quitting, drained physically and mentally. Conflicting images and messages rattled around my brain as I paced around our hotel room holding Elsie, who was barely three months old, in my arms.

I idly watched highlights from the opening day of Wimbledon as I lulled her to sleep, a comforting process with which any parent can identify. Alice urged me to stay with it, arguing that it was against my nature to give up. She was right. Stubborn to a fault, I didn't want to be known as a quitter. It was against everything that I had been brought up to believe and express.

Trevor Bayliss, the England coach, has a saying: whatever happens, the next morning the sun rises; you get up and get on with it. My sense of calmness and renewed purpose even survived a mortifying defeat when Jimmy Anderson, who had batted without scoring for eighty-one minutes during twenty overs in which Moeen Ali completed his maiden century, fended Shaminda Eranga to Herath at leg gully. Sri Lanka had won with a ball to spare.

I felt so badly for Jimmy, who, despite being named man of the series, was in tears during the post-match ceremonies. England's greatest bowler could not forgive himself for falling just short when his most singular achievement as a batsman was within reach. We might have been an odd couple when thrown together a decade earlier, but we have many things in common, including owing our promotion to the misfortune of others.

That tends to be the way of things in international cricket. I was first called up by England in 2005, when I was with the Academy squad at Loughborough, ironically training against reverse swing, a Pakistani speciality. I was indoors on the bowling machine before bowlers were introduced, to mind-blowing effect.

They used a ball with one pristine side and the other roughed up. It was doing all sorts, nigh on impossible to play. When I was pulled out and told to get to Multan because Michael Vaughan had injured his knee in the final warm-up match before the first Test, I momentarily panicked. I pleaded to be fed a diet of underarm deliveries, just so that I could get the feel of bat on ball again.

It was a surreal few days. It was the first time I'd heard my name on Radio 1, which was pretty cool for a twenty-one-year-old. I drove to Reading University to see Alice before submitting myself to the tender mercies of Pakistan Airways.

Within twenty minutes of reporting to the team hotel I was invited into the Harmison Arms.

Steve would suffer severe homesickness but here, in a hotel room that acted as the centre of our universe, he was in his element. He ensured I didn't have time to remain awe-struck at being alongside the Ashes heroes I had so recently watched on TV. I was quickly playing darts for the first time in my life and eating the sweets and snacks he had taken instead of his cricket gear. He basically travelled with his bat and his boots.

It was a very different experience, even before the horrors of the attack on the Sri Lankan team minibus sent the Pakistan team into enforced exile. On other tours, players splinter, visiting friends or restaurants. Here, we were all in it together, watching a lot of TV in team rooms. Culturally, we missed out, but to be honest visiting tourist sites loses its allure when you've had a four-hour practice session in 35-degree heat.

I didn't play on the three-Test tour, even when Andrew Strauss went home before the final match to attend the birth of his son Sam, but I was integrated immediately into the group. I might have been the rookie, in my first team meeting, but they wanted my insight into my Essex teammate Danish Kaneria, the right-arm leg-spinner who would eventually be banned for life for spot fixing.

Sport reflects the brittleness and uncertainty of life. I've never asked Marcus Trescothick about the illness which resulted in his departure from the 2006 tour of India and my unlikely Test debut. Our conversations tend to centre on the future, in the form of his coaching ambitions, rather than the past. I suppose it reflects the unspoken reality that one man's misfortune is another's opportunity.

When he returned home, citing a virus as a diversion from the terrors of what would eventually be diagnosed as clinical depression, I was on an England Lions tour of the West Indies. I'd scored 6 in the first innings of the initial unofficial Test at the Recreation Ground in Antigua when I received a tap on the shoulder from Peter Moores, our coach.

'Go and pack your bags. You and Jimmy are being called up to go and play in India.'

I'd never heard of Nagpur, our destination, and frankly dreaded the journey because Jimmy had abused me a fair old bit the previous September, when I got the treatment from the entire Lancashire team in a County Championship match at Chelmsford. I'd scored a double hundred against the Australians the previous week, and they informed me I was a posh boy who was 'strutting around'.

A bit harsh, and not entirely fair, but Jimmy gave me a particularly pungent send-off when he had me caught by Andrew Symonds for 19 in the second innings, after I'd made 64 first up. The memory was with me as we commandeered the team bus and headed to the beach, since we had time to kill before the evening flight.

We'd barely spoken on the tour and lay there, half pretending we were asleep. I thought I'd better break the ice, since we were about to fly halfway around the world and would spend the first seven hours of a two-day journey cooped up together in cattle class, on the way to London. It was a strange, short, exchange.

'You know that time you called me a c**t. Did you mean it?'

'Nah. I call everyone a c**t.'

'Oh, all right, then.'

With that we started chatting away, as you tend to do. It was the beginning of a beautiful friendship. The extent of the chance became clear in a Heathrow hotel during a twelve-hour stopover. I was flicking through Ceefax (ask your dad, kids,) got to page 340, the cricket page, and saw the headline 'Trescothick Flies Home'.

Up until that point, I couldn't really see a way in to a top six of Tres, Vaughan, Bell, Collingwood, Strauss and KP. I turned to Alice, who had popped over from uni, and said 'Oh, God. There's an outside chance of me playing here.' A twelve-hour stopover in Mumbai and two training sessions later, I was in.

Freddie Flintoff became captain when Vaughan finally lost the battle of his wounded knee. In what felt like a dream sequence, he saw me bat and announced: 'He's playing.' This wasn't great news for Matt Prior, who, as reserve wicketkeeper, was the only other realistic option for a place. Logic dictated that my status, as a specialist opener, gave me priority.

Wow. Here was Freddie, the big hitter, the hero who scared Australia, telling everyone I was his man. We would play together for three years before retirement from international cricket in 2010, following a year-long rehabilitation from knee surgery, broadened his horizons. Not for the last time, it felt as though I was turning the pages of a comic book, wondering what plot twist would next ambush the superhero. Life was not dull.

In this case the superhero clashed, rather predictably, with KP. It is rare for either of two alpha males to defer to the other, but if Freddie liked you, he stood by your side. He was a force of nature, a talismanic figure who loved laughing at his own jokes and drove himself to be a magnificent bowler by developing that elusive skill of hitting the back of a length quickly.

I look at him now, applying that natural determination to a hugely successful secondary career, and wonder whether he could have got more out of himself as a cricketer. He's a gym bunny, hasn't had a drink for something like four years, and is ripped to shreds, physically. He's ten kilos lighter than when he was a player.

That additional mass is the equivalent, for a bowler, of having forty kilos going through your knee and ankle. How much wear and tear would he have avoided had he maintained a slightly lower fighting weight? We'll never know, and, given his mocking self-promotion as 'a fat lad', we probably shouldn't ask. His legend is justifiably secure.

To give him his due, KP worked on his batting with greater intensity. He lacked Freddie's common touch, though the stereotype of the Northern lad who loves a pint was never entirely accurate. Freddie knew the power of his personality and remains a brilliant self-promoter. Good luck to the guy. He certainly helped me at a pivotal moment in my career.

I was one of three debutants in Nagpur, alongside Ian Blackwell and Monty Panesar. In one sense I had little to lose, because I was just off the plane. In another, as I walked out alongside Straussy, I knew I was about to confront the ultimate test of an English opening batsman, dealing with spin almost from the get-go.

The rhythm of batting in India is so different. Facing world-class spinners with men around the bat, especially once the ball loses its hardness, requires patience and focus. The subcontinent rarely offers the respite of an occasional nick through third man to get going, as is the case when you open in more accustomed circumstances, against pace bowling.

There's little certainty about conditions, but the process is regimented, which suited my character. Goochy captured the challenge perfectly, telling me 'you have the opportunity to set the game up'. I caught myself looking down at the three lions on my shirt in wonder a few times (my promotion was too quick for it to have been inscribed with my England number, 630), but did my job, being fourth out for 60, with the score on 136.

The fourth day began with the Indians threatening to field in casual clothes unless they were paid a 130-rupee laundry allowance. It ended with me unbeaten on 104, suitably grateful that Harbhajan Singh dropped a spooned return catch when I was on 70. For good measure I had received my first marriage proposal, scrawled on a piece of cardboard.

Alice was studying in Reading. I checked.

I scored only 17 and 2 in the second Test, which we lost, and missed the third in Mumbai, which we won, through illness. I was off and running. Though I tend to think the role is over-romanticized, because we will bat with the lower order if we do our job properly, Straussy was the first of my fifteen opening partners in Test cricket.

Since my sport is a statistical smorgasbord, someone has inevitably calculated that Sunil Gavaskar holds the record with nineteen. In human terms, the list forms an interesting case study of the collateral damage inflicted by the international game. It features different characters with contrasting strengths and weaknesses, united by the responsibility of providing firm foundations.

Disregarding dalliances with the likes of Vaughan, KP,

Trotty, Moeen Ali and Joe Root, it is largely a story of seeking Strauss Mark 2. Jarrod Kimber of ESPNcricinfo, who has rightly underlined the unfairness of the process, worked out that I had scored around 60 per cent of the runs in England's opening stands since our six-year partnership came to an end.

It's more nuanced than that. Over the past three or four years we took a strategic decision to play on home wickets that did a bit. There's no disrespect intended in that policy; Jimmy and Stuart Broad, principal beneficiaries, are extraordinary bowlers, whose ability to exploit traditional English conditions has enabled us to win Test matches.

The flipside is that with a brand new Dukes ball and a bit of grass on the wicket it became hard work for us to build an innings. The first twenty or thirty overs were tricky, especially given the level of scrutiny my less experienced partners were enduring. There were times I sensed their tension: they didn't have the leeway my longevity afforded me.

None of us are perfect, technically. Few sportsmen are so exposed to trial by slow motion and multiple-angled replay. Getting through the first cycle of Test appearances is fiendishly difficult, because there is no hiding place. Occasionally, as in the case of Michael Carberry in that train-wreck tour of Australia in 2014, a player is simply in the wrong place at the wrong time.

Once a flaw is identified it is worked on, coldly and with disconcerting effect. Alex Hales, employed for aggressive intent, became frustrated and couldn't duplicate his short-form impact. Ben Duckett struggled on tough turning wickets. Sam Robson and Keaton Jennings each scored hundreds without curing their problems outside off stump.

Adam Lyth looked terrific in scoring 107 against New Zealand in his second Test, on his home ground of Headingley, but struggled against Australia's fast bowlers in the subsequent Ashes series victory. My opening partnership with Mark Stoneman, which encompassed eleven matches, has the lowest average, 18.8 runs, in England's Test history.

But, again, statistics scratch the surface of the story. There is an enduring bond between opening partners, however brief or relatively unproductive the relationships. Shared experience helps to develop a unique form of friendships; Alice and I remain close to Mark and his wife Serene.

My instinctive reaction, when I first saw Haseeb Hameed in India in 2016, was, 'Blimey, this kid can bat.' I wasn't alone: Sachin Tendulkar offered him an audience and Virat Kohli predicted he would be a star in all forms of the game. Aged only nineteen, he scored 82 in the first Test at Rajkot and a half-century, batting with a badly broken thumb, in the second Test at Mohali.

Then . . . he fell off the face of the earth.

Technically, there is a hint of concern against short-pitched bowling. Temperamentally, there is a price to be paid for his obsessional approach, which carries the inherent danger of putting process before outcome. I have no inside knowledge, but sport has many examples of problems created by the emotional intensity of having a father as a coach. It is hard for the parent, too.

It is never nice to look down the wicket and see someone being consumed by their fears and neuroses. I have a lot of time for Nick Compton. Since he was the grandson of Denis Compton, a definitive post-war cricket hero, he bore the burden of the family name well. We played sixteen Tests together, in two spells. He helped us win in India in 2012 and scored a couple of excellent hundreds in New Zealand the following year, but the pressure eventually got to him.

Insecurity is insidious. Nick sought reassurance from too many people, and it worked against him, with his natural intensity. His explosive release of tension after completing his first Test hundred showed how much it meant to him, but you could see the game eating him alive. He took a six-week break after his final series against Sri Lanka, helped Middlesex win the County Championship in unforgettable fashion, and now combines photography with commercial and media activity.

Fitting, that, because cricket is a freeze-frame image of who we are. Why do we do it? Here's a hint . . .

5. The Zen of Opening the Batting

The effective distance between batsman and bowler when a ball is delivered is approximately 17.68 metres. When Shoaib Akhtar releases it at around 160 kph, there is fractionally less than four-tenths of a second in which to react. Whatever you do, don't blink, because that will waste a tenth of a second.

This means that, in the time it takes for a hummingbird to flap its wings about forty times, or a beam of light to cover in the region of 75,000 miles, you must read the ball out of the hand, judge the line and length, and detect, if possible, the degree of revolution. Talk about multitasking. It's not the moment to realize you left your keys in the car.

Not all bowlers are the same, of course. There's no one way to do what they do. Spinners are the three-card-trick merchants of the game. Sometimes, you can't pick them, no matter how long or how intently you study the video. You need human contact to read any clues in body language. You watch in real time to see which way the ball is revolving. No matter how good the bowler is, he can't release the ball so that it spins in an entirely different direction halfway down the wicket.

It's not like being in the nets, where you have the freedom to play attacking shots against slower bowlers. You are simply not going to run down the wicket and try to hit them out of the park the moment you see them, because of the pressure of the situation. To play spin well, you attack on your terms, and that requires trust in your ability to defend well.

Batting at the top of the order is an expression of individuality. When you're young, it is the equivalent of being the kid in the football team who plays centre forward. Opening is regarded as a bit of a status symbol, but as you progress the better players fancy going in at three or four. I had a spell, coming in first wicket down against Pakistan in the summer of 2006, and quite enjoyed it.

The openers' co-operative is convened in the manner of the goalkeepers' union. We are united by the disadvantage of fronting up when the bowler is fast and fresh, and the ball is hard and new. There are unspoken responsibilities to those who follow us to the crease. Our failure increases the likelihood of their failure; our success gives them breathing room.

We tend not to be show ponies. We have the hardiness of National Hunt racehorses, rather than the five-furlong flashiness of thoroughbreds on the flat. We're not dull, but we make a living through dependability. We live for the days when calmness settles, and something intangible suggests the scene is set for profit and plunder.

Such an experience also forms part of baseball's mystique, where batters deal with the deceptive angles and speeds of a ball thrown from a mound sixty feet away. Batters who have 0.413 seconds to react to a 100 mph fastball speak of 'feel', an instinct that defies deep analysis. It's a hard sport, one that doesn't encourage hippy-dippy romanticism, but the occurrence is commonly described as entering another dimension.

There's a lot of talk about mental toughness, but what does that really mean? To me, it involves wringing the maximum out of your natural ability at the most important moments on the biggest stages. Opening is suited to the more literal thinker, the individual who can place an innings, good or bad, in a box and hide the key. Failure must never be allowed to fester.

I took joy in finding the rhythm of my batting, the bass line that set the tempo. The job wasn't easy (that word rarely features in the vocabulary of any professional athlete), but it was occasionally effortless. I have a lot of moving parts to my technique, so I've got to get my hands and feet working in harmony.

A lot can go wrong in those four-tenths of a second. A lot must go right. That synchronicity is very, very enjoyable. You know, when you get to between 30 and 40, that a big score is on the cards. Suddenly, time accelerates, almost into double motion. Those are the occasions you look up at the clock and are surprised to see it is only ten minutes until the first drinks break.

Where did those last fifty minutes go? You can't really remember them, break them down into bite-size chunks for comfortable consumption. They've just happened. You have a drink, take on any messages delivered through the twelfth man, and go again. You're preoccupied by the practicality of batting, the actions that speak louder than any words.

Suddenly, something reminds you, from out of nowhere, to focus on the clock. Only five minutes to lunch? Another hour has disappeared. You can vaguely remember specific shots, mood swings and momentum shifts, but you concentrate on cashing in. There will be other days when you don't have the mojo.

Being out of form is like trying to push a concrete wall away when it is closing in and threatening to crush you, like some sort of fiendish ancient trap. You are out of sync, out of the pattern. Something isn't quite right, and your brain cannot compute. That's when the clock face seizes up. Time passes terribly slowly. It's hard work; half an hour seems like four.

This is going to sound weird, but the art of concentration is in being able to concentrate, and then not concentrate on concentrating. I did so through the routine I've described previously. Play the shot, scratch the line, walk away. Sometimes I'd go down the track and indulge in gentle gardening. Most times I would head in the direction of square leg.

I'd be digging myself in. Look around at the crowd, allow the bowler to have his say. If I'd been beaten, or had an ugly hack, I might wander down and have a chat with the non-striker, whoever it may be. We'd smile, I'd admit 'that was a shit shot' and the situation would be defused. I'd return to the crease, having rationalized what I had done, and let it go.

The sequence probably takes twenty seconds. I'd be consciously calm by the time the bowler turned from his mark to run in. We go again, and again, and again. When you are in form, it is metronomic. When you are out of form, you are fighting yourself. You start to worry about your foot position, how you've bent your knee, all the stuff you shouldn't be thinking about. If you can't get rid of that, you're in a skid that's extremely difficult to correct.

Maintaining concentration during the entirety of an interval is impossible. If I was set at lunch, I'd take my pads off, have a bite to eat and have a variety of conversations, some cricket-related, others inconsequential. I'd switch back into game mode six or seven minutes before resumption, when the mental checklist would once again be employed.

It's all about the maintenance of routine. I batted, without fail, on arriving at the ground. That might merely be facing underarm bowling from coaches, but I would always be wearing pads. Some players – Hashim Amla, for example – don't bother to wear pads, but we are all, at heart, creatures of habit. I have never forgotten being pulled up by Graham Gooch at the age of nineteen, when I netted wearing only a front pad.

'Would you do that in a game?' he barked. Obviously not. 'Well, don't ever do that again.' It was one of those 0.1 per cent moments that matter in professional sport, a reminder of acceptable standards that lead to marginal gains. We went on to develop a routine in which I'd ask him to throw down at me using the dog-stick to stimulate sharpness. It was our way of making sure we had done everything possible to prepare properly.

I used to enjoy my time as captain once I'd completed the formalities of the toss, especially if we were batting. Ten minutes were taken up with three interviews, with Sky, Channel 5 and BBC radio, leaving another ten or so for me to pad up, and be prepared. That gives the inner voice less scope to start yapping in your ear. The bowlers tap you on the back for postponing the workload, wish you good luck, and you're off.

There's not exactly a randomness about success and failure, but it pays to be pragmatic. It helps to remind yourself that sometimes the odds are simply not in your favour. Test bowlers are paid to take wickets and, by definition, they are the best in their country. They make the most of beneficial conditions.

I've not been out to that many unplayable deliveries, but in about 99 per cent of dismissals you might have done something differently. Some mistakes come with the territory: you could have been drawn into the new ball and nicked off, because it behaved more dangerously than a ball that's thirty-five overs old.

I was once told that Mike Brearley, the captain's captain, used to hum a Rachmaninov quartet when he was batting. My mental musical tastes are less highbrow, easy-listening earworms produced by the likes of Razorlight or Queen. I don't sing along, but occasionally hum a sequence, or work through the lyrics. Familiar songs in my head allow me to maintain rhythm.

Occasionally I remember scenes from certain films or have a sudden appreciation of the noise of the crowd. That's not a great sign, because it suggests the bubble of concentration has been punctured. My instinct is to identify the problem, accept what has happened, reorganize and reset. You will never fight it, because the brain can take you to random places. When you are playing well, you soon return to reality. When you are not in good nick, you're struggling for control.

That's when easy conversation with the bloke at the other end is important. It brings you back to the moment, delivers a reminder that it's the two of you against the world. It is a marriage of sorts. You get to know each other's funny little ways and learn to adjust. The manipulation of small targets is a common way to cope. Trotty, for instance, compulsively built his innings in five-run blocks.

Each to his own. The problem comes when errors are contagious. I'm fascinated by the psychology of batting collapses, even though it is one of the hardest phenomena to discuss openly, because doing so can be regarded as an admission of collective weakness. A dressing room doesn't usually have a Corporal Jones, barking out, 'Don't panic, Captain Mainwaring.' It is inclined to be eerily quiet.

Supporters share the paranoia. Whoever they follow, they are convinced their team is more prone to collapse than most. It's illogical, since with the occasional exception, we are all pretty much of a muchness. It's difficult to explain, but cricket isn't an academic exercise, an application of Artificial Intelligence. It is a game played by human beings, who are susceptible to mood and momentum.

It is simple to identify the problem, by the repetition of common sense. Don't lose wickets in clusters. That might appear to be a statement of the obvious, but to recap, that's exactly why I was immediately apologetic after being dismissed in my last Test innings. Joe Root and I had lazily put the onus on Jonny Bairstow and Ben Stokes to rebuild. They were subjected to unnecessary pressure.

Here's the way things can go: you've got a steady partnership, forty or fifty or so, and you're at the other end when your partner gets out. Suddenly you've got a new face in, and for no apparent reason you feel differently. Is it pressure? It is certainly a trick of the mind. Logically, you don't immediately lose shape or form. You know you've been batting well, but your mind is telling you that you can't get out, that you must not get out.

Those horrible negative words, can't, won't, mustn't, couldn't, are at the forefront of the brain. Predictably, you get out, leaving your teammate, alarmed by the sudden shift in momentum, to struggle through the hardest period of any innings, the first ten to fifteen balls. He succumbs, and before you know it, you've lost three wickets in less than thirty minutes.

The collapse is on. The opposition have their tails up. Bowlers are running in harder, with greater intensity. The fielders are sharper, more eager. It's a hard task to shackle the game, stop it from sprinting away from you, especially in Test cricket, where the players are better, tougher, stronger. It's like a supercharged tug of war.

You can never win a Test match in a single session, but you can certainly go a long way towards losing one. A palpable air of tension descends on the dressing room. Later, in the debrief, you may conduct a thoughtful review, and suggest it might not have been the best policy to go quiet and retreat into your shells. Yet neither is it the time or the place for bluff and bluster.

The last thing you need, when you've gone from 50–0 to 50–3 in what feels like a heartbeat, is someone blathering on, in jolly-hockey-sticks mode. You need a partnership. You're desperate for that partnership. Yet something seems to be happening with every ball. It's like watching an avalanche start to roll down a mountain. This is something bigger than any of us.

There are plenty of England collapses that belong in cricket's dungeon. Six wickets lost for three runs presented Australia with a win at Melbourne in 1990. England lost their last eight wickets for twenty-six against Pakistan two years later, after Graham Gooch and Michael Atherton had scored 135 and 76, respectively. (Remarkably, they still somehow managed to win.)

We replaced New Zealand at the bottom of the world rankings by squandering our last eight wickets for thirty-nine against them at the Oval in 1999. Shane Warne seized the bragging rights when he was instrumental in England losing nine wickets for sixty at Adelaide in 2006. Oh, and in case you are wondering, regrets, I've had more than a few.

My team lost six wickets for nine runs in ten overs at Brisbane in 2013 and compounded the problem by losing our last seven batsmen for forty-nine in the second innings. We lost seven for forty-three in a defeat by South Africa at Centurion in 2016. We were 27–9 in the first Test of my last series in New Zealand, at Eden Park in Auckland in March 2018. That was so bad it was like an out-of-body experience.

It was the first day–night Test in the country, played with a pink ball in swinging conditions. I was first out to Trent Boult for 5, with the total on 6, having batted as if my feet were encased in cement. Aggers, in the commentary box, offered the caveat that I had been lambing a couple of weeks previously. To maintain the rural theme, Trevor Bayliss, our coach, was closer to the mark in suggesting we were 'like deer caught in headlights'.

It was horrible. A couple more bad shots, a couple of good deliveries, and we were done. It seemed that no one in the team was good enough to stand up to them. The game was pretty much over before it had begun. We could talk around the issues by suggesting it was the result of a communication breakdown, but essentially, we had given their bowlers an unnecessarily easy day.

They would have come into the match with the mindset of being prepared to endure ninety overs in the field, six and a half hours of hard work. Their main guys would have been steeling themselves to bowl twenty-five overs. That hurts, incrementally, as the day wears on. Our batsmen failed to do their basic collective job: to hang around long enough so that the opposition bowlers tire, and there is less pace on the ball. Get them into their fourth or fifth spells and take advantage.

The lower order can do a lot of damage in that situation. I loved batting with Jimmy Anderson as a night watchman, because he was so diligent in his work, and visibly determined not to let me down. He listened to every word I said, which was a novelty. I didn't bat that many times with Stuart Broad, but our partnership in the Boxing Day Test at Melbourne in 2017 was a blast.

We led by only 46, with two wickets left, when he arrived at the crease. He knew his role was to drive home our advantage by building a partnership, and he willingly wore a couple of short-pitched deliveries. My role was to keep him sane and remind him of certain realities. The problem is that whenever tail-enders play a couple of fantastic shots – in Broady's case a pull through square leg and a sumptuous back-foot drive – they think they're Don Bradman.

Our plan was to make sure our lead grew incrementally, in batches of five runs. We worked on the theory that reaching a series of small targets leads to big gains. I managed to keep him in check, focused on the job in hand, so that we put on 100 in eighteen overs before Usman Khawaja was adjudged to have cleanly caught a top-edged pull off Pat Cummins. Broady made 56 from 63 balls and helped me to be 244 not out at the end of a day in which I passed Mahela Jayawardene, Shivnarine Chanderpaul and Brian Lara in the all-time run list.

Jimmy was out for 0 from the first ball he faced the following morning, and I carried my bat for the first time in Test cricket. Only two of my thirty-three Test centuries have been more substantial, 263 against Pakistan in Abu Dhabi in

2015, and 294 against India at Edgbaston in 2011. Funnily enough, the principle of that sort of achievement resonates across sports.

The Saracens guys were fascinated by the underpinning philosophy of daddy hundreds when the Essex squad visited them, to share ideas and experiences. Their team meeting was based on the imposition and continuation of dominance, since they were in the process of becoming England's best rugby team. Specifically, they wanted to pick my brains about the Ashes tour of 2010–11, when I scored a record 766 runs at an average of 127.66.

Firstly, they had to understand its context. The unbeaten 235 in Brisbane, in the first Test, was my first double hundred. It had taken me nearly five years, and a lot of growing up, to learn how to make it. The highest score in my previous thirteen Test centuries had been 173, against Bangladesh in Chittagong the previous March.

Opening the batting is a bit like walking in the Himalayas. The air is thin and you're climbing constantly. It is easy to make mistakes through inexperience. When I first started playing, scoring a hundred was such a big thing. Once you reached three figures, you felt the weight of the achievement lift, and switched off a little. It was almost 'job done'. It was a goal to be ticked off, rather like reaching the requisite level in a fitness test.

It took longer to identify the importance of batting for longer periods. I had to learn to deal with the troublesome Gimp on my shoulder, whose negativity was making me expend too much mental energy. With him in his cage, I had more resources to devote to my batting. I began to realize that a big hundred, 160 or 170, provided greater insurance against the bad days, when I would be out cheaply to the new ball.

The biggest opening partnership I had was 373, with Nick Browne against Middlesex at Chelmsford in June 2017. It fell just short of the overall Essex record of 403, set by Goochy and Paul Prichard for the second wicket in 1990. That was all my fault; Ollie Rayner had me caught at slip when I'd made 193. Nick went on to score 221, and, with Simon Harmer taking fourteen wickets, we won a rain-affected match by an innings with two minutes to spare.

In psychological terms, I was colour-coded as a 'cool blue', a so-called introverted thinker. I was depicted as being very analytical and had to be aware of the danger of overthinking, when the tendency was to become too mechanistic in my batting. In another simple metaphor, used by Mark Bawden, England's psychologist, I was characterized as an 'assassin'. My strength was my ability to stay within my bubble and utilize repeatable skill.

So, in tennis terms, I was Bjorn Borg. KP was John McEnroe, a 'yellow' and extroverted 'feeler'. He had a 'warrior' mentality, emotional and aggressive. Players can switch between the modes, as in the case of a confrontational fast bowler like Stuart Broad having occasionally to think a batsman out, but the common denominator is the development of the ability to remain in the moment.

Scoring a hundred is almost arbitrary. You play as well to get to 99 as you do to get to 101. It means little in the run of the game, but everything, psychologically and practically, to the batsman. In our enclosed, statistically driven world, you are judged on centuries, not near misses. I was once told no England player has scored more nineties, but to be honest, it is such an arcane record I haven't bothered to check. It's probably true, because I have played more games than anyone else.

Would it change things? Obviously not, and that's one of the stupid things about cricket. The only time I felt I messed up unforgivably in such circumstances was against Australia at Lord's in 2015 when I attempted a big drive and played on to the leg stump, off the inside edge, to Mitch Marsh when I'd made 96. It was a schoolboy error, a submission to the situation.

I was spewing about it because I allowed myself to be undone by the proximity of the second new ball. I wanted my century as insurance against a delivery with my name on it. If I had played the same way as I had for the previous six hours I would have achieved it, but I succumbed to outside influence rather than backing myself.

It was a terrible mental mistake, at a critical juncture. You didn't want to be inside my head in the endless seconds when I slumped forward on one knee in disbelief at what I had done and stared at the ground as if inviting it to swallow me whole. That was a long walk back, to sympathetic applause I didn't merit. I had failed a basic test, in being controlled by the environment.

Is it any wonder superstition is rife in cricket, when failure can be so infuriating? I've lost count of the number of times I have sat on a dressing-room chair and wasn't allowed to move. If someone does so, and someone gets out, you're like, 'Urghh . . . what?' It is almost a betrayal. Some people, including Trotty, Jimmy and Graeme Swann, used to just lie there.

Swanny wouldn't watch many balls live. He'd be on his

back, in front of the TV. My kit used to be an organized mess, Trotty's was immaculately laid out, like a still-life painting, but Swanny's was a public health hazard. He had his lucky pink shorts, which were white until something leaked colour in the wash, and bowled in the same cycling shorts for days on end.

The undercurrent of such eccentricity is the inherent seriousness of Test cricket. I spoke in the previous chapter of my opening partners. Some had a technical fault, exacerbated by a perceived inability to adapt under scrutiny. Did that mean they weren't quite good enough at that stage in their careers, and should have been allowed to incubate in county cricket? Did they get a raw deal?

It's debatable. But one thing that cannot be challenged is the scorebook. When you strip away the extraneous stuff, the noise and the political posturing, if you are scoring a lot of runs you won't be dropped. Some people who feel hard done by look for the excuse that they weren't treated properly, or given enough opportunity.

Sorry, but if they had scored four centuries in their seven or eight matches, they would have played more. I realize that sounds dispassionate, callous even, but that is the harsh reality of professional sport. Produce with occasionally undue haste or repent at your leisure. The cut-throat nature of Test cricket is what makes it so hard, so intense, and ultimately so rewarding.

There can be anomalies. James Taylor, for instance, spent a long time outside the England set-up because Andy Flower and the selectors came to a certain view on him. It was nothing personal and didn't reflect badly on Andy, but it took a long time for them to be convinced James had the skillset required to progress from being a prolific county cricketer.

A teenage prodigy at Leicestershire, some had deemed him too small, though he was taller than Sachin Tendulkar. In technical terms, he had a dominant bottom hand, which led to his working the ball across the line to the leg side with a twist of the wrist. At the highest level, this is seen as an exploitable flaw.

Another coach, a different set of selectors, could have come to a contrasting decision, and trusted a natural talent. Conversely, James could have been promoted prematurely and been found out. Ultimately, after about three years on the fringe, he was given his chance, and excelled in seven Test matches before, at the age of twenty-six, fate intervened.

He was forced to retire after being diagnosed with a serious but rare congenital heart condition known as arrhythmogenic right ventricular cardiomyopathy (ARVC), which can be fatal during vigorous exercise. He described the sensation of having his heart shocked back into a normal rhythm by an implanted defibrillator as like being hit by a ball delivered at 100 mph.

He has since been appointed as a full-time independent England selector, so he will understand the onerous nature of the process. I've been in selection meetings, judging batsmen with as much objectivity as I can, when the sense of responsibility has been almost overpowering. Decisions are hard, sometimes horrible, and often final.

It is sometimes easier to judge a bowler than a batsman; that's why they seem to have fewer games in which to prove themselves. If they bowl thirty overs in each innings, across three or four Tests, you get a fair idea of the parameters of their potential. A batsman, in the same time frame, can get out unluckily to two or three very good deliveries. The temptation is always to offer another chance.

Whether that's deserved is open to judgement. As captain I've been in selection meetings where we're not exactly ending a bloke's career, but we are giving it a big old dent. I know what a struggling player is going through, the fears and frustrations he is trying to contain, because I have been there myself.

6. In the Bush

A condemned man is supposed to enjoy a hearty last meal, but my dinner seemed flavourless, a nutritional necessity rather than a source of pleasure. It had nothing to do with the food at the team hotel near Tower Bridge; the palate of a struggling batsman cannot be teased, even by a kitchen staffed with Michelin-starred chefs. He is desensitized, from his taste buds to his toes.

It might almost have been a subconscious act of self-sabotage, but after the table had been cleared I sat there alone, flicking through a newspaper. Sure enough, I was being nailed as beyond my sell-by date. I had lasted only seven deliveries in the first innings of the third Test against Pakistan, and my time was assumed to be up.

It was the evening of Thursday, 19 August 2010. I was 0 not out, England were 6 for the loss of Andrew Strauss in the second innings, and I would be walking out at the Oval with Jimmy Anderson on the third morning. Things were so bad Jimmy had sacked me as his unofficial batting buddy.

As I headed for the lifts, I passed Mark Bawden, who was having a drink with a friend. Months later, he would tell me I looked as if I had the weight of the world on my shoulders. 'You all right?' he asked. Apparently, I smiled thinly. 'Well, not really,' was my deadpan response. 'I'm about to go and play my last innings for England tomorrow.'

With that, I walked off, mentally calculating the worthiness of my international career. I had scored twelve Test centuries to that point, not bad but no protection when you can't buy a run in a long, hot and wet summer, where the ball moves more than usual. I was deep in the bush, my shorthand for being psychologically gone.

I went back to my room and lay on the bed, staring at the ceiling in my five-star cell. There, amidst a jumble of images, I acknowledged the magnitude of my mistake nine months earlier, when I'd modified my technique with the intention of enjoying long-term success against Australia. I changed my trigger movements and became very rigid.

I have a lot of movement in my usual technique, with a double backlift. In layman's terms, my hands start the trigger. My feet then move, my weight goes back, and I go back and across towards the stumps. My front leg floats, so that if the ball is short, I have the flexibility to push off it. If the ball is full, I can plant it.

I had developed what I called the Jacques Kallis method, named after the South African all-rounder. Again, in basic terms, that involved pressing forward with my right foot first, before going back and across with my left. I had my bat tucked in very straight and waited for the ball to come. It worked initially. I scored 118 against South Africa in Durban on Boxing Day 2009, and made two centuries, 173 and 109 not out, in my first Test tour as captain, in Bangladesh.

It wasn't pretty, and the results were ugly. By the time I fell into a fitful sleep that Thursday night, I had decided to revert to my old technique. I would play naturally and aggressively. I would not die wondering. I would take quiet inspiration from Paul Collingwood, and his pugnacious innings at Trent Bridge.

There is always one player under pressure for his place in

an England batting line-up, and it was Colly's turn in 2008. He had gone twenty-three innings without a Test century and hadn't reached fifty in any form of cricket in that wet summer when he joined Kevin Pietersen at the crease. Michael Vaughan, sitting next to me on the balcony, murmured, 'Fuck me, if Colly gets runs here it will be one of the great achievements.'

Colly ran down the wicket to reach his hundred with a six and was last out for 135 following a brilliant fifth-wicket stand with KP, who succeeded Vaughan as captain in the aftermath of a series defeat clinched by Graeme Smith's retaliatory unbeaten 154. He played forcefully, with the body shape and fluidity that so often signals new-found freedom.

I took note of his resilience in producing the big innings when he needed it most. It chimed with another performance earlier that year, when Andrew Strauss was popularly assumed to be playing for his Test career in New Zealand. Distracted and struggling to sleep, he reached his lowest point in the first innings at Napier, when he batted at three and was caught in the gully, off debutant Tim Southee, for 0.

He had dinner that evening with his wife Ruth and told her he was playing his last Test match. Ironically, in a delicate situation where offering advice to a teammate can feel intrusive, Colly provided unlikely impetus by telling him to concentrate on his natural game, the pull and cut shots. Straussy scored 177, set up a 121-run win and was England captain within a year.

What did I have to lose? I reached the conclusion I would rather play a massive drive and nick off, than briefly delay an inevitable dismissal by defending obsessively. It was a good pitch, and I had been fortunate to survive an edge through the slips the previous evening. I resolved not to make what had become a familiar mistake, in failing to get forward, and being trapped on the crease. I hit the first ball of the day, outside off stump, through midwicket for four. The shackles were off.

My footwork was sharper, my form more fluent. Though I edged a couple, I was 76 not out at lunch, and dominating what would be a partnership of 116 with Jonathan Trott. In an eerie foretaste of what was to come nine years later, I reached my century in bizarre fashion, when Mohammad Asif, the bowler, returned the ball over my head for four overthrows.

That 110 was enough to secure my place on the subsequent Ashes tour, where Bawds gave me a book called *The Confidence Gap* by Russ Harris, an exiled English psychologist and life coach whose CV includes stints as a stand-up comedian, sex therapist, filmmaker and novelist. It used the concept of Acceptance and Commitment Therapy to introduce me to the Gimp, who had so often been sitting malevolently on my shoulder.

I have a natural aversion to motivational mumbo-jumbo but this was a little different. I didn't read more than twenty pages but it was enough to set me thinking. I realized self-doubt was a common thread, linking someone as externally resolute as me to a supposedly supreme example of self-confidence such as President Obama. Human beings are apparently hard wired to think negatively; it is a basic survival instinct.

How, and why, could that be related to cricket? I mulled it over for a couple of days. Then it was off to a pub in Adelaide, to complete a conversation with Bawds that had started, very unsteadily, at the back of the team bus on the way to

Potchefstroom for a warm-up match against South Africa A, a little less than a year earlier.

I can say this now, because he is a trusted adviser who has my complete respect, but on that day he looked like a competition winner. Slightly overweight, glasses, a geek sent from central casting. No one had seen him before yet there he was, trying to negotiate the invisible minefield of seating arrangements on the bus. Everyone, coaches and players, has their own spot.

Fortunately, we had taken only twelve players; I was twelfth man because of a back twinge and was at the back of the bus, to the left. Since Jimmy and Swanny were off duty, there was space to the right of me for the hour-long journey. Bawds plonked himself down and, since I don't really listen to music on headphones, I steeled myself for polite conversation.

He was nervous, a little too eager, as he immediately outlined his thoughts on the relevance of his trade. To be honest, I was standoffish. I knew the advantages of training the brain but had never really thrown myself into it. I preferred the more literal benefits of a biceps curl, bench press or squat in the gym.

The theory of sports psychology was introduced in Under-19 training camps, but I had still to be convinced of its practical application. That wasn't a reflection on Bawds's professionalism; scepticism is invariably deep rooted in sport. Some of the rah-rah, happy-clappy slogans passed off as leadership maxims in the corporate world would, frankly, be laughed out of an international dressing room.

I played the role of slightly sour old pro. We were about to pull up to the ground when I presented the psychologist with a challenge: 'I want to have more confidence. I want to feel able to back myself more. When you've watched me work, come back with something that is relevant to me, not token bullshit.' With hindsight, it was probably no surprise he confided to friends: 'Crikey. He's going to be hard work.'

I probably hid my self-doubt better than most. The guy who is struggling, deep in the bush, usually gives himself away. He has an almost hollow-eyed expression, the vacant stare of someone who is searching, worrying, losing trust in himself. He doesn't consciously detach himself from the group, but there is a subtle difference in outlook and approach.

Sometimes, the intensity of international cricket acts like a depth charge. A newly promoted player sustains his county form through a heady mixture of euphoria and adrenaline. Then reality is detonated. His faults are analysed by the opposition, the intensity of accountability builds, and confidence is hammered. Before he knows it, the international game has beaten him.

Sam Robson is a case in point. I was very impressed when I first saw him at close quarters. He was well organized, gutsy. He scored what was to be a solitary Test century in his second appearance against Sri Lanka in 2014 but was quickly worked out in the subsequent series against India by Bhuvneshwar Kumar, an English-style bowler who could swing the ball both ways.

That was puzzling, since Sam had faced similar bowlers, operating at around 80 or 81 mph, for Middlesex. Generally, new players are surprised by the extra pace and bounce of international cricket, since the ball in the county game comes through lower, between knee roll and hip, but he kept getting out in the same way. He was under pressure for his place on the winter tour in the last Test at the Oval.

I sensed him alongside me as we were going through final preparations on that glass-fronted dressing-room balcony. I looked out of the corner of my eye and saw, to my alarm, that he was transfixed by a TV screen along the corridor, which was showing his dismissals in sequence. It was almost as if his fate was sealed by auto-suggestion. He got out in familiar fashion and was unfortunately dropped.

My rudimentary understanding of my fear of failure was expanded by Bawds on an Ashes tour that began with the familiar ritual of a serious night out after getting off the plane in Perth. We had a couple of hours' sleep before, apart from Straussy – our captain and token grown-up – we reported for action at 6 p.m. The group straggled back to the hotel between 3 and 5 a.m.

Spare the sermons, because this was team bonding in its purest form. Without exception, we were running in the park at 11 a.m. that day. A snapshot from the session remains one of my favourite photographs; it is obvious we are hanging, but everyone is committed to putting the hard yards in. A cricket team isn't formed in a pub, but good habits and practices can be confirmed there.

No one had been less forthcoming to our team psychologist than me, but over ninety minutes or so I opened up to him for the first time in that bar in Adelaide. I was honest about my battles with myself. Everyone talked about my mental strength and thought I had cracked the most difficult aspect of the game, but I had big doubts each time I went out to bat.

It was strange. For someone who consciously struggled to articulate deeper thoughts and personal motivations, the words flowed like a torrent. I admitted to walking out thinking,

'I don't want to be here today. I can't be bothered with the effort of scoring runs.' That inner voice would tell me: 'We're on a green seamer. It's not flat, it's not your day. They're going to get you out.'

I had issues with public speaking and was astonished to find in the book that someone as accomplished as Obama, a new president at the time whose speeches were characterized by their fluency and emotional impact, had admitted to underlying unease. 'Is it normal?' I asked Bawds. 'It can't be, surely?'

It was.

We talked about the private trials, during the night before and on the morning of a game. I confessed to an ache, deep in the gut. A poached egg on toast for breakfast felt like it had the consistency of cardboard. I relied on my natural stubbornness to get through the first half hour of an innings, when I would settle down, but the anxiety never truly left me.

When I was out cheaply, I had too much time to think, because my chance to atone might take two or three days to arrive. I maintained the façade of strength and imperturbability, but the game regularly beat me up. My life as a batsman was black and white: if I scored runs, I was a success; if I didn't, I was a failure.

I just offloaded. Bawds explained I had become consumed by what I couldn't do, rather than dwelling on what I could do, what I had done. He sought to reconnect me, remind me of the virtues that had made me a good player. Everyone suffers from fear and self-doubt. My values, my love of family and trust in friends, were still strong. My priority was to reset and rebuild my relationship with myself.

Bawds asked what I wanted to achieve. That involved

coming to terms with the facts of an athlete's life. The nerves would always be there. Why waste energy trying to fight them? It sounded so simple and basic. I confessed that I longed to be free, to push aside the negative thoughts and be able to concentrate on the most important thing, the ball coming towards me.

Commit and watch the ball.

I wanted to be decisive. I wanted my battle to be not with myself, but with the opposition collectively and the bowlers individually. I couldn't go on being stuck in the crease, neither forward nor back, not committed to a defensive shot or an attacking flourish. I was half-hearted, unresponsive and unsatisfied.

Bawds asked me to expand on my feelings, to explain what I experienced when I was at my most confident. I answered flippantly but revealed a central truth. I felt most secure in bed, the night before an innings. It was my refuge; nothing could get me there. Though Alice stayed with me from time to time, I was usually alone. There were no distractions.

I felt at peace, savoured the silence. It was the lull before the storm. Bawds stimulated my imagination by suggesting that in those moments of respite I should start to write down who I wanted to be, what I wanted to do, the following day. How did I want to bat, knowing that the nerves would still be there, nibbling at my stomach lining? The sense of liberation was immediate.

I just want to score runs.

I want to be able to clear my mind, so I can concentrate on the ball.

I want to be decisive, go out there with my shoulders back.

I want to leave the ball well.

I want to fight.

Bawds told me to go through the checklist when that dread came over me. I added technical details to the mantra, relating to individual bowlers and distinctive situations. To give a specific example, I reminded myself to open up to an inswinging bowler, to concentrate on hitting the ball in certain areas, rather than being obsessed by playing straight.

It may sound almost pedestrian, but it worked for me. Two days later, I scored a century in the Adelaide warm-up game and felt renewed. Sometimes I would read the piece of paper containing my inner thoughts, screw it up and throw it in the bin. Other times I would take it to the ground, secrete it in my kit and study it when those familiar doubts began to bite.

Psychologically, Bawds felt I had forgotten what made me successful. My immediate response was to suggest my unnecessarily flawed technique didn't allow me to do so. The aim of playing straighter, being more still at the crease, might have worked on flat wickets in Bangladesh, but as soon as the ball moved, I needed greater dexterity.

When it nips about you have to ride it, adjust your hands. I was so rigid I was nicking it, with hard hands, to the slips or gully. I was trapped between theory and practice. I kept finding the fielder, banging balls at mid-on and mid-off. I had lost that intrinsic skill of being able to work the gap. I needed not to improvise, as such, but to rediscover the balance between risk and reward.

As a team we began to focus on what Andy Flower described as our super-strengths. These were definitive aspects of our talents, that separated us from the rest. Mine, as a batsman, were the consistency of the cut shot and the pull shot. How had I adapted those strengths as my career had progressed?

My leg-side play was efficient. If they bowled short at me, I didn't get out that often and generally hit the average ball for four. If they bowled straight, at the line of middle stump, I wasn't hitting the boundary as often as I had when I turned up on the scene. Certainly, in those early days, anyone who bowled at my legs was punished.

It was time to confront the Gimp, the imaginary tormentor who had been on my shoulder since childhood. He had grown with me from those games in the back garden, where he'd whispered idly about the shame of losing to my brothers. At that stage in our lives, though, he was a little more innocent, markedly less intense.

Rationalizing my relationship with self-doubt was the key to the longevity of my international career. I stopped stubbornly fighting it, grinding away at it. I knew the Gimp would continue to play devil's advocate and attempt to sour any success. He's a cheeky bastard who won't leave you alone, a cartoon figure who dusts himself down and springs back at you when you've punched him a thousand times.

Everyone has one.

It had taken eight years, from 2003, to understand him. I accepted him without welcoming him. It's no longer a case of flight or fight. There are days when I'm better than him and days when I go to bed angry because he has beaten me. He will never stop telling me I've lost it, that everyone will notice when I don't get runs tomorrow.

I've gone through a lot as a cricketer, managed to deliver decent results under intense pressure. I had a clearer mind, a rediscovered ability to concentrate completely. By focusing solely on the ball, and the conditions, instead of being deflected by self-imposed distractions, I began to enjoy the battle of the game of cricket. It was engrossing, fulfilling.

That doesn't mean to say Bawds and I agreed on everything. His insistence that it didn't matter whether I got 0, 10 or 100, so long as I had followed The Plan, was a step too far. In his world, I can take off my pads having made 3 and be satisfied. In my world, if I score 3, or something similarly underwhelming, ten times on the trot, I haven't got a job.

It is all very well trusting the process, but results matter. It is a numbers game, and that involves delivering for the team. I understand the concept of the scorebook not telling the full story, but reality is telling me something entirely different. Once the umpire gives me out the circumstances are irrelevant. I'm out. It is how I deal with results that is most important.

I appreciated the underlying strategy, of attempting to reduce fluctuations in form. We all ride the wave scoring runs; the better players crash off, climb back on, and re-establish themselves quickly on the next wave. I knew what Bawds was getting at when he tried to draw a distinction between a hundred in which I'd played relatively poorly, being dropped four times, and a fluid twenty, when I was beaten by a brilliant delivery, but I spoke from experience.

I used my 105 against Pakistan at Lord's in 2006, in my first Test in England, as a reference point. I was dropped twice, the first time on 0, by Imran Farhat. Danish Kaneria spilled a simple return catch. Umpire Steve Bucknor failed to detect a thin edge off the spinner when I had made 43; there was no DRS and walking wasn't in the playbook.

Those escapes, lucky or not, ultimately didn't matter.

Having three figures against my name helped me, as a young player, to feel I belonged. I wasn't very accessible in those days. Even such a lovely guy as Marcus Trescothick, who opened with Michael Vaughan in that Test, mentioned to me, 'You don't do pleasantries very well, do you?'

I'm not that bothered about pleasantries in my cricket. I've always been single-minded, driven by doing things my own way. I shared my deepest thoughts with Bawds in 2010 because I trusted him. He wasn't what I'd call a tick-the-box psychologist. He wasn't giving me cliché after cliché. He really understood where I wanted to be and how to get there.

He put me in touch with Nick Matthew, the former world number one squash player, calculating that we were similar characters. I had played the game a lot as a youngster and understood the nature of Nick's success. Like myself, he got the most from his natural ability. He worked tremendously hard and ground down the opposition. He had an innate durability to work through unpromising situations and daunting deficits.

I became increasingly self-aware. I was suited to a team environment, since I was one of those characters who was rock solid 99 per cent of the time. I had learned to develop a game face after watching Michael Vaughan and Andrew Strauss; you could never tell, at first glance, whether they had made a duck or a century.

I realized that was so important. The last thing a team needs is for a bloke at the top of the order to be too up or down. There are a lot of times when the odds are against you, and you can't give away too much about private thought processes. I think such self-containment comes from my mum. My dad is very sociable but self-effacing; he once went an entire tour of Sri Lanka, sharing rooms in a travel group, without telling any of his companions that I was his son.

My parents gave me the space as a boy to become my own man. Choir school taught me about an individual's responsibility to the group. Boarding schools were hierarchical, but I never experienced the bullying that characterized earlier generations. That's not to say it didn't exist, but sport was my passport, spiritually and socially.

As a leader of men, I tried to set the example of being low maintenance. I rarely saw the physio, unless I had an obvious problem. I identified most closely with the bowlers, who were prepared to act selflessly and put the hard yards in – I barely had a massage, because I believed they needed the release more than me.

Captaincy entailed dealing with emotion, which is so often a by-product of stress. It also involved an investment of faith. In the most pressurized moments, basic themes, such as trust, unity and generosity of spirit, came to the fore. They won us a pivotal Ashes Test match, at Trent Bridge in 2013.

Australia began the fifth day needing 137 runs to win, with four wickets remaining. What transpired also involved the application of a combination of learned skills, raw cunning, natural talent and nerveless defiance. It was tense, relentless and draining. My role initially involved the learned skill, slip catching.

Mark Waugh and Graeme Swann spring to mind, but there aren't that many natural slippers, who have an innate sense of movement to get into the right position for the catch. It looks easy, but you must work at it. The ball is coming at 90 mph, and you might not have had a sniff all day. The natural thing is to snatch at it.

The ball does hurt, incidentally, especially when it hits the end of your fingers on a cold day. April cricket in England can be horrendous; it explains why our catching techniques are worse than those of the Australians or South Africans, who field in warmer conditions, where the sting is not so painful. It is no surprise we are starting to integrate catching gloves into training.

In simple terms, your hands have to be relaxed, yet firm. You need to move your body, keep your weight forward and align your eyes to the line of the ball. Our eye-testing programme at Loughborough confirmed I had very good lower vision, but I struggled getting to the ball low to my left because of a basic lack of flexibility.

I was a pretty efficient catcher when the ball came to me at shoulder height but dropped more than I should in the bread basket. Though I struggled with some of those easier chances, I forced myself to improve through repetition. I would take literally thousands of catches, from machines, off the face of a bat or off a trampoline net. I fielded at gully, short leg and mid-on with England before settling on slip because I felt, as captain, I could exert greater influence standing there.

So much for the theory. The outcome, on that particular morning in Nottingham, was that I took three slip catches, to remove Ashton Agar, Mitchell Starc and Peter Siddle. They were all off the bowling of Jimmy Anderson, whose unbroken thirteen-over spell was only curtailed by cramp. Natural talent, you see, is never enough.

Jimmy's willingness to sacrifice himself is as fundamental to him as the accuracy of his orthodox and reverse swing, cutters and slower balls. It gave us insurance against the defiance of Australia's final pair of Brad Haddin and James

Pattinson, who took them to within twenty runs of victory at a delayed lunch interval.

That was where the raw cunning kicked in. Jimmy, as the senior bowler, demanded to know who was going to bowl on the resumption. I deliberately said nothing, and smiled, knowing the message would get through. Jimmy understood, and broke into a huge grin. Words were superfluous; we both knew he was restored, relaxed and ready.

Sure enough, Haddin drove away from his body at Jimmy's eleventh delivery of the afternoon session. Matt Prior claimed a catch behind. I reviewed it when umpire Aleem Dar turned down our appeals. We formed a joyful scrum when the giant screens revealed a faint hot spot mark on the bat. We had won by fourteen runs and were being mentioned in the same breath as the boys of 2005, who had a two-run cushion at Edgbaston.

Jimmy, having secured his second five-wicket haul, was rightly named man of the match. Would things have turned out differently had I been sitting in the dressing room at lunchtime, stressing, fiddling and fussing? Probably not, but I was at ease with myself. Bawds approached me afterwards and asked if I had deliberately limited myself to a smile at that key moment.

Again, words were unnecessary. I merely smiled at him as well. I was getting the hang of this psychology lark.

7. Honesty

Truth can be toxic in international sport, if expressed thoughtlessly. Emotion is a potentially dangerous commodity if it is unchecked in a team meeting and criticism becomes personal. Yet, when the alternative is deception, wilful ignorance of broken relationships and collective weaknesses, the risks are worthwhile.

We did not know it at the time, but the Honesty Meeting, called immediately after we had been bowled out by the West Indies for 51 to lose by an innings and twenty-three runs in Jamaica in February 2009, marked the moment England's ascent to being the best team in world cricket began. It was harsh, horrible at times, but cleansing in its candour.

Andy Flower and Andrew Strauss, a new head coach and captain appointed on an interim basis, had every right to be livid after a terrible performance in their first Test in charge. There could be no hiding place, no room for self-deception, since defeat exposed divisions and demanded a fundamental change in approach and attitude.

It was probably the first time I had spoken with true honesty and openness in such a situation. It could have developed into a free-for-all, because some people had been bitching about others being more interested in haircuts, cars and clothes than serious training, but I felt it was time to make a simple statement of fact and commitment.

I was very emotional, on the edge at times, but tried to be

rational. I acknowledged I hadn't been scoring enough runs for England. I'd been out for thirties and forties, and hadn't scored a hundred in fourteen months. That wasn't good enough. I'd been falling down on my job, as an opener, to score big runs to set up wins.

'If I don't start scoring runs I will be dropped,' I told the room. 'I don't care what anyone else is doing, but I'm not doing my job for the team. I'm putting pressure on number three, four and five. I need to buck my ideas up and deliver the goods. Everything is in place for it, but it is down to me to bat, to front up, to stand up. We can talk all we like about achieving, blah, blah, blah, but if I do that, we'll all be better off.'

Andy, who was chairing the meeting, seized the moment. He said it was the first time anyone in the group had admitted to vulnerability and put their contribution into a team context. That sort of honesty, he insisted, was essential if trust was to be restored, and talent was to be explored. Change is only possible when people are prepared to admit the need to change.

We left the room, after several hours, with a determination to draw a line under a difficult period during which Kevin Pietersen and Peter Moores had been sacked as captain and coach, respectively. We had been all over the place. There had been too many excuses, too much distraction. We needed to be more honest in our assessment of where we were, and what we did.

Our skill levels needed to improve. We had been too casual in our debriefing. The remnants of a drinking culture needed to be tackled. There had been too much blame and bullshit. Our fitness levels and mental durability were not good enough. Our decision-making under pressure was flawed. Were we tough enough? That's not macho posturing, but an essential asset when you are building a long innings or remaining sharp for hours on end in the field in 40-degree heat.

Our training became more physical; instead of the sanitized setting of the gym, we did weight sessions on the outfield. We started boxing, using pads. We consciously challenged ourselves. Were our minds truly open? Successful teams have greater willingness to share experience proactively and to think positively.

The farce of the second Test in Antigua, abandoned after ten deliveries because the outfield resembled a cross between quicksand and one of the island's 365 beaches, provided almost light relief, and marked a turning point of sorts. I proved something to myself by scoring an unbeaten 139 and 94 on a very flat pitch in Bridgetown, and the West Indies showed admirable resilience in saving two Tests with one and two wickets in hand.

There was something salvageable from what remained a naturally talented group that needed direction. At a post-tour meeting at Loughborough we set the collective goal of being the world's best. We needed the certainty of that target. A home Ashes series beckoned that summer, and beyond that, in the winter of 2010–11, lay the acid test of a series Down Under. It was a relief to concentrate on cricket, knowing that Flower and Strauss had the authority to take things forward.

The group had been fractured during the preceding tour of India by the magnitude of events and the misplaced force of personality. Dressing rooms inevitably breed alpha males, and friction had become wearing. KP's relationship with Freddie Flintoff was extremely difficult; the tension between KP and Moores was equally marked.

Comfort is an alien concept in elite sport, which cannot be allowed to become too relaxed because it is by nature intense and all-consuming. Our issues had been complicated immeasurably by the fallout from the terrorist attacks in Mumbai in November 2008. We had suffered a fifth consecutive defeat to India in a scheduled seven-match one-day series when news filtered through.

I had been recalled to the team and opened with my county teammate Ravi Bopara. Since we had never done so for Essex, let alone England, it typified a squad searching, with increasing urgency, for balance and impetus. It was a quiet, hour-long journey back to the team hotel; like many, I dozed fitfully. Mobile phone coverage was intermittent, at best, but I suddenly received a text from a friend: 'Are you OK?'

Others were obviously getting the same sort of messages, because people were whispering, 'Oh my God, have you heard?' without being entirely sure what was going on. All became clear a couple of minutes later when, as the bus pulled to a halt, our security guy, Reg Dickason, stood up and announced the attacks. A group of us, including Jimmy, Swanny and Freddie, headed for the communal TV and spent the next four hours or so watching events unfold.

We could barely have been further away from the incidents while being in the same country, since we were staying in the satellite city of Bhubaneswar near Cuttack on the east coast, some 1,000 miles from Mumbai on the west coast, but watching the Taj Mahal Hotel, one of our tour bases, burn was eerie and disturbing. The Middlesex team had been due to arrive the following day; it was all too close to home.

Coverage was graphic: you saw people dead and dying in the streets. The ramifications were horrifying. Indian TV anchors were blaming Pakistan for the terrorist outrage, which killed 170. Breaking news is the same the world over: it feeds off itself. What was going to happen next? There was talk of war and retaliation. It didn't seem right to be sitting there; we all had anxious conversations, reassuring loved ones back home.

We still had gear in the Taj Mahal, and pressure increased when reports emerged that terrorists originally planned their attack for earlier in the month, when we were staying there. They apparently abandoned a recce due to the intensity of the security. Understandably, we were ordered not to leave the surreal setting of our palm-fringed resort.

I felt for KP. His first tour as captain had been far from easy, even before he was subjected to the strains of an international incident that had political and diplomatic dimensions. Like most of the players, I wanted to take the common-sense option of leaving the country and allowing things to settle before deciding whether to resume the tour.

I was still relatively inexperienced, a little naïve in the ways of international sport. With the hindsight of my experience of captaining England, I can now appreciate the consideration given to the financial implications of cancellation by the respective cricket bodies in India and England. TV income was in jeopardy, and a Test tour was under threat. As a figurehead, KP would have been under pressure to take the party line.

KP addressed a team meeting and insisted we should stay. He argued that he wanted to do so because, as a fierce competitor and a proud captain, he hated the thought of being unable to stem a losing run. To be frank, in such a frenzied atmosphere, a lot of people didn't believe that. They wondered about a potentially ulterior motive, of maintaining popularity in India at a time in which the magnitude of the IPL was inescapable.

That competition could have been created for someone of KP's charisma and technical brilliance. He can be a compelling performer and knows how to play to a crowd. But, privately, he was struggling to sustain his authority. There was no overt hostility, but cricketers, like all athletes, are sensitive to mood. It probably wasn't the smartest thing to do, but Freddie called a team meeting from which the captain was excluded. He was insistent we should leave.

We departed after a two-day hiatus and spent four days at home before flying to Abu Dhabi while Reg assessed proposed Test venues in Chennai and Mohali. He was joined at a pivotal team meeting in the UAE by Hugh Morris, managing director of England Cricket, and Sean Morris, chief executive of the Professional Cricketers' Association.

Reg insisted it was safe to return and promised blanket security. I had been digging around, researching the situation as best I could. Indian newspapers were talking about us being protected by a phalanx of 300 commandos and 5,000 other security personnel. A thousand police were assigned to enforcing a lockdown at the team hotel – superficially reassuring, but hardly likely to encourage a settled state of mind. Knowing Reg as I do now, a decade on, I should have trusted him. His responsibility, his priority, has manifestly been our safety. Yet, at the time, I was cynical about the influence of the Indian cricket authorities on the world game. They were certainly not short of financial muscle.

Cricket had been in the crosshairs before. Three New Zealand teams had been caught up in terrorist suicide attacks, twice in Sri Lanka, in 1987 and 1993, and again in Pakistan in 2002. As things turned out, we were little more than three months away from the attack on the Sri Lankan team bus in Lahore, which sadly succeeded in its primary political aim of isolating Pakistan from the rest of the world.

Something didn't feel right. Freddie and Steve Harmison were dubious about returning. Jimmy and I were the last to agree to do so. It was a hugely sensitive situation; Graeme Swann spoke of waiting for ten years for a chance to make his Test debut and was determined to fight for the opportunity. He told us: 'This could be my only chance to play Test cricket, so I'm going.' Such passion swayed many of the team because they identified with the force of his ambition.

I'm so glad we did so, because we saw at first hand the healing power of sport. On arrival in Chennai each of us was presented with a garland of flowers and marked with a *tilaka*, the traditional Hindu red spot placed on the forehead to signify health and prosperity. The sense of respect and gratitude from the Indian public was almost overpowering.

Cricket seemed an indulgence, and character had a different connotation, but Straussy showed his substance by trying to carry us over the line in Chennai with scores of 123 and 108, supported by Paul Collingwood's second-innings 108. Swanny made his debut and featured in a footnote of cricket history when India chased down 387 to win by six wickets on the final day.

Fate kindly placed him in the company of Sachin Tendulkar, who had been promoted as a symbol of national unity and resistance in the wake of the attacks. His call for the nation to come together had been replayed endlessly on TV. An impassioned address ended with the words: 'I play for India. Now more than ever.' On 99 and needing four to win, he steered Swanny's delivery to the long leg boundary. The place went nuts.

We drew the second Test in cold and foggy conditions in the north of the country and flew home for Christmas Eve. It was not entirely the season of goodwill to all men. The personality clash between KP and Moores required a solution, though the captain was not the only player to doubt the coach. I had known Peter from his Academy days, loved his enthusiasm and responded to his intensity. Several others, including Straussy, felt his approach masked certain shortcomings.

Things were coming to a head as the New Year approached. I parked up near my home at the time, in the village of East Hanningfield in Essex, to take a call from Hugh Morris. With very little preamble he asked: 'Who should go, KP or Moores?' His tone suggested it was not his first conversation along those lines. It seemed a deceptively simple summary of a complicated situation.

Culture change in sport is rarely straightforward. This transition had to be placed in the perspective of Duncan Fletcher's eight-year spell as England head coach, from 1999 to 2007. He was hugely influential, extremely successful, very dour. A hands-off coach, whom some believed gave senior players too much power, he was, in emotional terms, the antithesis of Moores.

I told Hugh that Peter was a very good coach who would respond to the lessons of his retention. I didn't think KP had the temperament to remain as captain, though I stressed the importance of his playing presence. As it turned out, the fate of both men was sealed. Moores readjusted in county cricket and KP returned to the international ranks.

It had not been a tight ship. There was no common, over-arching goal. Individual agendas led to inconsistency. As we approached the 2009 Ashes series, we craved an anchor point, something to hold on to. Andy Flower used statistics to back up his argument that we had fallen below the standards demanded and delivered by the Australians.

The group contained strong characters, very talented cricketers, once-in-a-generation players. Freddie was approaching the end of his career, but a powerful team could, and would, be built around Strauss, KP, Paul Collingwood, Ian Bell, Matt Prior, Swann, Broad and Anderson. Jonathan Trott was waiting in the wings to make an indelible mark by scoring a maiden century at the Oval to set up the series win.

The skill of leadership is to respect the stridency and experience of senior players while nurturing younger members of the group who might not have the confidence to be vocal. There is no Utopian solution, but when it came to team building, we set great store by actions rather than words. We had the honesty to concede we were nowhere near our capacity.

We split into groups of four or five, with the task of returning to the group with our vision of what we wanted to be. The seeds had already been planted, subtly, by the management group, but the players felt empowered. When shortcomings were pointed out, they were couched not as accusations but as evidence-based reflections.

It was a democratically led dictatorship, a contradiction in terms that felt perfectly normal from the moment Andy and Straussy, in conjunction with team psychologist Mark Bawden and statistician Nathan Leamon, put things in black and white. They provided the parameters for our professed ambition, of becoming number one.

Our bowlers were performing close to the capacity required of a world-leading team. As a side we were conceding 2.9 runs an over; the target was just under 2.7. Our batsmen collectively averaged 37; we had a bigger gap to bridge, since that would need to be improved to around 45 if we were to fulfil our objective.

Nathan, known as 'Numbers' to all and sundry, loved this sort of stuff. He wasn't, and isn't, your average geek. A former maths teacher with eight, largely self-taught A levels, he played rugby league for Cambridge University, wrote poetry and had a novel, which centred on a dysfunctional Test dressing room, published in 2017. Hmmm . . .

As vice-captain, I had been able to play a minor role in challenging him during the formation of the strategy. I played devil's advocate, insisting he was merely stating the obvious in numerical form. His response was swift and effective: he produced a series of potentially positive outcomes in the forthcoming Ashes series, ranging from a 5–0 whitewash to a narrow 2–1 victory, and extrapolated the consequences.

He calculated it would take between two and three years to become world number one, if results went the way he expected, and we delivered our promised levels of commitment and performance. This, remember, was at a time when analytics in cricket was in relative infancy. By the time of the 2017 Ashes, 'Numbers' was breaking down the pitch into twenty blocks, each 100 × 15 cm, to illustrate the optimal block for each bowler to target against individual batsmen.

Modern players devour the video footage sent to their online Dropboxes. Coaching staff utilize a match-specific dossier, combining video and statistical analysis. Computer simulations factor in weather forecasts and analysis of the pitch surface. Though our game still lags behind Major League Baseball in this area, since MLB's 162-game regular season is a more comprehensive sample size and their sport has fewer variables, it is catching up fast.

A mathematical equation still can't be framed to include the influence of mutual trust and respect. Human factors require greater sensitivity, more subtle consideration. The Ashes series in 2009 was the first time I had been in an England team with a truly common purpose. We needed only to look around the room to realize our aspirations were realistic.

Most of the group had been through the initial cycle of international cricket, which features success, failure, survival and revival. That process is vital, because anyone who emerges with his game intact and his mind fresh has a good chance of longevity and substantial success. The principle applies across sport; England rugby union coach Eddie Jones points out that the profile of a World Cup-winning team features players who have won a total of between 750 and 800 caps.

In my first Test, against India in 2006, Michael Vaughan had made fifteen Test hundreds, and Andrew Strauss seven. Ian Bell and KP had two apiece. Paul Collingwood, like myself, made his maiden hundred in Nagpur. The core of the Indian team had scored between ten and thirty centuries each. Not quite men against boys, but maturity offers an obvious advantage.

It took less than half an hour to appreciate the logic of the next phase of team development, focusing on the notion of our so-called super-strengths. This had its greatest impact once we had reclaimed the Ashes, following a warm-up series at home against the West Indies, where I played myself into a modicum of form by scoring 160 in the second Test at Chester-le-Street.

I was nowhere near my peak and failed to make another century that summer (the next would come on Boxing Day, in Durban). However, without making any assumptions of selection, I felt secure within the group. It had the usual loud characters, like Swanny and Matty Prior, though they were capable of sober reflection. We drew on the emotional energy of Freddie Flintoff as he played through the pain of a chronic knee problem after announcing his impending retirement before the second Test, at Lord's.

There was a point of difference, though. Intriguingly, and perhaps decisively, the group that went on to become number one consisted mainly of introverted characters. That is extremely unusual in an elite male sports team. Strauss set a measured tone as captain. Senior players, key achievers like Jimmy Anderson, Stuart Broad, Ian Bell, Paul Collingwood, myself and, latterly, Jonathan Trott were inclined to withdraw into ourselves.

Critically, we were alive to the challenges of character. We each knew our default mechanism under pressure was to keep our own counsel and concentrate on making the very best of ourselves. If those instincts were unchecked, we would hesitate to contribute in team meetings, preferring to internalize information rather than share deeper thoughts. When things were tough, we consciously forced ourselves to speak up, because that was what the side needed.

This was where the paradox of Kevin Pietersen became apparent. He applied himself superbly, following his demotion, before being forced to withdraw from the second Test, and the series, after surgery on his right Achilles tendon. He had put himself on the line when the injury flared up in the spring, but a regime of rest and pain-killing injections had only short-term success.

He came across to me as a fusion of two different personalities. The introvert – let's call him Kevin – is driven, a deep thinker about the technicalities of his batting and the intricacies of the game. The extrovert – the alter ego we will refer to as KP – is a colourful, compelling character, thrilling in his intensity and creativity.

I'm no psychologist, but any captain learns to read people. My hunch is his insecurity flicked the switch and made him extroverted almost to command. If he felt under threat, he would be the peacock strutting around, showing his multi-coloured tail feathers. He probably needed that exhibitionist streak in order to bat at his best.

That's no criticism, by the way. We should celebrate our differences, since in psychological terms we are all colours of the rainbow. I've already mentioned I was defined a cool blue, fond of structure, discipline and organization. Greens were earthy people who cared deeply about personal relationships. Swanny was an obvious yellow, brash and insistent.

In current terms, Ben Stokes is a classic red, fiery and emotional, but personality colours can bleed between boundaries. We learned over time to accept Andy Flower as a blend of blue and red. His attention to detail underpinned his coaching style, but he responded aggressively if he felt standards were slipping.

He made a pivotal intervention in that Ashes series, after we surrendered the initiative, and the series lead, in the fourth Test at Headingley. We failed to live up to our promises to ourselves. It was an ugly defeat, by an innings and eighty runs, that threatened to undo all our previous application and adventure.

The tone of our work had been set in the initial Test at Cardiff. Once Colly's admirable resistance, in scoring 74 runs with soft hands and hard-headed defiance, had been broken, Jimmy and Monty Panesar batted memorably for sixty-nine excruciatingly tense deliveries to save the day. That unbroken last-wicket stand was like a buddy movie – part comedy, part drama.

We built upon that reprieve in the second Test, our first Ashes victory at Lord's since 1934. I was trapped leg before by Mitchell Johnson for 95 after an opening stand of 196 with Straussy. His monumental 161, combined with Freddie's five-wicket farewell to HQ as an international cricketer in Australia's second innings, set up a 115-run win that augured well.

The loss at Headingley represented everything we wished to exclude from our game. We were sloppy and submissive. We didn't have an immediate 'naughty boys' meeting' in the dressing room, but Flower had his say later, back at the hotel, before he threw the floor open. As in the Caribbean, he enabled us to speak openly, honestly and harshly. It cleared the air and renewed our focus. We admitted to the collective mistake of envisaging the outcome, winning the Ashes, instead of focusing on the process. It didn't go unnoticed that outsiders couldn't wait to write us off.

I didn't mind the occasional bite and bark. I never regarded Andy as particularly fierce, because I had the advantage of having played with him at Essex. I saw the softer, more collaborative aspect of his nature as a youngster coming through, but had also witnessed the fiery side of a man who could snap and have an argument.

There were times when he consciously placed us under pressure in training. Boxing was one of his ideas. He liked to see us sweat, and deal with a little adversity. The group respected that, and dealt with the highly organized aspects of his approach. Team meetings can be a pain, and repetitive work is usually boring, but they breed an understanding of what is expected.

Rewards, when they arrive, are all the sweeter. We had a ten-day break to digest the lessons of Leeds before we took to the field at the Oval, that traditional stage for the last boys of summer. Broady made initial inroads with a trademark, consistently hostile five-wicket spell. Trotty became the eighteenth England player to make a century on his debut, and Australia needed 546 to win in little more than two days.

Freddie, writing his own script to the last, was responsible for the turning point. He broke a troublesome fourth-wicket stand of 127 by running out Ricky Ponting with a direct hit from mid-on. As we closed in on victory, I was sent to Boot Hill, short leg to the uninitiated. It is not a place for the slow-witted or the faint hearted.

You are taught to stay low and to stay alert. My first experience of being hit on the head in Test-match cricket came against the Australians in 2006. It was nearly my last. Adam

Gilchrist, a brilliant sweeper of the ball, splintered my protective helmet, which went flying. It gave me every incentive to learn from my mistake, in turning my back instead of having the presence of mind to duck.

The key is not to tense up, and to anticipate the shot the batsmen intends to play. You try to read body shape in a split second, but occasionally make yourself look silly in unnecessarily taking evasive action. That's when everyone laughs at you and why, when you've done your time, you tend to look for safer pastures.

Slower bowlers who are harder to sweep, like Swanny and Monty Panesar, are appreciated. The thrill of the chase, when they are attacking, with victory in sight, compensates for the occasional perilous drag down. Swanny secured the Ashes in trademark style, forcing Mike Hussey to nick one to me at short leg after a 328-minute vigil for 121.

I still smile when I see the photograph that captures the moment. We are running madly, indiscriminately, in triumph, arms aloft and screaming with joy. What the image doesn't reveal is my animal cunning, in putting the ball straight into my pocket. I had not forgotten the enduring regret of my old schoolmaster, Derek Randall, in throwing the ball away in similar circumstances.

Swanny spent the next hour pleading for the ball, promising undying love or never-ending enmity. He was wasting his breath. I made great play of offering him a ball, and he chased me around the changing room when he discovered it was a random practice ball. I'm not one for memorabilia, but I instantly formed plans for it to be mounted and given pride of place in my house. I didn't realize it at the time, but I was prey to the power of posterity.

I couldn't refuse when I was asked to donate it to the Lord's Museum (on Swanny's suggestion, inevitably). On reflection, it was one of the few times that a player sees the bigger picture. Normally, you envisage little beyond the next training drill, the next catch, the next innings or the next gym session. Flower tried to get us to appreciate we were engaged in something bigger than ourselves.

He tried to accelerate culture change by connecting us with British history, and the bloodline of the England cricket team. England rugby players under Stuart Lancaster did similarly before their disappointing home World Cup in 2015. We went on a field trip to the trenches in Ypres. Celebrated former England cricketers began to do the honours, in giving caps to debutants.

Most contentiously of all, players and management teams were packed away to a five-day hardship camp in Germany, run in the hills outside Munich by Australian special-forces personnel, the morning after the Professional Cricketers' Association dinner. Phones were banned, and people answered only to their surname. An abbreviated version of their internal training programme, it was designed to break us down and build us back up again.

When I arrived late, after being granted leave of absence for my elder brother Adrian's wedding, the players looked as if they had been brutalized. They spoke with a strange mixture of horror and amusement, of regimented press-up sessions, wearing hiking boots, in the middle of the night. An hour-long exercise involving a chariot race, with teams of four carrying a teammate up a hill on an improvised platform, had obviously left its mark. I wasn't there at the time, but the lads told me that KP was ordered by the organizers to be the passenger after he complained of an Achilles problem. He was mortified by the burden he suddenly represented, but was not allowed to change his role.

Other exercises tested leadership skills. Sleep-deprivation techniques were used as a training tool. The link between playing cricket for your country and being woken at 2 a.m. to do hard, physical work, carrying bricks across a forest, may be tenuous but it has a scientific basis, in the response of the brain to shared experiences.

The programme built upon the collective experience of visiting the concentration camp at Dachau before the 2009 Ashes. That had reinforced the power of perspective. No one emerges untouched from such a profound occurrence. It preys on the mind and challenges the conscience. I began to understand the team-building theory, that trust is enhanced when you see those close to you being pushed to the edge, physically and psychologically.

It was enriching in hindsight. Hardship bred a renewed sense of what could be achieved together. People reminisced fondly about carrying out menial tasks in the pouring rain at three in the morning. Jimmy Anderson's broken rib, sustained in a boxing match, entered dressing-room legend. We were ready for the relative sanity of an Ashes tour in Australia . . .

8. Baggy Green

Picture the scene. Manuka Oval, in Canberra, is an old-fashioned ground, ringed with cypress, poplar, oak and elm trees planted nearly a century ago. Also used for prominent Aussie Rules matches, it is the venue for the tour's traditional one-day fixture against the Prime Minister's XI. Not quite cream tea and cucumber sandwich territory, but pretty civilized, right?

Wrong.

Willing pupils in the dark arts of mental degradation, some straight from primary school, wait to ambush an unthinking, unsuspecting England player. If their victim is as naïve as I was, on my first Ashes tour, he is an easy mark, and ridiculed as a cross between Mr Bean and the Upper Class Twit of the Year.

Older tormentors gather in small groups of twenty or so, to sledge in unison when England are in the field. They think they're big and brave, and they're certainly brutal. The abuse is crude, rude, relentless and acutely personal. It's not even leavened by humour, acidic or otherwise. International sportsmen are no one's idea of blushing innocents, but the invective is genuinely shocking.

When I first experienced it, in 2006, my first thought was that I was going to hate Ashes cricket. My second, on getting out for 4, caught behind by Tim Paine off Ben Hilfenhaus, was to long for the release of the local airport, ten minutes down the road. I didn't have time for a third thought, because the other delight of the day was upon me.

The lad was in my line of vision, waiting with a pen and a piece of paper in familiar fashion. As I approached, the trap was sprung. 'I don't want your stupid autograph,' he said, pulling the paper away with a flourish as I stood there, looking silly. Oh, how they laughed. Suddenly, another boy appeared, as if out of nowhere.

He, too, was waving a piece of paper. 'Go on, sign it for the kid,' the adults in the crowd crowed, relishing my dilemma. I knew what was coming and kept walking, to general derision. It was the ultimate no-win situation. You can't have a go back, because it is pointless and unbecoming. Why expose yourself to further ridicule simply because you play for a certain team or country?

Australians are big on theatrical patriotism. I admire the intensity with which the nation identifies with its athletes, and, to be fair, Andy Flower's broader strategy as we set out to climb the world rankings sought to connect the England team with the aspirations of supporters, and our traditions as fellow citizens.

I've felt the emotional pull of those bonds, and can understand the veneration of the Baggy Green. It has captured the imagination of the Australian public and seeped into the global consciousness. Various sweat-stained incarnations, worn by such bona-fide legends as Steve Waugh, are presented in museums as if they are holy relics. But part of me agrees with Jimmy Anderson when he observes: 'It's just a fucking hat.'

It's a brand, built on imagination and history. Its timeline can be traced back to the Don and the other greats. I'm proud that my England cap links me to Hutton in the way Waugh's is supposed to link him to Bradman, but we haven't made a point of embracing the wider significance of what is, after all, a piece of kit.

That doesn't mean the 161 times I walked out to play for England in a Test match weren't very special, acutely personal occasions. I know where my caps are, apart from one, which appears to have been spirited away by the Borrowers on the farm. They are associated with my debut and other milestones, since they were presented in twenty-five-Test blocks. My mum has one. They carry my England number, 630.

They are important, but they are not intrinsic to my pride as an England player. I recognize the yearning for meaning that leads to all the talk about symbolism, but could honestly give away all my kit, because it is just a representation of relationships. The real emotional power lies in memory, flashbacks to those winning dressing rooms, celebrating with my mates.

That idea, of satisfaction gained through the knowledge you have given everything to the group, offers a clue to why we do what we do. An appreciation of playing your part, understanding what the achievement means to others, creates an amazing high. Some might see the 2010–11 Ashes tour as a personal statement, enshrined in the record books, but it wasn't undertaken alone.

International sport stimulates the senses, not least your hearing. Two contrasting moments, against Australia at home and away, are a private soundtrack, playing in my head. The first explains why one of the items on my post-retirement bucket list was to spend the first day of the Lord's Test watching from the Long Room.

I knew I wouldn't be able to recreate the tension and

pressure of personal expectation but wanted to be able to experience it from an alternative angle. You never lose the sense of privilege, playing there, but when there is a job to be done you have tunnel vision. You simply don't notice the portraits and the chandeliered splendour.

Walking out to bat at HQ carries the same mystique for a cricketer as driving off at St Andrews has for a golfer. You're surrounded by ghosts, touched by history. The difference is that players do not access the first tee from the R&A clubhouse. No walk to the wicket has greater resonance than that which takes you right, out of the first-floor dressing room, down two flights of the mahogany staircase, left through the Long Room, then right through the double doors and into the daylight.

I still get goose bumps when I close my eyes and recall that experience in the first innings, against Australia in 2009. The noise the MCC members made, packed together in the Long Room like a strangely colourful army awaiting inspection, was extraordinary. It was the sound of posh people cheering. You may laugh, but that's the only way I can describe it.

There's a moment's peace as you walk to the middle with your mate. On that morning, Andrew Strauss and I looked at each other, awestruck. 'What was that?' he asked, aghast. 'Jesus, that was special, wasn't it?' To be honest, I felt like babbling, but knew we had to recalibrate. 'Yeah,' I agreed. 'How good was that? Come on. It'll mean nothing if we don't score runs.'

Those are often moments of truth. Michael Atherton tells a similar story, of walking out with Mark Lathwell for his second, and final, Test appearance, at Headingley in 1993.

Lathwell was known on the circuit as 'The Natural', a Somerset batsman touched by genius. 'Good luck,' said Atherton. 'The crowd are rooting for you.' Lathwell shot back: 'They won't be in a minute when I'm on my way back.'

Sure enough, he was dismissed third ball. He loathed the fanfare, loved nothing more than a game of darts in the pub. He retired prematurely and is still spoken of as one of the great wasted talents. Alec Stewart, a consistently shrewd judge of character, believes that, of his generation of England cricketers, Lathwell was the only player who 'just didn't want to be there'.

Being alone, when your opening partner has been dismissed three balls into an Ashes Test match, is a disconcerting experience. When that happened to me at Brisbane at the start of the 2010 tour, it triggered another tidal wave of noise, with an entirely different tone. Straussy held his head in his hands after being caught in the gully by Mike Hussey off Ben Hilfenhaus.

I could see him thinking, 'What have I done? *What have I done?*' He carried the responsibility of captaincy like a concrete overcoat. It was a nothing ball, delivered in an area that Ricky Ponting acknowledged played to Straussy's strengths, but was fractionally too close to his body to safely attempt the cut shot.

No words were necessary, though they would have been impossible to hear, in any case. The Gabbatoir was living up to its reputation. There was something primeval about the tribal howl that accompanied him back to the pavilion. I turned and looked at the mob scene of Australian players at the other end of the pitch and felt like the loneliest man alive.

Everything is built up to that first ball, that first over.

Brain fades, such as Steve Harmison's opening delivery in 2006, which went straight to second slip, enter folklore. While I was waiting for Jonathan Trott to join me, I was thinking, 'Nought for one. Big series. Oh my God.' I suspect I fooled no one with my stilted attempts to radiate inner peace while practising a forward defensive.

Here's the funny thing: my mind was very clear. The Gimp never takes a day off, but I had him under control. I didn't have to listen to his snide whispers, his mocking insinuations. He had been hammering me, but I simply stepped around him. I knew he would still try to cause me grief when pressure was applied, but the release of being able to manage him allowed me to concentrate on my batting.

We'd had more than three weeks to acclimatize. I failed in the first warm-up game, but something clicked when I scored a century in the second, at Adelaide. It never ceases to amaze me how confidence feeds off itself, so that it feels self-generated. I scored another ton in the final warm-up; I had averaged 26.21 in ten Tests against Australia up until then, compared to an overall Test average of 42.78, but I felt ready.

Looking back, that first morning marked a turning point. It was the first time in my career that I consciously stood up to the pressure. I delivered. I picked the length. I refused to dart at anything wide and waited patiently for anything steered into my pads. It wasn't a flawless innings, a copybook century. I was dropped at point by Xavier Doherty on 26, and had made 67 when I was fifth out, setting up a hat-trick by my current Essex teammate Peter Siddle.

Most immediately, my feeling of freedom helped sustain our spoiling operation once Australia had taken a 221-run first-innings lead. The fallout from the final ball of the fourth day was another indication that I belonged. Though my execution was nothing special – a full toss by Doherty despatched through a big gap for the boundary that took me to 132 not out – I was operating on another level.

When you are on that sort of score overnight, you allow yourself a Happy Hour. It's a very special feeling. You know you are delivering. You allow yourself the luxury of enjoying the warmth of the welcome back to the dressing room, and scroll through the congratulatory messages on your phone without getting carried away by the back-slapping. You permit yourself the simple pleasure of a beer, and burger and chips.

There are not many days like that in Test cricket, so make the most of them. I went to bed around 9 p.m., absolutely knackered from being on the field almost four days straight, but woke before midnight, and never got back to sleep because my mind was racing. When I got up the next morning, that familiar ache, in the pit of the stomach, reminded me it was time to do it all again.

Cricket is like snooker, in that the trick is being able to reset after periods of inactivity. A snooker player is defined by his production in the World Championship, where games can extend to more than ten hours over two days. He needs the discipline to avoid concocting disastrous scenarios when he is in his chair, waiting for the other guy to clear up, or make a fateful mistake.

Andy Flower cut to the chase in the team meeting on the fifth morning. 'Lads,' he said, 'we haven't saved this game yet. Cookie and Trotty. You've got a responsibility to set the tone. That first hour is so crucial. If we get through that they'll start to go. You know the job isn't done yet.'

There we were, straight back under the pump. Little more than twelve hours after sitting contentedly in that dressing room, nerves were kicking in. We were on the edge of the precipice again, living on the thinnest of lines, operating on the finest of margins. It is stressful, but seductive. Of course, it is uncomfortable. That lack of comfort is comforting, if that makes sense.

Someone unaccustomed to high-performance sport might criticize Flower's intervention as a coach applying unnecessary pressure. I regarded it as a routine reminder, a statement of the obvious. I did have a responsibility to others. It was my turn to carry the load, just as others carried me when I was out of nick. It is the essence of being an individual in a team game.

Australian culture is built on the concept of mateship, an acceptance of unconditional assistance that historians have traced back to the first days of settlement. The term was even considered for inclusion in the Constitution. I have huge respect for that aspect of their national heritage, and identify with it strongly, because it distils an important element of what we do for a living.

We walk miles in one another's shoes. Deeply hidden aspects of Trotty's character emerged only in extremis, but I had a natural affinity with him when he described the experience of playing well as a drug. During a long innings we're all chasing the dragon, the natural high of excelling without conscious effort. The craving fluctuates, as pressure surges and recedes.

The rearguard action in Brisbane was a case in point. Trotty was in the nineties just before lunch on the fifth day. I got a couple of bad balls and suddenly accelerated to 197 not out. I could see him looking at me intently. His inner monologue might as well have been written in neon, across his forehead: 'I wish I'd get one of those . . .'

It was a flat wicket. We were well set, against an old Kookaburra ball. Yet he suddenly became a little skittish. I got to 199, clipped what should have been a simple single into the leg side to bring up my double hundred, but we both stuttered because he couldn't immediately envisage the run, though it was obvious.

He avoided running me out, and I repaid the favour by running as hard as I have ever done to turn a comfortable two into the three that completed his century. Tension sprayed out of him. He was punching the air, with his bat in his hand, halfway down the wicket on his third run.

That's international sport, right there. Happiness, insecurity, joy and fear, a mixture of contrasting emotions endured or enjoyed in the space of a couple of minutes. We are always teetering between success and failure: before that innings Trotty had been practising privately with Graham Gooch on a bowling machine, deep in the bowels of the stadium. He was seeking a ray of light in semi-darkness.

Those disparities explain why I love my sport so much. Trying to suck the marrow from the bones of your career is a complex process. Perversely, it is easier to talk about the negative stuff, the hard times, because the accompanying emotions are so raw that they are easily understandable. It is much harder to put it into words when things go well, because the feelings are so individual and intimate.

You strive to be the best you can be, knowing you will never play a perfect innings. You are living to gauge your response to the game's harshness. The pressure of applying your skills in daunting circumstances is a challenge, a buzz. The feelings are irreplaceable, and impossible to reproduce. That's probably why so many sportsmen struggle at the end of their career.

People talk about respect in sport, as if it is a demand to genuflect before the athlete. It's much more subtle than that. Peers express it too, through actions rather than words. You can inspire by example, even in an international dressing room. When we saved that Brisbane Test, you could sense others in that room thinking, 'This tour and this team will be different.'

At the highest level, sport strips away superficialities, and reveals the essence of the individual.

Confidence bubbles to the surface in unlikely ways, at unexpected junctures. We lost the toss in the next Test, at Adelaide. It was blisteringly hot, and the prospect of a long day in the field was daunting. Within thirteen deliveries, Australia had lost three wickets for two runs. The Brisbane bounce had squashed them.

Matty Prior had been nagging Trotty to work on his fielding. His point, that the standards he set in county cricket were inadequate in the international arena, paid dividends on the fourth ball of the day. An inside edge on to Shane Watson's pads leaked into the leg side; he set off to run, hesitated, then bolted down the wicket.

Trotty took four paces to his right, swept up the ball on the run, steadied himself, and hit the stumps on the full, from just in front of square leg, with a right-arm throw. Simon Katich was well short, out without scoring, and Trotty was rewarded for hours of solitary practice. No wonder he ran around with his arm in the air as if he had scored the winner at Wembley. It remains one of his favourite moments.

Jimmy Anderson had, together with Steve Finn, bowled brilliantly without due reward on the third morning at the Gabba. It was payback time. With the following delivery he had Ricky Ponting caught, first ball, at second slip by Graeme Swann. Again, there was just enough swing to take the edge from the first ball of his second over. Swanny's safe hands swallowed up what remained of Michael Clarke's confidence.

That was the process of psychology in action. The scorecard in Brisbane refused to recognize Jimmy's excellence, but he gained inner strength from the small moral victories and narrow margins of supposed failure. He carried self-belief and a secret sense of security in the next game, when the theories played out spectacularly well.

To repeat that old line, trotted out by coaches since time immemorial: you can't win a Test match in the first hour, but you can certainly lose it. Michael Hussey and Brad Haddin helped Australia to 245 and left us with a single over to survive before the close. For some strange reason, the terms of engagement for that series had shifted, so that the final over had to be completed. Normally, if a wicket fell in that time, it was close of play. No offence, but I wasn't having the theory that Jimmy should go in as night watchman, in case of early calamity.

I said to Straussy, 'Fuck it. Let's front up.' He normally took first ball, but I offered to do so. He refused, after a bit of confusion. I was relieved, deep down, because I reasoned he wouldn't get off strike that evening. The first ball hit his thigh pad – *Wham!* – so we jogged a single. Instead of being a spectator from the other end, I had to grind through the final five deliveries. Flower's determination to put us under pressure in training had paid off, because we didn't want to take the easy option of delaying that pressure by asking Jimmy to give another demonstration of his darkest art.

It is all too easy to put back that appointment with destiny. I lost count of how many times the Gimp whispered: 'I hope we lose the toss and bowl.' The law of Sod being what it is, Straussy left a straight ball and was bowled with the second delivery of the following day, when the heat eventually took its toll.

Trotty's face was grey, almost waxy with tiredness, when he got out just before tea after we had put on 173 for the second wicket. During that interval I lay on the floor of the dressing room in a foetal position, completely drained. If there ever was someone to come to the fore in such a situation, it was Kevin Pietersen.

He was brilliant. He had been sitting for hours with his pads on, a showman in full make-up waiting in the wings for his cue. He hadn't been in the greatest touch on that tour, but when he emerged, he had an aura about him. He had clearly decided that this was his time. It is how I wish to remember him: expressive, powerful, creative, and so, so competitive.

We proved the attraction of opposites. By the close of the second day I had progressed to 136 not out, having broken the England record for runs scored and minutes at the crease without being dismissed, 371 in 1,022 minutes. When I was eventually out for 148, he had completed his first Test century in nearly twenty-one months.

My skill was in setting games up. His was in finishing off

the opposition. He could single-handedly turn a game in four hours. He absolutely hammered them down, making a personal best 227. When he was on, he was extraordinary. There was a savage beauty to his batting. It was honestly a pleasure to be alongside him. Boy, could he run. His cricket brain was fantastic, calculating angles and recognizing space. He played shots beyond my scope.

My modus operandi when I was playing well was to suck up the pressure, wait for the bowler to stray into my area. Soak it up, take them down. When I batted with KP I concentrated on accumulation, rotating the strike with singles and hitting the occasional boundary. He would typically take between 60 and 70 per cent of the deliveries.

The opposition focus would be on him, which is just how he liked it. He was a big bloke, a massive presence. This isn't a show of false modesty, because I enjoyed applause as much as anyone, but I never really wanted to be the centre of attention. Kevin wanted to be the big shot, the star on centre stage. There's nothing wrong with that. It's just what makes him tick.

He's the actor who wants to be in the spotlight, delivering booming lines and memorable speeches. I was happy to be the stage assistant. That's why our partnership worked so well. People with his capacity to dominate an occasion are few and far between. They are invaluable when they are fully focused.

The disparity in our philosophies of life was underlined by the subsequent week off, in Melbourne. I asked to play in a low-key two-day game at the MCG, because I wanted to maintain the synchronization of my batting. I was in the form of my life, and Goochy reinforced the value of simply hitting the ball, to keep the rhythm going. Flower readily excused me from fielding duties.

KP was certainly different. He hired a lime green Lamborghini, which he parked outside the Langham Hotel. I am a bit of a car nut but would be wary of Mother Cricket biting me on the arse for having the nerve to do that. I loved KP for doing so. The last thing I would want to do is shout about a double hundred; he drove around town in a motor that demanded attention.

In his brightest moments he had a zest for cricket, for living to the max. I still smile when I recall his childish glee at taking a rare Test wicket, with the final delivery of the fourth day at Adelaide. I caught Michael Clarke, going backwards from short leg, and KP nearly flattened me with the ferocity of his embrace. It was like being hit in the midriff by a tightly packed hay bale.

That Adelaide Test revealed other aspects of character. Straussy shielded us from the worst of the weather forecasts on the final day: the ground was under water within an hour of Swanny guaranteeing victory by bowling beautifully on a turning wicket. The Barmy Army, congregated around the scoreboard, went, well, barmy.

They were unaware of the background to another definitive performance by Stuart Broad, who bowled in the first innings with a two-inch tear in a side muscle. The public perception of him as an impossibly handsome, occasionally petulant, preening blond couldn't be further from the truth. He is as tough as they come; that act of self-sacrifice put him out for two months.

If anyone doubts him, just because he is a pretty boy, they are making a fundamental mistake. He is a hard nut. I've never forgotten his resistance to pain in India, where he forced himself to play despite detaching the fat pad on the sole of his foot. The specialist who scanned the injury said he had never seen anything as bad. He should not have been walking on it, let alone going out there, on hard ground, day after day, putting the miles in. Outstanding.

Why, then, did we get hammered in the subsequent Test at Perth? As in Kingston, and Headingley, we power-washed our working principles and practices with a no-holds-barred dressing-room debate. Flower chaired it brilliantly, asking challenging questions of individuals without being confrontational. It wasn't a destructive 'you were shit' distribution of blame; we analysed things honestly, collectively and with appropriate humility.

We reached a consensus that we had probably made the classic mistake of thinking we were a better side than we were. We had one eye on the outcome, rather than the process. The experience within the group meant there was no panic. It was a harsh reality check, but it didn't affect mutual trust or confidence. We looked around, and still believed.

We discovered we were not yet good enough to answer the spell of bowling that can change a Test match. In this case, we were blown away by Mitchell Johnson. He bowled very badly at Brisbane, was dropped for Adelaide, but was nigh-on impossible to combat at Perth, where he had the Fremantle Doctor, the area's cooling afternoon sea breeze, coming in over his shoulder.

Again, fine margins were decisive. He canted the seam slightly, at an angle of no more than five or six degrees, to produce devastating swing, back to the right-hander and away from the left-hander. I'm still not sure he meant it, because I was looking for certain clues in his wrist action that never materialized, but he got it spot on.

The following fortnight was our sliding-doors moment. Had we failed to stand up as a side, and forfeited the Ashes, we would have been lost, taunted and tainted by an historic missed opportunity. Not many England teams had gone into the Boxing Day Test at Melbourne with our chance to prove our progression.

First, of course, we had Christmas Day, my birthday, to negotiate. It's weird, being in work mode on a day most of the world takes off. It's the only day when both teams train simultaneously. It doesn't feature the sort of Christmas spread where you can gorge yourself silly, but there's still turkey, oysters, and pizza and chips for the kids.

Andy Flower ruffled a few feathers by hosting a pre-tour lunch for wives and partners, at which he expanded on their responsibilities and explained the practicalities of an international cricketer's life. There would be times, for instance, that we would travel ahead of our families, because of recovery programmes and training schedules. Alice would never cause an issue for me but found it something of an eye-opener.

The party hat was on, but my mind was elsewhere. As cold as it seems, you've got to have a very clear appreciation of boundaries. There were days when I'd get back from the ground and want to slob out, even though Alice had looked forward to dinner. There were other days when she kicked me out of the door; I enjoyed the release of normality, instead of hiding away.

It is easy to forget we are dealing with people, rather than cartoon characters. Australia as a nation yearned for

1. My final Test. 'Just go out and enjoy it,' they told me. 'It doesn't matter how many runs you get.' Sorry, but it did.

2. Reaching my final Test hundred was just the most amazing way to finish.

3. My first time playing against an international side as a nineteen-year-old against the West Indies, at Arundel.

4. New kid on the block. People sat up and took notice when I scored 214 for Essex against Australia, at Chelmsford in 2005.

5. A magical feeling; it doesn't matter if it's your first or your last. Not much has changed in those twelve years, perhaps just a few more grey hairs.

6. Trevor Bayliss and Paul Farbrace: a complementary coaching combination.

7. With Peter Moores, a friend in hard times. I argued against his sacking as England coach, the second time around.

8. In the nets with Andy Flower. When he made me England captain, he reminded me, 'Just because you've got the armband it doesn't mean you know everything.' He was right.

9. Jimmy and I, walking off during my last Test match. My best friend in cricket and an absolute pleasure, standing at slip and watching a genius at work.

10. England v South Africa. My twentieth Test century.

11. Never the most elegant mover! Doing everything I can to make my ground, including a terrible dive!

12. Home is always close to my heart. Loading sheep with Tess the dog, closely supervised by Elsie.

reassurance in the build-up to that match, and turned to Ricky Ponting, as a symbol of hope. He was front, back and centre of the papers. They recreated him as Punter, the superhero who would save the day by batting through the pain of a broken finger.

Since their media can be vicious in the event of disappointment, that wasn't an entirely comfortable place to be. They had named a seventeen-man squad, which suggested they didn't seem entirely sure of their best side, and we had been decisive to the point of brutality. Steve Finn, our leading wicket taker, was told he was dropped on Christmas Day.

Happy holidays . . .

It's professional sport. It's hard and harsh. It shouldn't really matter on what day the big decision is taken. He was left out because he was being hit for four runs an over. It was the equivalent of dropping your most productive batsman for scoring too slowly, a brave call, made after exhaustive discussions between captain and coach.

Tim Bresnan came in. Straussy gambled on the accuracy of our seamers, deciding to bowl on winning the toss. If that lager company ever did Boxing Days, this was it. It was just bloody marvellous. Australia made their lowest total against us for forty-two years: 98. They chased the ball and, excepting two early drops, we caught everything behind the wicket.

I had the best gig, watching carnage unfold from mid-off. Conditions were English, with a little rain around at lunchtime, and our bowlers were relentless, exceptional. The anticipated partnership didn't develop. There aren't many moments when serenity settles, but I looked around and thought, 'This is it.'

It felt almost fated, a reward for faith and application in

those stressful net sessions searching for a semblance of form. We felt as if the ball would also nip around when we batted, but conditions caught the deadened mood. Straussy and I didn't feel the need for words when we walked off at the close, with an unbeaten partnership of 157. We simply touched gloves.

The MCG is a great stadium, but doesn't feel like a traditional cricket ground, because of its scale. It's a concrete bowl, and lacks the charm of Adelaide or Cape Town, where the scene is softened by the grass banking. I'll leave you to insert your own joke, but Straussy and I cleared it. The Barmy Army sang 'We can see you sneaking out' at the locals. There were 84,000 in at the start of play; by the end there were about 30,000 Englishmen left.

Memories were created, but nothing had been confirmed. I had a momentary flash of alarm when someone in the dressing room shouted, 'Bat properly here, and we've got the Ashes,' as we prepared to go out after tea. Don't tempt fate. Don't look too far ahead. Simply do your job. I was out quickly the following morning, for 82, and Straussy lasted little longer, but others took our places in the trenches.

Trotty was metronomic, forming adhesive partnerships with KP and Matty Prior, who was reprieved after being mistakenly given out to a no-ball early in his innings of 85. He was unbeaten on 162 when we were bowled out with a first-innings lead of 415. Australia were six down entering the fourth and final day and though Brad Haddin and Siddle put on a few, we were soon doing the Sprinkler Dance on the outfield.

It's simple enough – put one hand behind your back and whirl the other arm – and legend suggests it was originally performed in the eighties. Paul Collingwood rediscovered it; Graeme Swann's video diary ensured it went viral. The occasional fossil, back in England, saw it as another death knell for cricket's dignity, but most saw it for what it was, harmless fun.

The MCG's dressing rooms are cavernous, due to the AFL's need for internal kicking areas, but the ferocity of the celebrations made up for the lack of traditional intimacy. A few of the lads headed out to share the night with the Barmy Army, but something held me back. We had retained the Ashes for the first time in twenty-four years, but I wanted to win them, outright.

I'm puritanical when it comes to performance. Losing in Sydney would have meant a drawn series, which wouldn't have felt right. Would we lapse into old habits? Would we be up for it, mentally? Had we retained our hunger? Sad, perhaps, but I was nervous, even as I watched the New Year's Eve fireworks from an apartment overlooking the Sydney Harbour Bridge.

Ricky Ponting and Ryan Harris were injured. Australia were in disarray, but they still had their oath of allegiance to the Baggy Green. We were in for one of those tug of wars, when weakness, once sensed, builds before it bursts. They got to 105 for the loss of one wicket before Brez had Shane Watson caught, and defiance seeped away.

The best teams take pride in their superiority, reinforce it in pivotal phases. Straussy seized the initiative from the off, and I made the most of my good fortune, in being caught off a no-ball. I was in unprecedented rhythm and cursed the lazy drive that cost me a double hundred. Ian Bell and Matty Prior compensated with centuries; once we were out for 644 it was a matter of when, not if.

We were taken into a fifth day, warmed by the memory of the previous evening's skewering of Mitchell Johnson. The crowd were living it; they, too, sensed it was our time and their place. An entire stand serenaded Johnson with his song all the way to the wicket, once Chris Tremlett had bounced Haddin out.

'He bowls to the left. He bowls to the right. Mitchell Johnson, your batting is shite . . .'

Chris was a big, intimidating guy, but wasn't express pace. As I delivered the ball to him from mid-on he murmured, 'I'm just going to try and bowl this as fast as I can.' He produced an absolute jaffa, which swung in and splayed the stumps. The next few seconds were almost surreal.

It was bedlam. The crowd's roar could have been heard in Auckland. Johnson, accompanied by TV's cartoon duck, was serenaded all the way back to the pavilion. He would exact his revenge, three years later, but you couldn't do anything other than laugh. When I saw Henry, my brother-in-law, later, he summed up the mood by saying he never needed to see another away Test match.

There was the usual champagne-soaked scrum in the changing room before we decided to take a few beers out to the square for a debrief. We knew the symbolism of sitting in the middle, in the spiritual home of Australian cricket, and events took on a life of their own. The cigars were passed around, and everyone spoke from the heart about what the achievement meant to them.

Sport at the highest level doesn't encourage emotional growth, but no one held back. I was in a panic when it came to my turn to speak, worried about failing to do justice to the magnitude of the moment. Somehow, I came up with the words to express the essence of being an international cricketer.

'Ten weeks ago, I still felt I shouldn't have been selected for this tour,' I said. 'Four months ago, I was one innings away from not being here. Being named man of the series, winning the Ashes, is mad. I've achieved something I didn't think was possible. We have achieved something that will be with us for the rest of our lives.

'So, never give up. No matter how bad it is, never give up. It will turn if you keep doing the right things . . .'

9. View from the Mountain Top

It takes time, on emerging briefly from the bubble of international sport, to get used to the light and shade of life. You think you can gauge the public mood by looking at online trends and talking to friends, but it is not until you are confronted by the impact of your achievements on a human level that you appreciate their deeper meaning.

The English are generally reticent about approaching recognizable figures, but I lost count of the number of people who came up to stress how happy we had made them feel by winning the Ashes in Australia. So many confessed, like guilty schoolchildren, that they had stayed awake all night during the previous six weeks and snatched surreptitious naps in the office.

My depressurization process began in a pressurized first-class cabin, to which Alice and I were upgraded on the way home. That twenty-four-hour journey, free from phones, email and Wi-Fi, allowed me to reflect and reset. I had never felt such personal satisfaction. That deep ache of insecurity had gone – for the moment, at least. I knew I could not have done any more.

As a team, we were in rarefied air, close to the summit of our Everest. We still had a home series against India to negotiate, the equivalent of the deadly Hilary Step, before we could call ourselves the best team in the world, but we were relentless. We reached the peak at Edgbaston on 13 August

2011, precisely 918 days after that honesty meeting in Kingston, Jamaica.

India's spirit, weakened by heavy losses in the first two Tests, was finally broken on the third day of the game. This may sound silly, but there are very few occasions when it doesn't matter how long you bat. I was 182 not out overnight and woke up with a single thought in my head: 'This is your chance to go massive.'

The pitch was flat. I had dispelled doubt, created by averaging only five in the series going into the game. The Indians, who had required late-innings defiance by MS Dhoni to reach 244, knew defeat was inevitable. It was Test cricket at its most brutal. It is rarely as obvious as football or rugby, where dominance is reflected by six-goal or sixty-point winning margins. Distress signals are subtle, but instantly recognizable at close quarters.

The Indian bowlers steamed in for the first hour, but I sensed a slight sag in the shoulders, a realization they each faced another thankless twenty-over shift across another long day. Their intensity level fell by a fateful fraction. My partnership of 222 with Eoin Morgan was cricket's equivalent of water torture. I scored only two boundaries in two sessions; a mid-afternoon power cut was the opposition's only release.

They spread the field in the hope of delaying the declaration, which we planned to make if I got 300. Runs came steadily through midwicket, or behind square on the off side. I was on 294 with the field spread, and everyone on the boundary, when I attempted to hit the ball too hard. I couldn't believe it when I top-edged a loose drive and was caught at deep backward point.

History turned to dust. At that moment it didn't matter that my innings of 294, which lasted seven minutes short of thirteen hours, was the highest in Edgbaston's 116-year Test history, and England's biggest since Graham Gooch's 333, twenty-one years earlier. As in my final Test innings, public acclaim couldn't deflect private reproach.

Perspective, of sorts, was quickly reasserted by the manifestation of my worst nightmare, a king pair in Test cricket. Virender Sehwag had nearly three full days to digest the consequences of gloving off Stuart Broad to Matty Prior in the first innings. He seemed almost beyond caring in the second. A massive drive at Jimmy Anderson's first delivery, an away-swinger, sped to Andrew Strauss at first slip.

Victory, and number one status, was confirmed the following day, when Kevin Pietersen caught Shanthakumaran Sreesanth in the gully, off Tim Bresnan. There's a lovely painting of our response, running to form a huddle with arms aloft. Though the consistency of the reaction is subconscious, the symmetry of the image is strangely appropriate, since it captures the nature of the team.

We were moving parts in a highly efficient machine. Our ruthlessness and resourcefulness were innate. We were operating the 2 per cent rule, continually seeking subtle ways to gain marginal advantage, especially away from home, where we struggled when the ball wasn't moving around. That attention to detail extended to Mushtaq Ahmed, our spin-bowling coach until 2014, teaching us the reverse swing.

He had done so, with Matty Prior, at Sussex. My job, as the principal shiner of the ball, was to monitor the moisture on the rough side. Matty would throw it directly to me, rather than going through the hands of the fielders, because their sweat could dampen the dry side. It is amazing, if you don't touch the dry side for two or three overs, how rough it will get, even when it is thirty or forty overs old on hard ground.

Fielders consciously threw it seam up to me, so I could catch it on the shiny side. There were unavoidable complications – sometimes someone with sweaty hands would make a diving stop or roll on the ball – but as soon as the ball is moving sideways on a good wicket you are back in the game.

Another trick to accelerate the process is skidding the ball in from the outfield on a lower trajectory so that its rougher side hits the ground. Footmarks left on previous wickets are a favourite target. If the ball is reversing, though, you never throw it on the ground. For instance, if it is hit to the boundary the fielder carries it forward until he is sure of the return throw reaching mid-off on the full.

This also helped mentally, through the placebo effect of knowing we had done everything to look after the ball. So much of sport is played in the mind; reaching the finite goal of being number one, faster than we expected, was dangerous. Andy Flower spoke of setting mini-targets, reinforcing and renewing habits. He was the main driver of cultural change and continued to talk of a higher calling than the fleeting sensation of victory, but such all-encompassing ambition was not easy to sustain.

That big-picture policy had already included an evolution of authority. I had been appointed one-day captain in May 2011. Stuart Broad simultaneously assumed leadership of the T20 team, leaving Straussy clear to concentrate on the Test group. The setting for my introductory speech, Churchill's

War Rooms, tied into an overarching theme of identity. We did something similar in the Tower of London, with a military speaker.

The underground bunker, beneath Westminster, from which the War Cabinet operated, was evocative, though my speech was hardly Churchillian. I had thought long and hard about its tone and content. As in Jamaica, I thought honesty the best policy. I spoke passionately about my competitiveness, of not letting down those close to me. Sure, we could inspire others. But first we had to look to each other.

That's the three-card trick of managing a dressing room. It must be big enough to accommodate the larger characters, and small enough to breed the intimacy that enables you to show how much you care. Differences should be celebrated, because no successful team contains identical personalities. That's the theory, anyway . . .

Reality tends to set ambushes. We were number one in the world, hoping to push on, and suddenly lost all three Tests in the winter series against Pakistan, who were ranked fifth in the world. Chasing 145 to win the second Test at Abu Dhabi, we lost all ten wickets for fifty-one runs on the way to being bowled out for 72. It was a chastening setback; the subsequent series in Sri Lanka was drawn, and we still had to prove our mettle in Asian conditions.

Fault lines that existed, largely unnoticed and completely unprotected, opened during the main summer series, against South Africa. KP's exclusion from Andrew Strauss's 100th Test, at Lord's, mirrored his idiosyncrasies and inconsistencies, and raised fundamental issues of trust.

Perversely, we were engulfed in that particular controversy after one of KP's most distinctive innings, 149 in the drawn second Test at Headingley. That was a work of genius. His individualism in playing with the nerve and aggression of a baseball slugger was extraordinary and, in hindsight, revealing, since it seemed to be a release of frustration.

He hinted at retirement in an interview, and then recommitted to the team. The tone was strange, but I understood what he meant when he famously observed, 'It's not easy being me in that dressing room.' He is a man of great gifts, compelling passions, soaring highs and puzzling lows. A psychologist will tell you that anyone with such a strong sense of self is inclined to introspection and liable to view the world with a narrow focus.

His suspension was inevitable, once an investigation was launched into his sending of what were described as 'provocative' messages to South African players on his BlackBerry. He would later admit in his autobiography to agreeing in one exchange that Strauss was behaving like a 'doos', a colloquial Afrikaans insult for 'dick' or 'idiot'.

He had laughed along with us at the 'KPgenius' parody account on Twitter, lampooning public perceptions of his character in the build-up to Headingley. Suddenly he seized on it as evidence of poor faith from his teammates. It transpired the account was owned by a friend of Stuart Broad, but he and Graeme Swann, who was also implicated, swore on their lives they weren't involved.

As so often happens in these situations, views became polarized. The debate generated more heat than light. Had KP initially been more transparent and shared his phone records as soon as the investigation was instituted, a lot of problems could have been avoided. As it was, what would be

Straussy's farewell to Test cricket was overshadowed by rancour and suspicion.

A week after that match at Lord's I was in Southampton, killing time before a day–nighter against the South Africans. I never slept late, so was watching *Homes Under the Hammer* in T-shirt, shorts and flip-flops, when Andy Flower called. 'Where are you?' he asked. 'I need to see you.' His manner was bland, as if he was working through a final pre-match checklist.

I twigged what had happened when I walked into the downstairs meeting room and saw him sitting with Hugh Morris of the ECB. They clearly weren't interested in small talk about Dion Dublin's vision for a semi-detached in Sidcup, but it's funny how big decisions, and huge career milestones, seem so matter-of-fact.

Flower wasted no time: 'Straussy is resigning the captaincy and is going to announce his retirement from the game tomorrow,' he said. 'I would like you to become the new England Test captain. Will you do the job?'

'Absolutely,' I replied. 'I'd love to. It's a huge honour.'

And that was that, a schoolboy fantasy reduced to a statement of the obvious. I turned to leave the room and paused before opening the door when Flower added: 'Don't tell anyone, and don't let it distract you from the game tonight. You've got a big game.'

'Oh, I won't,' I promised. 'Don't worry, I'll be on it.'

Of course, I got 0, bowled second ball by Lonwabo Tsotsobe, who would go on to become a DJ after being banned for eight years in a match-fixing scandal. We ended a run of ten consecutive wins and enabled South Africa to become the first side to be ranked number one in all three formats. I told Alice about my promotion, but otherwise kept the following day's headlines to myself.

Straussy sent us all a personalized letter and we bought him a hundred bottles of wine in return. I love the bloke. He embodies everything you wish for in a leader: calmness, fairness, fierce pride and consistent purpose. He's the rock-solid guy everyone looks up to, whether you are walking out to bat with him or asking for quiet guidance.

My abiding loyalty towards him couldn't be fairly factored into my first decision as captain: whether we could, or should, bring back KP. I didn't go out of my way to talk to Straussy about it, first, because I couldn't be distracted and, second, because I didn't want to be influenced emotionally by the respect I had for him. I was trying to do what I thought was best for the team, not best for me or my mate.

While I privately weighed up the pros and cons, I had my public initiation as England captain in the arena I liked least: the press conference. The question I hated most arrived on cue: 'What leadership style can we expect from you?' Put simply, it is hard to answer when you don't truly know. You get picked for the job because people see leadership qualities in you, but it's hard to put into words, beyond an appreciation of the honour and the intention to do what comes naturally.

I eventually relaxed into the role after about eighteen months, but was worried about how I came across as a public speaker. I panicked initially, when I had to articulate ideas or strategies in front of the squad. I was uncomfortably aware of Swanny giggling in the corner because I'd misquoted a saying or put my words in the wrong order in a jumble of thoughts.

Media training is useful, to a degree, but sport involves operating on instinct. I knew what I wouldn't do following a leadership seminar in the City of London at which a prominent chief executive stood up and said: 'I tell my employees to reach for the stars. They might not get the stars, but they get the moon. That's a bloody long way.'

If I had come out with that tosh, I'd have been laughed out of the dressing room. The truth is that nothing can prepare you for the England captaincy. Experience of doing the job in county cricket might offer tactical experience and acumen, but it has limited relevance because of the magnitude of daily decisions, which are second guessed by people with minimal knowledge of the situation.

It's like a football manager walking into a changing room to address his players for the first time. He must meet questioning eyes. He knows what is going on behind those eyes. Every player is watching intently and wondering what change will mean for him. Ultimately words are of secondary importance to actions.

When I took the job, I had a short but significant exchange with Andy.

'What kind of captain do you want to be?' he asked me.

'I want to be an honest captain.'

'Honest?'

'Yeah. You've got to be honest.'

'Well, what happens if you drop a player. Are you going to be honest then?'

'Yeah, yeah. I'll tell the truth.'

'So. You're going to drop this player because he isn't bowling well, or he can't hit it off the square. You're going to tell him, in so many words, that you can't trust him.'

'I'm not sure if I'd say that.'

'But what happens if there's an injury, and you need that player for the next Test match? You've just told him you don't trust him, because you're honest.'

He had a point.

It was a crash course in the value of relationships, which become more interdependent on tour, when captain and coach pick the team. A selector is normally on hand, in case you don't agree, but there is a constant need to manage, firmly but sensitively, the five or six players who are on the outside, looking in.

It involves straddling the age-old credibility gap between practice and theory. You must be truthful, because otherwise they won't respect your authority. You can't tell lies, because they will come back and bite you on the arse. But the truth, the whole truth and nothing but the truth? You learn quickly that idealism is a luxury.

Dealing with disappointment is the hardest part of the job. My compromise was to have what I used to call the toilet chat, a private conversation away from prying eyes and ears. I always offered the dropped player the option of revisiting the conversation, though not many took up the offer. Most decisions are clear cut, but borderline choices can prey on the mind.

Flower and Prior played pivotal roles in helping me reach the decision to reinstate KP. Neither deserved KP's subsequent criticism. We exchanged views in three- or four-day cycles, after mulling over the issues. Matty was opinionated, but team orientated. I trusted his views, having spent a lot of time on the field chatting as slip fielder to his wicketkeeper. He strongly supported Kevin's return.

Andy had more to juggle. He had built a close relationship with Straussy over the previous three years and had dealt with recurring tensions. Kevin was high maintenance, difficult to manage, but worth the extra effort because of his special talent. Loyalties were entrenched, and I knew I would have to sell his return to his teammates.

Above all, Andy is a principled man. His clashes with KP are a matter of public record, but he thought rationally, and suggested I could make the reunion work. I wasn't a particularly close friend of Kevin and can count on one hand the times I went for dinner with him in our eight years together, but I saw potential for progress.

We were polar opposites in terms of personality but had never clashed. As batsmen we suited each other down to the ground. Left hand, right hand. A sponge and a top gun. My fondness for going under the radar worked well, because KP fed off my calmness. Andy was right. We did make it work, in my eyes at least, for a while.

We both laughed nervously when Andy said: 'This will go one of two ways, but it is definitely going to be better than ending a bloke's career for good.' I was armed with a list of questions when I met KP in London to chat through things. It was awkward, initially, but he talked a good game, in stressing his eagerness to carry on playing for England.

He gave all the right answers. He knew he needed to clarify his commitment and playing for England built his brand. I prided myself that my teams worked their bollocks off, even on the shittiest of tours, and he had to buy into that. I never had a direct issue with Kevin, though I didn't like the way he attempted to manipulate Strauss. He's a man of fascinating, sometimes bizarre contrasts and, to be fair, did go to Andrew's house to apologize personally, for ruining his final Test.

That's the paradox. Someone summed him up as the bloke you would buy a drink for without hanging around for him to buy you one back. That's why he was naturally suited to franchise cricket. Everything's new, fresh and exciting for three weeks, and then he breezes off, into another town, to do it all again with another team. Spending ten months of the year with him is an entirely different proposition.

The warning signs were obvious. Kevin felt misunderstood, rightly or wrongly, for long periods in his career and preferred love to be unconditional. Lines of communication had to be clear and unambiguous. As a captain, I tried to treat people individually, and sensitively, within certain boundaries.

He was always going to be on his best behaviour in India, which was a phenomenal tour on which to bed in as captain. It is a personal challenge, as much as anything, since it is a tour when you spend too much time in your room. Security had increased following the Mumbai bombings, so wandering through crowds excited by their proximity to an international cricketer was impractical.

I was brought up to treat people fairly and with respect. The adulation you receive as an England player in India is difficult to justify, but logical, if you see what I mean. Cricket assumes exaggerated importance because it enhances everyday life. It costs nothing to be civil. A smile or a quick conversation with the lift attendant or the breakfast waiter can make his day.

If India's people are captivating, its poverty is overwhelming. Sometimes you get morally confused by it. One of my great strengths as a cricketer is compartmentalizing my game, not being dull or dense, but refusing to overanalyse things. Yet it is impossible to sit in a grand, spacious hotel and eat fine food with the knowledge that on the other side of the hedge children are washing in polluted ponds.

It is difficult to get your head around such extremes. You are never immune to the suffering of a fellow human being; I've found that in India emotion seeps out in surprising ways. When we were in Ahmedabad, playing our third and final warm-up match before the first Test was staged there, I watched the box set of *The Pacific*, an American mini-series that followed a band of soldiers through Second World War battles in the Pacific rim.

The storylines were compelling and the characters believable. I'm not usually one to cry at fictional TV but was tearful immediately after the final episode, in which two main characters, turned into cynics stripped of compassion by the horrors of war, prepared to return home following the atomic bombing of Hiroshima and Nagasaki.

I was looking out at the sprawling city, imagining unseen lives playing out beneath me, when there was a knock on the door. Jimmy and Swanny burst in and looked at me, red-eyed, with a mixture of amusement and alarm. 'Thank fuck you guys have turned up,' I said. We were in a dry state, Gujarat, with a two-phase, three-month, four-Test tour stretching ahead of us. A beer would have gone down well.

In such circumstances there is no alternative to throwing everything at it. Kevin and I each scored centuries in the warm-up matches, but we were hammered by nine wickets in the first Test. Sehwag got a quick hundred, Cheteshwar

Pujara announced himself with an unbeaten 206, and we followed on, trailing by 330.

We had done a lot of work on playing spin in the nets. The skill lies in not getting caught playing half forward, half back. It is the most mentally challenging aspect of the game and hitting without consequence in practice can be deceptive. A delicate balance needs to be struck. We had spoken of being positive, putting the pressure on the bowler, and trained assertively.

When the pressure is on, aggression can be self-destructive. Training in the nets, with lots of sweeps and big shots, can sometimes disguise a batsman's deeper lack of trust in his defensive technique. Ian Bell, for instance, is accomplished facing spin; he ran down the wicket to Pragyan Ojha, the slow left-armer, didn't get to the pitch of the delivery and was out first ball. That signalled a bit of a scrambled mind.

There were mitigating circumstances, because he was preparing to return home for the premature birth of his son Joseph. Maybe we were over ambitious, in seeking to put the pressure back on the Indian spinners. As captain, I had to lead by example. I batted for 556 minutes for 176 in the second innings, sweeping consistently and choosing my moments to use my feet. We avoided an innings defeat and at one stage, when Matty Prior was similarly resistant, I sensed we had them worried.

Batting in India is a mental challenge. The first twenty or thirty balls are very hard work. Everyone is around you, chatting away. Bowlers specialize in pinning you down. It doesn't take long for the Gimp to ask, 'How are you going to score a run here?' You must be at ease having fielders clustered around the bat. You must learn to manipulate the field, to milk runs carefully but decisively. It is a case of low risk, high reward.

Once I demonstrated what was possible, my words carried additional authority. Batting against spin has certain certainties. It's picking length, watching the revolutions on the ball. It's reading the drift, responding to variations, especially the one that goes straight on. You either want to get as close as possible to the pitch of the ball and smother, or as far away as possible, on the back foot, to allow the ball to spin before you select your shot. My message at the end of the game was disarmingly simple: we had to learn to trust our defence, and when to attack on our own terms.

India were a very good side, with stellar players, but they weren't in their pomp. I saw the first signs of self-doubt – we call it 'getting nippy' – and they gave away their underlying thinking by producing another turning wicket for the second Test in Mumbai. Usually they deliver a series of flat pitches after going one up in a series; here they were desperate to avenge their 4–0 whitewash in England.

Even the net wickets ragged. We selected Monty Panesar because we needed to play our two best spinners. He promptly took eleven wickets in a match that crystallized KP's capacity to destroy the opposition. His 186, against a ball that spat and spun, was one of the greatest innings by an England player.

There was an element of playing the percentages, since the ball was turning so much. That involves rationalized aggression, designed to knock the bowler off his length and rhythm. Because I am a left-hander, left-arm spinners aim at the rough outside my off stump. It can spin, bounce, or keep low. You can't retreat into yourself because you will be a sitting duck.

KP defended calmly and resolutely before attacking viciously and joyfully. He played with discipline, concentrating on the sweep and the slog sweep. We put on 206 for the third wicket. I ground out 122, by sweeping, nudging and nurdling, but my innings was colour-by-numbers stuff compared with his Impressionist masterpiece.

Sometimes captaincy is simple. Monty and Swanny were doing their bit by bowling brilliantly, and Jimmy Anderson was providing reverse swing, I didn't have to be a tactical genius. In Kolkata I lost the toss for a third time, and got my head down for eight hours, scoring 190 before enduring one of the biggest brain fades of my career.

I had shared big partnerships with Nick Compton and Jonathan Trott. I was well set, and ready to play the foil to KP. I was backing up to him and turned back to the crease after realizing a run wasn't on. Virat Kohli moved round to short midwicket, threw at the stumps . . . and I stupidly lifted my bat out of the way to let the ball through.

Dopey, but not disastrous, because of the reverse swing employed by Jimmy and Steven Finn, who had come in for the injured Stuart Broad. We needed only 41 to win; I was stumped, fourth ball, after a rush of blood, followed quickly by Trotty and KP. At 8–3, I was so nervous I literally could not watch. I sat on the toilet until Compo and Belly put me out of my misery.

We won the toss in the final Test, on a flat pitch at Nagpur, and didn't bat particularly well in occupying the crease for 145 overs, scoring just 330. It was attritional, soporific cricket, though I managed to be sufficiently alert to run out Dhoni on 99 in India's reply. Trotty and Belly scored centuries in a second innings we stretched to 154 overs, and the series was ours.

It took me a long time to appreciate the significance of that win. Playing in India is an immersive experience, since the game drives a billion people absolutely barking mad. The gods of their game, Tendulkar, Dhoni and Kohli, live surreal, detached lives. I've rarely spoken to them deeply, because they have become distant figures by the nature of their fame.

How they perform under such extraordinary pressure is incredible. When Tendulkar went out to bat, electricity surged around the ground. It felt as if the world had stopped to watch, and wait, for its portion of perfection. When he got out there was a deathly silence, as if the world had stopped turning.

Scoring a hundred hundreds under that sort of pressure is an almost unbelievable achievement. My fear of failure drove me on, but what he went through, on a daily basis for twenty-five years, was of another magnitude. No one is immune to self-doubt, but he was a prisoner of his genius. The responsibility of pleasing so many people, so often, demanded a barely credible inner strength.

We should have done the double, by winning the one-day series, but lost it 3–2. The noise in the opening match, on Dhoni's home ground in Pune, was off the scale. I was at first slip and couldn't hear James Tredwell, who was alongside me at second. It was ludicrously loud. Screeching assaulted the ears like feedback from an electric guitar held up to an amplifier.

In England, I cherish my freedom to roam as I wish. In

India, leaving your hotel involves a calculated gamble. Before the final game of that one-day series, in Dharamsala, Ian Bell, Chris Woakes and I went out to a pizza restaurant recommended by Trevor Penney, our former specialist fielding coach. The plan involved a slice or two of deep crust, washed down by a couple of bottles of Mexican beer as we watched the sun set over the Himalayas.

Dharamsala is a beautiful place, ringed by cedar forests. The air is so clean and fresh. Appropriately, since it is home to the Dalai Lama and the Tibetan government in exile, it is a tranquil contrast to the teeming cities we are used to visiting. The three of us reasoned that we would get away with the expedition because we are not instantly recognizable folk heroes in the mould of KP.

It was Friday, and traffic was strangely heavy. Without exaggeration, our car was surrounded by around a thousand people as soon as it pulled up at the restaurant. I don't know how they knew we were going to be there, but once we were bundled through the crowd, they decided to storm the place. It was absolute bedlam.

Armed security guards took us upstairs and locked us in a bedroom, where the occupant's underpants were still on the double bed. They devised a secret door-knocking code to smuggle the pizza and beer in, so we sat there for an hour or so, giggling at the absurdity of eating with guys who were waving guns.

And then we tried to leave.

I'd never seen anything like it. There were now five thousand people there, waiting for us. The most adventurous were blocking the stairway, phones at the ready. They were desperate for any form of contact. It wasn't particularly dangerous, apart from the fact someone could easily have been hurt in the crush, or during the subsequent stampede after our car, but it was surreal.

We never got the chance to relax and enjoy the serenity of the mountain top. Perhaps there was a moral there . . .

10. Decline and Fall . . .

'You, or your team, will reveal themselves.'

Andy Flower's summary of the challenge of Test cricket, articulated in clipped tones that disguised his sensitivity, stayed with me throughout my England captaincy. He was right; the highest form of the game exposes who you are, individually and collectively. It takes no prisoners. It spins you round and spits you out.

It is diametrically opposed to the one-day game, where the mathematics of the occasion dictate your approach. Test cricket offers greater opportunity to impose yourself on the situation, because of its length and intricacy. It doesn't tell you what to do, through force of circumstance. To survive, you must find a way that works for you.

It can suck the life out of you. Not many batsmen who go straight back to county cricket after being found wanting bounce back immediately. They endure what is almost a period of mourning; it takes time to rediscover the mental fortitude required if they are to regroup. On the way up, or the way down, your promise or failure is emphasized by the TV news ticker, a snapshot that sums up your performance in a few words or numbers.

It is a dive into very deep, extremely cold and invariably murky water. What is talent? Can it be defined only by its reproduction on a regular basis? Skills are nothing without application, and delivery of results. Certain players have obvious attributes – the ability to swing the ball both ways or to bat with conviction and imagination – but they lack that intangible force to fulfil themselves.

I've lost count of the times I've heard people around the game exclaim, 'God, he's so talented!' Sometimes that expression is tinged with exasperation. On other occasions, such as in the case of Joe Root, it reflects the emergence of a special player. He announced himself in the final Test of that Indian tour, at Nagpur.

I knew, instantly, that he was made for international cricket. He's naturally cheeky, and walked to the wicket for his first innings with a broad, beaming smile. He wasn't going to be overawed by the occasion. We probably should have selected him sooner, but that transitional stage, being exposed to the environment in training, held him in good stead.

I benefited similarly at the start of my career as an unused squad member in Pakistan. His inner belief, bolstered by the knowledge he had been picked as a fantastic player of spin, manifested itself in a first-innings 73. It came as a surprise when he offered a return catch to Piyush Chawla because he was so obviously comfortable.

The most improbable highlight of a drawn three-match series in New Zealand in the spring of 2013 was provided by Steve Finn, who erected the Watford Wall on the fifth day of the first Test in Dunedin. He had come in as night watchman the previous evening, when I was out after sharing a first-wicket partnership of 231 with Nick Compton, who also scored a hundred.

Since the match remained in the balance, an unorthodox approach was required. Quite simply, I 'incentivised' Finny. It began before the start of play with the promise that I would pay for his evening meal if he survived the first hour and ended just before tea with me ordering him a case of wine for making 56 and, more importantly, eking out 203 deliveries in 286 minutes at the crease. Had he reached a century I would have been in real trouble.

We warmed up for the Ashes in the return series against the Kiwis, winning both Test matches. Rooty scored his maiden Test hundred at Headingley, where I contributed 130 in the second innings and Graeme Swann took ten wickets. The sense of anticipation was tangible; unfortunately for Compo it was too much. He just went, mentally.

Promoting Joe to open in his place was the only major selection decision. The pundits, who have the privilege of not having to back up such statements, forecast victory as a formality. Beefy Botham, never one to gather splinters from fence sitting, proclaimed that we would beat the Australians 10–0: not bad going in a five-Test series.

We were in a pretty good place as a team but weren't from another planet. Australia weren't Luton Town, my team, turning up at Manchester City in damage-limitation mode. Margins were narrow and matches were decided by players who possessed the confidence and experience to seize the moment. The first Test, at Trent Bridge, was a kaleidoscopic example of long-form cricket.

The fairytale of Ashton Agar, the teenaged tail-ender who made 98 in his first Test innings, didn't quite make it to the publisher. Stuart Broad somehow made himself a marked man by refusing to walk when an edge ricocheted to slip from the gloves of wicketkeeper Brad Haddin. Jimmy Anderson, another Aussie irritant, bowled himself to the point of exhaustion on a slow, low pitch before his tenth wicket of the match, confirmed by DRS, clinched a fourteen-run victory.

We ran around like headless chickens, but the quietest member of the group had made the biggest noise. Ian Bell came of age in that series, scoring the first of three centuries at Nottingham and raising his game to a different level. He was a beautiful player, an aesthetically pleasing cover driver, but naturally insecure and easily overshadowed.

It takes strength to admit weakness but, by working with Mark Bawden, he reached his optimal level. He was sensational, almost lyrical on occasion, but as someone saddled by expectation since the age of sixteen, when he was selected for England A, he was temperamentally a slow burn.

It took time, and careful self-analysis, for the golden child to truly believe in himself. He acknowledged the pressure, rationalized it, delivered and dominated. I owed him so much because appearances were deceptive. The win by an innings in the second Test at Lord's, where Belly changed the tenor of the match by scoring 109 after coming in at 28–3, signalled the beginning of the end for that team.

We never again reproduced the ruthlessness that spawned articles with headlines such as 'How Does One Beat a Team of Robots?' The journalist, who had evidently decided to flog the analogy to death, suggested removing my battery, apparently inserted by ECB scientists. He hoped fervently that I would be found, wandering around, intoning, 'Does not compute! Does not compute! Error! Error!'

This wasn't science fiction, or even a rom com. It was a kitchen-sink drama, coming to a climax. We were lucky with the rain in Manchester and won a tight Test in Durham through Stuart Broad's personal momentum. His six-wicket spell, following a heated dressing-room row at tea sparked by Matty Prior's scathing summary of declining standards, was decisive.

My form had certainly cooled, and I felt I had to take the lead by speaking passionately and harshly about what we were in danger of losing, without allowing emotions to contaminate relationships. The draw at the Oval, when bad light intervened controversially to prevent a 4–0 series win, merely emphasized the unforgiving nature of international cricket.

What turned out to be a flawed selection, that of Simon Kerrigan, proved to be another sobering example of flying too close to the sun. I had first faced him for Lancashire two years earlier, when he struck me as a serious bowler in the making. He was competitive, skilful, knew his own game. He also had that stubborn, arrogant streak you look for in a player from whom much is expected.

Jimmy agreed with my instinctive conclusion that he was a goer. In that blunt Burnley way of his he described Kerrigan as 'the first young spin bowler I've seen who knows what he is doing'. Perhaps we should have both paid greater attention to those whispering that he bowled too slowly to thrive at the highest level.

It would become critical, once he was psychologically damaged by Shane Watson in Australia's warm-up game against the England Lions at Northampton the week before his senior debut. Watson is a fantastic cricketer, a brilliant batsman in the shorter forms of the game, and since the pressure was off, was able to unload. He scored only 45 but hit Kerrigan hard and consistently in the general direction of Milton Keynes.

The logic of Kerrigan's selection, that we wanted a left-armer to turn the ball away from a right-handed batsman in spinning conditions, began to look shaky in the build-up, where he simply didn't look the same bowler who, at first glance, exuded authority and self-belief. He seemed nervous, and though I was conscious of the danger of him bowling at Watson, it was unavoidable.

It was another of those sliding-doors moments. Had he made an immediate breakthrough the course of his career could have been drastically different. As it was, those eight wicketless overs, which went for fifty-three runs, are his solitary contribution to Test cricket. He was released by Lancashire at the end of the 2018 season and is developing a coaching career.

On a personal level, that match was one of my most memorable experiences. Being an Ashes-winning captain is very special. It meant everything to share it with Alice and my parents. I don't care about the relative merits of that Australian team; they never go quietly. Who, for instance, remembers the weakness of the side beaten by Mike Gatting's 'can't bat, can't bowl, can't field' England in 1986–87?

It's in the book, part of the bloodline.

I had set up the series by telling the team that it was their chance to enter folklore and link their names to an historic rivalry. We didn't want an open-topped bus parade and the keys to the Downing Street drinks cabinet, but I find it puzzling that our 2013 win should be regarded as the forgotten Ashes. The sudden familiarity of victory, after a quarter-century of Australian domination, worked against us.

Of course, there is an element of remorse. It is part of a captain's responsibility to look after people and I felt for Simon on a human level. I occasionally wonder what he thinks of those celebratory pictures, with the champagne spraying and the tinsel cascading, where I'm holding up a replica Ashes urn taken from the Lord's shop.

The original artefact, of course, is far too fragile to be entrusted to a bunch of cricketers eager to get on the sauce. It even had its own first-class seat when flown to Australia, for only the second time, in 2006. The romance it represented, as an old perfume bottle given to England captain Ivo Bligh in 1882 by Lady Clark after defeat to Australia prompted a mock obituary of English cricket, didn't survive our celebrations. That night ended, infamously, with Pee-gate and online images of myself and Matty, still in our kit, attempting to flag down a London bus. I was carrying my England blazer on a hanger; it is one of my favourite photos.

I deeply regret the urination on the square that night. It was not meant to be disrespectful; it was simply a case of a group of young guys being carried away by the moment. The characteristics of a successful team, in our case intensity, repeatability, self-assurance and an insularity tinged with arrogance, can mutate, and accelerate its downfall.

International sport is cyclical, and we weren't alone in underestimating the underlying issues. It happens to the best. Australia, under the coaching influence of Darren Lehmann, were brash, verbally aggressive and pushed the boundaries of acceptable behaviour until their reputation was scoured by sandpaper. Where once they were praised as being assertive, they were criticized as being amoral.

Don't get me wrong. I'm not Mr Nice Guy 24/7. To put it into a context the Australians can understand, sometimes you have to have that bit of dingo about you. Paul Farbrace says there is something flinty, something slightly different, about myself, Rooty, Broady and Jimmy. We are not hard to manage, but we know our own minds, and are ready to fight our corner.

I try to be considerate in my dealings with the general public. I'm continually ready to offer my advice, if requested, to younger guys working through the challenges of their cricket career. But I'm far from perfect. I tend to be prickly when my standards are challenged and was often sharp when I felt we were training suboptimally.

I can be sarcastic. I'm not particularly proud of my impatience with a cameraman, trying to rig up a GoPro camera in the net when I returned to play for Essex after my knighthood. He took maybe thirty seconds, but I was waiting, as were the bowlers. 'Mate, hurry up,' I said, making things worse. 'You can't just have a net, can you these days, without being fucking filmed?'

He was just trying to do his job, but I eventually asked him to stop 'because I'm wasting my time here'. At one level, I was wrong in making him flustered and embarrassed. But on another, my training was being compromised. He was eating into the fifteen minutes I had scheduled to hit. In an ideal world, I would have apologized, and had what Farbrace calls 'one of those leave your beer and walk away moments'.

Swanny can be sharp and stubborn. He spent part of that evening at the Oval wandering about with a soft toy swan on his head, but there were weightier matters on his mind. In hindsight, he probably should have stuck with his original plan to retire there and then.

He had always dreamed of going out on an Ashes win, but

the landscape was changed by the decision to stage back-to-back Ashes series to rationalize the cricket calendar so that the World Cup would not be a competing attraction. Players weren't consulted and were correctly concerned about intensified physical and mental strains. It should never happen again. That the plan was thrown out for 2019 tells you everything you need to know about the expedience of the modern cricket administrator.

We play too much international cricket. Gambles are being taken that can shorten careers. I was rested for the one-day series against the Australians following the Ashes win. In hindsight, the same consideration should have been shown towards a struggling Jonathan Trott. He was bounced out first ball a couple of times, which deepened his problems. KP, too, should have been given room to breathe.

My final words to the group at the end of that Oval Test were intended to act as a punctuation mark between summer and winter. 'I want everyone to be as fit as a butcher's dog for the tour,' I told them. 'That's the only thing we can control between now and Australia.' Those words had greater relevance, and consequence, than I realized at the time.

Swanny was in pain but got a little greedy. He loves Australia, and gave his son Wilfred the middle name Sydney, so saying farewell at the SCG as part of another winning England team was tempting. His elbow injury was severe and had required two operations. One, in America, was conducted by a specialist in baseball injuries. Swanny spent fifty minutes of every hour in an electrically charged sling for two days and nights after surgery.

If that was storing up trouble, our decision to stage another pre-tour hardship camp was a big mistake. The boys looked back at the one we'd staged in Germany with fear, amusement and a strange sense of satisfaction. To this day, Ravi Bopara talks about it. He loved every press-up, each carefully planned humiliation.

If that one was Teutonic, this one, held in Stafford, was shambolic. Other than knowing it was designed to be less physical, in order to reveal different aspects of character and alternative styles of leadership, Andy Flower went into it as blindly as the rest of us. It transpired that we would be trained in surveillance techniques in an operation that would climax with a firefight.

The prospect brought out the little boy in us all. Who wouldn't want to learn how to install tracking devices on a car, and to tail it in traffic? How devious would we be when ordered to act as a spy, following someone into a pub and reporting back overheard snippets of conversation? It all seemed harmless fun.

It was terrible. All hotels in the area were fully booked, so we had to travel for more than half an hour to the rendezvous point for the daily mission. The food was awful. We were briefed for hours, sitting uncomfortably in parked cars, before undertaking a farcical set of exercises. On one occasion, when we were tasked to secretly film a stash of plastic guns in the middle of the night, our patrol leader dropped his mobile phone and alerted the enemy. Half of the team got lost before the final firefight.

We can look back and laugh at the absurdity of it all, but it certainly got the 2013–14 Ashes tour off to a bad start. Poor planning was exacerbated by questionable selection decisions. Individually, several players were past their best.

Collectively, we lacked the cohesion that defined the team that climbed to number one in the world.

Warning signs were ignored. I was as enthusiastic as anyone when we called up Boyd Rankin, a 6ft 8in fast bowler who had transferred allegiances from Ireland, at the age of twenty-nine, after a nine-year, 82-cap career for his home country. A strapping farmer's son, he had a distinctive action. Though evidently prone to bouts of cramp, he caused batsmen a different set of problems.

Initially selected for the one-day series after the Oval, he was unplayable in practice. Ashley Giles, who had come into the England set-up, had coached him for Warwickshire. We wanted to let him loose in the first match at Southampton, but he was forced to withdraw the night before with a back spasm.

By the time he made his Test debut at Sydney, four months later, the Ashes tour had collapsed. It was his first match for five weeks. He admitted to being consumed by nerves, reported a back spasm on the first morning, and was twice forced to limp off with cramp. His only Test wicket for England, when he incited Peter Siddle into a top-edged pull, came from his last delivery.

Australia went into the series on their worst winless run since 1986. They were blighted by injuries that ruled out emerging quickies Mitchell Starc, James Pattinson and Pat Cummins. Mitchell Johnson was deemed to be chronically wayward, a caricature gunslinger. We were unbeaten in thirteen Tests and forbidding favourites.

I'm not going to shy away from the depth of our problems, but credit where it is due. Johnson's speed, hostility and accuracy exposed weaknesses in our technique and temperament. I spoke to him after the series, when he admitted to being initially nervous about further ridicule. To come back in that manner showed the psychological strength of a champion.

Nathan Lyon, Ryan Harris and Peter Siddle bowled at their best. Michael Clarke scored early hundreds and proved to be a very impressive, tactically astute captain. Brad Haddin was a nuggety batsman who led several significant fightbacks when our bowlers, principally Stuart Broad, were on a roll. Some of the sledging was below the belt but I enjoyed a beer with them once it was all over. They're very similar to us, beneath a different badge.

We were in trouble, almost from the get-go, and fell apart under pressure. So many things went wrong. It all came to a natural end, with bewildering speed. Andy Flower had become jaded by the incessant demands of international coaching. Chris Tremlett struggled badly and was dropped after the first Test. Steven Finn lost his rhythm and confidence.

Monty Panesar was at his most enigmatic. His form was so unpredictable he could not be trusted. He was, on his own admission, on the rebound from alcohol problems, and withdrew into himself. He seemed especially troubled by Trotty's issues, and later sought medical advice after suffering anxiety and paranoia that stemmed from a loss of confidence and self-esteem.

He hadn't reached out to the group, and you do worry about someone you don't see on tour. I tried to coax him out of his room but, to be honest, he was erratic. Was his self-containment a necessary shield we had taken away briefly, albeit for all the right reasons? All I know is his decline was sad, and deeply affecting.

He had quickly become a cult figure on coming into the England team. He bowled beautifully, with a lovely shape on the ball, massive hands, great control, a very repeatable action. A couple of steps in, arms up, good pace. His skill was just to bowl the same ball, one after the other. He held an end up, and rarely bowled a bad delivery.

Whenever he fielded the ball, he received a huge cheer. He worked very hard on his batting and would get a standing ovation for a forward defensive. He had a loveable simplicity in that he knew about little else than bowling and Sikhism. Were people laughing with him or at him? Did his exposure, as one of the most recognizable figures in the country, exacerbate underlying problems? Was he ready for the pressure, the scrutiny, the expectation, the celebrity, the fame? There were, for the time being, more questions than answers.

Swanny came to me, admitting that he expected to be dropped in favour of Monty after bowling poorly in the second-Test defeat at Adelaide. I asked him, as one of my senior lieutenants, to help generate the energy we required to stop the rot in Perth, which is rarely receptive to spin. He agreed, but in his head, he had already retired.

Perth was my 100th Test, and one of my most dispiriting. Swanny picked up three wickets but told me it had been the longest five days of his life. The last place he wanted to be was on a cricket field. His elbow hurt badly, but there was more to it than that. I looked into his eyes and knew that, mentally, he had gone. A light had been extinguished. He had hidden his hurt from his teammates, but the bubbly guy to whom everyone gravitated was consumed by sadness and frustration. I agreed to an announcement in Melbourne but, given my time again, would have asked him to keep our conversation confidential, and remain on tour for appearances' sake.

He wasn't stupid. He knew the uproar he would create. He accepted he would be portrayed as a bottler, a bloke who abandoned ship. No one has a divine right to play for England. Representing your country, reflecting your culture, is a special honour, to be treated with appropriate respect. His decision, in the middle of a series, was far from ideal, but I didn't feel fundamentally let down.

To go back to Flower's central point, Test cricket is quite literally a test of individual character. Who am I to say that Swanny hadn't made the harder, more courageous decision? He knew he had lost the necessary edge. The spark had gone. Instead of bottling it, had he simply realized he had nothing left? Maybe he just took the brave decision.

There wasn't time to process the answers, because problems were multiplying. Matt Prior, a stalwart of the team, was dropped for the final two Test matches. I had that so-called toilet chat. He was out of form and not doing himself justice. It suggested, to me, that he had been worn down by the intensity of international cricket.

It hurt, because he had turned up for the tour in the best physical shape I'd seen. He retained his hunger and ambition, but even those admirable qualities created tension because KP objected to him taking a leadership role in team meetings after his demotion. I felt his comments were a supportive gesture, and an indication of his devastation; Kevin appeared to be more suspicious.

Relationships were splintering. KP had a massive fallout with Graham Gooch on the balcony at Perth, after he had tried to hit Lyon out of the ground, into the wind, and was caught at deep long on by Harris. I sat between them, all too aware of my first-ball dismissal, as Goochy repeated, 'Shit shot, shit shot,' and Kevin replied with a few choice words of his own.

Damage was creeping from the field to the changing room. A team that once had a unique form of resilience was falling apart. We shied away from answering the toughest questions. Were we hiding from Mitchell Johnson? Why hadn't we, as a leadership team, addressed his threat properly, instead of expecting people to play him as they wished?

Flower had been meeting KP on a weekly basis since 2012, to discuss potential problems as part of a proactive managerial strategy. It wasn't as disruptive as has been claimed, but KP was high maintenance. He aired the possibility of flying home from Perth because of soreness in his knee but was talked down by Mushtaq Ahmed.

To be fair to him, he applied himself well in the final two Tests, without answering wider doubts about his motives. He was studiously engaged in public, helping less experienced players in the nets. Some saw ulterior motives, a politician creating a favourable impression. On balance, I preferred to give him the benefit of the doubt.

It was an extraordinarily febrile time, and mistakes were made under pressure. Joe Root had only one score over 26 in the first four Tests, but our batting was collectively poor. My 2010 series average of 127 certainly seemed an anomaly. Joe didn't deserve to be singled out and dropped for Sydney; it proved a pivotal moment in his career. He used his disappointment and resentment positively, as motivation never to allow himself to be in that situation again.

Goochy, old school to the last, thought I should have administered more bollockings in team meetings. It wasn't as simple as shouting. I had my head down, re-evaluating my approach, and realized I needed to take greater control. That meant easing my reliance on Flower, whose approach was criticized fiercely by KP in an intense players'-only meeting after defeat in Melbourne.

I'd depended on Andy too much and needed to drive the group in a different direction. As players, we needed to take ownership of our plight. That change of emphasis didn't startle or intimidate me, because successful teams tend to have strong captains, assisted by coaches who drive behind-the-scenes improvement. My apprenticeship as a captain was complete.

The buck stopped with me. I tried to hold my head high and made a point of going out to see the Barmy Army in Sydney, but the loneliness of leadership hit home. Failure, on that scale, is an extremely public process. Press conferences were brutal, though I sensed a degree of respect because when the story is that big the captain is only one of many characters to consider.

Everyone had a view. Opinions were being formed on little or no knowledge. I understood the process, accepted that cricket was part of the national conversation and promised myself never to react impulsively. Some of the second-hand stuff I heard or read was nonsense, but I ignored it. All I could do was act on one of international sport's truisms and attempt to control the controllables.

Paul Downton arrived in Australia to evaluate the mood, and consult those closest to the issues, prior to taking up the role of the ECB's managing director on 1 February 2014.

I spent a couple of hours with Ashley Giles, coach of the one-day side, in his room, trying to rationalize what the future looked like.

Andy's time as Test team director was clearly coming to an end. He'd had enough. It was an obvious opportunity to reassess and rebuild: I still wanted to lead and was told I retained the confidence of my employers. There were signs of promise, in Ben Stokes and Joe Root, but discussions kept returning to the thorniest issue: what should we do about Kevin?

KP had returned home after the Ashes series. I spoke separately to Downton and Giles Clarke, the ECB chairman. Giles has a polarizing personality, but I found him intelligent and impressive, especially in board meetings. I realized the gravity of some of the conversations, and wanted to give a balanced view, without excessive emotion.

Should I have shared my thoughts, in depth, with KP as part of that process? Probably so, though the atmosphere was not conducive to mutual trust. He was publicly bullish about his desire to help us regain the Ashes in 2015, but my sense, over the previous twelve months, was that his ambition had waned. I thought he'd had his fill of playing for England.

As a captain, I had to cut through the noise and glitter of the KP brand and analyse his impact on those around him. Managing him on a day-to-day basis was fine. Small issues, such as his expectation that he would occasionally be given special dispensation, were dealt with relatively smoothly, though prone to potential complication.

Kevin, an imposing figure, had a major impact on the dressing room. If he didn't particularly care about something, or if, conversely, he had powerful views on a certain issue, he had the capacity to drag people with him subconsciously. A senior player, particularly one of his stature and aura, has a profound responsibility to the group.

He was never nasty, but had been in hundreds of team meetings during a glittering career. If he didn't want to be there, he made it pretty obvious. Over time, that became draining. Even his staunchest supporters would concede that, to paraphrase the mischievous chat-show host Graham Norton, he was an individual in a team sport.

Helping to decide his future was the hardest aspect of my career as England captain. I had huge respect for him as a cricketer, and was determined to judge him from personal experience rather than the myths and legends that had been built around him. I had never, for instance, heard him issue the supposed 'him or me' ultimatum during his dispute with Peter Moores, so I refused to allow it to influence me.

I factored in Kevin's achievements over 104 Tests and 136 one-day internationals. Although this was strictly relative, given our collectively poor form with the bat on that Ashes tour, he had been our highest run scorer with 293. Yet I felt strongly, as captain, that we had reached the stage where we would get more out of up-and-coming players who were desperate to prove themselves.

I recommended that he should step away from the England team. All that remained was for the firestorm to break.

11. Fallout

Ending anyone's international career is a horrible, hateful experience. When it concerns a globally renowned, passionately admired figure you have played alongside for eight years it is uniquely uncomfortable. There is no easy way to express the hardest truth of elite sport, that everyone, to a lesser or greater degree, lives on borrowed time.

We didn't need *Wisden* to measure Kevin Pietersen's stature. Statistics, 8,181 Test runs at an average of 47.28, incorporating thirty-two hundreds for England across all forms of the game, merely hint at the majesty of the memories he created. Ultimately his personality was as integral to the decision as his waning powers of performance.

Andy Flower, as expected, had resigned as director of the Test team a couple of days earlier. Kevin had never really convinced him that he bought into the principle of being a team player without reservation. A consensus had emerged during the one-day series in Australia, and on our return home, that a statement of intent and a reaffirmation of trust were overdue.

Kevin was centrally contracted but, like all of us, had no guarantee of selection. Simply not picking him was a theoretical option, but I supported Paul Downton, the ECB's managing director. 'I don't want that cloud hanging over us,' he told James Whitaker, the national selector, and me. 'I don't want every press conference to start with the question, "*Is KP coming back?*" I don't want us to get bowled out cheaply and have everyone asking, "*Is KP coming back?*"'

Paul was my boss. He had the authority to confirm the big decision and wanted to make a clean break. As captain, my opinions carried weight. I had a responsibility to communicate the views of other senior players. Like me, they felt it was time to move on without Kevin, so that we could all have breathing room. It was not a final banishment, because in international sport no one can say never, but on a human level I felt a sense of dread. We were dealing with someone with whom I'd shared some magical experiences.

I met Downton and Whitaker in the coffee shop of the Danubius Hotel in St John's Wood, opposite the Nursery End at Lord's. No one was entirely sure how Kevin was going to react when we called him into a first-floor meeting room. I knew what was going to be said. As a player you learn to cope with nerves, but I can't lie. It was a deeply unpleasant experience.

Formalities were icy, as they tend to be in this type of situation in any job. Downton thanked Kevin for his service to English cricket, paid due homage to the magnitude of his career, but ended a brief summary with the words 'we are no longer going to pick you for England'. Kevin was poker-faced, stood up and said, 'OK, thanks,' and walked out of the room.

The meeting had lasted, in my estimation, no more than three minutes. Kevin would later describe me as a 'company man' who looked down at his shoes throughout the process. It's true there were moments when I studied the carpet, because this was not a decision taken lightly, but I made a point of making eye contact. I didn't say a word because there simply wasn't time to do so.

Kevin was a barrier to progress, a source of distraction, and I suspect he knew what was coming. There was a momentary silence when he walked out, a brief calm before the storm. Downton's public suggestion that 'the time is right to rebuild not only the team but also the team ethic' set off a predictable chain of events.

The dignity of Kevin's initial statement, in which he spoke of his pride and honour at playing for England, didn't last. What followed was a classic example of the 'pile on', a social-media phenomenon fuelled by egotism, ignorance, smugness and often superficial anger, which feeds off itself until it assumes a significance out of all proportion to the subject. Just a few people can be very, very noisy.

The campaign against us was well orchestrated and floated on hot air. Its principal cheerleader called me 'a repulsive little weasel', which might have had greater impact had it been said to my face. Matty Prior was accused of 'backstabbing' and Andy Flower was unfairly attacked. We faced a modern dilemma: would responding to such unwarranted slurs merely add to the hysteria?

Probably so, but the abuse was so personal, and the situation so tawdry, that the Professional Cricketers' Association, our union, in conjunction with the ECB, felt impelled to act. An ECB statement referred to 'a breach of trust and team ethics'. It supported both my captaincy and the culture we were attempting to create. Confidence was also expressed in Prior and Flower.

The over-riding irony was that the three of us had done everything possible to make the relationship work. We had driven the decision to bring Kevin back in 2012, and gave him the chance to extend his international career. That was lost on those swept along by inaccurate perceptions of betrayal. At times, they seemed beyond reason.

The vehemence of such personalized attacks is disturbing, and there would be moments in the months to come when I felt isolated and persecuted, scapegoated by people who gleefully picked at the scab of an ultimately pointless debate. I must admit I didn't see any evidence of Kevin's sensitivity to others, which seemed so central to his supporters, but I'm not one for bitterness.

Others in the firing line, principally Andy and Matty, had also done nothing to merit such denigration. Claims of a bullying culture were completely wide of the mark, but as contracted players we were ordered by the ECB not to respond because they didn't want the situation to be further inflamed. We weren't allowed to provide context. I am all for keeping a dignified silence, but it was a mess.

Was the atmosphere in the England dressing room uncomfortable at times? You bet. That's inevitable when you have highly competitive people who don't conform to the so-called norm striving for the sort of success that's very public but acutely personal. These were once-in-a-generation players, driven by the intensity of a consciously created climate.

Of course, there was piss-taking, which exists in every dressing room at every level of the game. It's politically incorrect, most of the time, often childish, but harmless because it is not vindictive or intended to be taken seriously.

Of course, we were imperfect. Of course, there were moments of tension. Jonathan Trott flew at Matty Prior when he criticized a mistake in the field. 'Don't you ever speak to me like that again!' he yelled. 'Well, you're fucking fielding for England, mate,' Prior replied. They had a stand-up row, sorted out their differences like adults and moved on immediately.

As captain I was comfortable with allowing senior players their head in the dressing room. These people cared. It is not a place for tra-la-la innocence. No one walks in trilling, 'Morning, everyone. What a wonderful day.' Mockery is delivered on a give-and-take basis. Nicknames, such as 'Cheese', which Prior picked up at Sussex, tend to stick.

Flower inherited chaos, and imposed order with greater sensitivity than his authoritarian image suggests. I enjoyed working with him, even though things ended badly. I'm happy to march behind anyone who possesses the cojones to call out Robert Mugabe as the man who ruined Zimbabwe, Andy's country. That takes a rare form of moral courage. The stability he brought gave us the extra 2 per cent that is so often decisive. He strengthened the bubble, acted as a doorkeeper to our world. Andy might not have been as good at empowering players as someone like Trevor Bayliss, who is skilful in fostering a spirit of independence, but I valued his directness, shrewdness and honesty.

The relationship between captain and coach is pivotal. Each must be comfortable with his role and responsibilities. Differences, in terms of selection strategies or training plans, can be dealt with if there is mutual trust and respect, but ultimately the coach is there to support the captain. Andy was the perfect guide in my early days, because he managed my workload and allowed me to concentrate on my game. As I grew stronger as a leader, I knew I needed to take greater responsibility.

We all develop. Andy didn't like grey areas, and if you spoke to him today he would perhaps accept he could have been a better listener. He admitted to me recently that, given his time again, he would still coach the player, but pay more attention to coaching the person. On one thing he cannot be challenged, however: he helped to maximize talent and developed a team through his willingness to confront difficult issues. His skill as a coach was to ask uncomfortable questions of his players.

All too often such questions go unasked. They prompt awkward silences but are never designed to belittle the individual. Singling someone out in front of twelve or fifteen of his peers is the worst thing you can do, as a coach or a leader. If there is an issue to be thrashed out, it must be done on a one-to-one basis.

Andy's style was to frame everything in a team context. Typically, he would say, 'Well, what went wrong this week? I thought we took our eye off the ball.' He'd then ask a player for his thoughts. It took me back to those days at school, when you are day-dreaming in class, and snap back into the present thinking, 'Shit! I hope the teacher doesn't ask me a question now . . .'

As we gained more confidence in each other, developed trust and ease in each other's company, those awkward silences became shorter. We weren't afraid to be self-critical, or critical of others, within reason. Obviously, the management of that is hard, because once you throw a meeting open you don't know what is going to be tossed back at you.

Failure is a touchy subject. Occasionally, an argument is going to be created by a loose word or a thoughtless comment, but that comes with the territory. I resolved to rebuild faith through the infusion of new players and coaches. Different personalities can help to restore a sense of momentum, provided they are loyal to the common themes of the group.

I had no active role in the selection process but was happy when Peter Moores was appointed as Andy's successor in April 2014, before the summer series against Sri Lanka and India. He was a familiar figure who offered a different voice and had re-evaluated his approach following his first spell in charge. I liked him as a person, already related to him as a coach, and he understood what made me tick.

I had come up with a list of non-negotiables for what I regarded as the second stage of my captaincy. These revolved around the principle of being an England player 24/7. It didn't involve a grand gesture, a PowerPoint sermon. I'd seen enough of those to doubt their effectiveness. It was more intimate, a renewal of our vows to one another as tried and trusted teammates.

My plan, scribbled in a little black book, included a commitment to reconnecting with the cricket public. We needed to rediscover our sense of freedom, reaffirm what it meant to us to play for England. We had a team charter that had run its course, but we still needed a simple set of rules to live, play and work by. This wasn't revolution. It was an evolution that recognized strengths we hadn't made the most of. No one was going to come riding in on a cloud of glory to save us. We had to do it for ourselves. Live it, think about it, revise it if necessary. Players improve themselves as people, coaches become better teachers; everyone benefits.

Peter acknowledged he pushed too hard in his first stint with England and took too much on himself. We worked collaboratively, to enable players to discover where they were, and what they needed to do, either technically or personally, to progress. I was disappointed he only lasted little more than a year, but coaching is an unforgiving business. The best cricket coaches, like the best football managers, rarely have long cycles in charge. There is a huge burnout factor; travel is constant and pressure rarely relents.

Looking at senior players on the verge of making the transition today, I can see Marcus Trescothick and Ian Bell being successful coaches. They are both low-key characters, hugely experienced players, bonded by a deep love of cricket. Their lives are based on the game, and they have a deceptively fierce drive. They don't hang around to admire the view; they want to climb upwards, safely and effectively. They have the level-headedness to appreciate that the art of coaching is incredibly hard.

Ultimately, success or failure is down to the player. You can't always hold his hand, though there will be times when you are forced to do so. He must make his mistakes, put his fingers in the fire and get burned. Graham Gooch, in his old-school way, understood the power of pain. Whenever I made an error in my batting, he expected me to learn from it.

The tenor of coaching is changing, in all sports. Back in the day, the 'tell me' coach held sway. Now it is fashionable for the player to be asked to find the solution. Theoretically that makes sense, because he is in the middle thinking for himself, looking for the answer, but I wonder whether the pendulum has swung too far.

Sometimes you just need to be told. The player may insist on personal preferences, but if he is wrong, he must be challenged. It is a balance; the coach has to be strong but could cause damage if he is misguided. We're back to that common currency, trust. Does the coach have the eye of a batsman, for instance? It obviously helps if he has experience at the highest level.

Even though we decided we needed a new voice in his area of expertise, Goochy spoke with the authority of a fantastic Test career. He held the view that cricket is a game that cannot be tamed, though its contrasts and contradictions can be tolerable. Elementary mistakes can be minimized, through the incremental improvement that comes with experience, but if the player has a poor mental attitude he is often beyond help.

Cricket produces very few Mourinhos or Wengers, hugely influential coaches with minimal playing pedigree. The closest comparison I can come up with is Paul Farbrace, who worked as assistant to both Moores and Bayliss. A wicketkeeper-batsman with a modest career average of 18.23, he played only forty first-class matches, for Kent and Middlesex, over eight years.

Occasionally fallibility, or experience of marginal lack of fulfilment at the highest level, is an asset. Mark Ramprakash exemplifies the latter, Marcus Trescothick the former. He and Trotty have, through their individual trials and tribulations, done current and future generations a great service, by highlighting issues that too often remain unspoken.

The second phase of my captaincy was conducted under the toxic cloud we feared, because of the inability of the ECB to put the KP affair to bed. The campaign on Kevin's behalf was shrill, ceaseless and spiteful, but it was very efficient in highlighting the limitations of a governing body that lacked expertise in key areas.

I became frustrated with communications staff who failed to communicate and by edicts that left me in an impossible position. On one farcical Essex press day, every question to me was about KP but I wasn't allowed to answer. It was extraordinary that the situation had become so convoluted, and mired in legal complexity.

The ECB board couldn't deal with the power of social media. There was an inability to follow a consistent line of thought, impotence in the face of clever cyber-warfare, waged by proxy. Interested parties promoted the myth of KP's victimhood and turned the debate into one of perception of personality rather than principle. I felt like public enemy number one, and lacked conspicuous support from my employers. We weren't the first team Kevin had fallen out with, yet he was being portrayed as the good guy, a martyr to his art. The elephant had broken out of the room and was rampaging around the outfield at Lord's.

The situation was out of my control. I lost count of the conversations I had with the ECB, who didn't possess the quality of leadership the current CEO, Tom Harrison, provides. His predecessor, David Collier, who retired at the end of the 2014 season before taking up a role in rugby league, sat firmly on the fence. The hierarchy agreed privately that Kevin could not be recalled, but never said so publicly. They hung me out to dry.

Sport moves on quickly; the controversy had very little relevance to our priority, fashioning a new team. It was wearing and distracting, a waste of mental energy since it was the only thing most people wanted to talk about. There were times I longed for the simplicity and purity of attempting to score as many runs as possible.

Though we lost that summer's opening series against Sri Lanka, in such gutting fashion that Alice had to talk me out of walking away, the first green shoots of recovery were detectable. Five of the six changes we made from the team that surrendered in Sydney contributed positively to the drawn first Test at Lord's.

Joe Root made a powerful point with an unbeaten 200, Matt Prior scored 86 and provided the solidity and direction expected of a senior pro. Gary Ballance contributed a second-innings century. Moeen Ali, on debut, played with the dexterity and assurance of someone vastly more experienced. Chris Jordan, an effervescent presence, took a wicket with his third delivery in Test cricket. Liam Plunkett, recalled after seven years, showed fantastic stamina.

Newer guys were free from scar tissue. They had everything you would want as a captain, inherent talent, rawness around the edges balanced by hunger and a willingness to listen. Ben Stokes, who had scored a wonderful maiden Test hundred on a cracked pitch at Perth, came into the side for the subsequent series against India.

It was still open season on me. Shane Warne was chirping away, and KP, a markedly similar character, turned up to watch us from a hospitality box in the second Test against India at Lord's. Inevitably, he was a magnet for the cameras. I trust I am not being unkind in suggesting his appearance was orchestrated.

We were back to the old routine, of Test cricket testing character.

We bowled too short after preparing a green wicket and were about eighty runs under par when we batted, despite another Ballance hundred. My captaincy was justifiably criticized, since I was too slow to change tactics. We lost, as badly in our own conditions as India did in Mumbai in 2012, but I looked around the changing room and felt a tightness of spirit we had not had for quite a while.

My relationship with Moores was acquiring depth and substance. He went above and beyond the call of duty to help me find some consistency in my batting, simulating the pressures of a ninety-over innings by throwing 540 balls at me during a concentrated three-hour training shift at Loughborough. We only took a short break, every thirty overs; I needed to lose myself in the process, forget about being a captain, and concentrate on my batting.

We drilled down into the numbers, which revealed we were winning the majority of sessions in our early matches. We were close to a breakthrough but didn't complete the job. Such niceties meant nothing to the usual suspects, who didn't need to tell me that I would have been out of a job if England had lost that marquee series.

There was, mercifully, a little light relief, in the form of my first Test wicket, which I'd like to think of as the highlight of the drawn Test at Trent Bridge. Ishant Sharma nicked off, was caught down the leg side, and I was away, doing my best Alan Shearer impression. I ran around, pointing at the balcony to remind David Saker, our bowling coach, that I had managed something he never achieved as a proud Australian.

Sakes has a one-word description of my bowling: 'Shite.' But if you have a spare hour, I'll happily go through my eighteen deliveries in Test cricket, as a study of unaccustomed excellence. I average seven as a bowler, which is none too shabby. I took my wicket with a seamer but also served up an over of spin. Imagine if I had taken being an all-rounder seriously . . .

Garry Sobers, eat your heart out!

I received quite a few texts after taking that wicket, mostly along the lines of 'it's good to see you smiling again'. I was still being hammered but viewed it as another examination of my resilience. I had come close to jacking it in after the Sri Lanka series but as the summer progressed, I acquired a strange, if temporary, serenity.

My stubbornness saved me. I wouldn't allow myself to be worn down. I wouldn't give my more hysterical critics the satisfaction of knowing how deeply I had been hurt. I was being tested as a person and felt a responsibility to those around me. My form was suffering, but it was my job to ignore the noise and lead from the front.

Rod Bransgrove, the Hampshire chairman, intuitively understood the intensity of that inner struggle. I didn't know him that well, but when we had dinner, in the build-up to the third Test at his pride and joy, the Ageas Bowl in Southampton, he assured me, 'You're going to have a good week with us. Don't worry, we'll look after you.'

I took it all with a pinch of salt, to be honest, but when I walked out to bat, on winning the toss, I was given a standing ovation. The crowd's warmth was tangible. It suggested that, for no apparent reason, the tide of public opinion had turned. I was still scratching around for runs, like a hen scrabbling in the dirt for scraps, but they cheered me to the echo when I reached 48 by lunch.

Maybe the silent majority had found their voice. Maybe it wasn't all about shouting from tabloid pulpit and Twitter feed. Maybe, after all the bluff and bluster, people were prepared to take us on our own merits. It was galling to get out for 95, to a good leg-side catch by MS Dhoni off a bottom edge, but a pressure valve had been released.

Ballance and Bell got big hundreds, Jimmy Anderson was man of the match and Mo took six wickets, in the second innings. We were nowhere near the finished article, but momentum was gathering. That 266-run win at Southampton was followed by victories by an innings at Old Trafford and the Oval. When I got home, Alice sensed immediately how much that sequence meant to me. She felt the same, since we had gone through so much together. We made the most of that week's grace before, once again, I was under the pump.

I was really looking forward to the one-day series against India, as a release from the stresses of the Test summer. I hadn't been in the best of form but was eager to express myself by playing an attacking innings. There's nothing like feeling ball on bat. Thanks to good old British rain on a Bank Holiday, I was completely blindsided by criticism from an unexpected source.

The first ODI, at Bristol, was rained off by 1.30 p.m. By that time, Graeme Swann had set the hares running by suggesting on *Test Match Special* that I should quit as one-day captain. Talk became increasingly cheap as we waited for the inevitable abandonment; Michael Vaughan piled in by implying I was doing 'half a job' as a batsman.

Bad news travels exceptionally fast. The controversy dominated the news feed on my phone, once I retrieved it from the anti-corruption officers. I understand the need to fill airtime, and the danger of issues being hyped out of all proportion, but when I read Swanny's tabloid newspaper column the following day I was livid. He had doubled down on the original comments. I didn't have an issue with his view, as such, because he had every right to an opinion, but I expected greater understanding from someone who knew what I had gone through in the previous eight months.

I regard him as a good friend. We'd shared beds in India, shared dressing rooms around the world. I had his back when he wanted to retire midway through an Ashes series. I now have even greater cause to understand the inevitable conflict when a senior player pursues a secondary career in the media, but at the time I felt genuinely let down.

'Couldn't you just see it from my point of view?' I asked him. To be fair, he apologized, but the agenda had been reinforced. Moores felt he should have been more proactive with the media, in explaining the thinking behind the transition to a new generation of players shaped by the limited-overs game. Our plan was to introduce them gradually, rather than all at once.

I was obviously vulnerable. Results, the ultimate arbiter, weren't good. We had brief bursts of success but lost consecutive one-day series to India and Sri Lanka. I wasn't producing the goods. I was assured that the selectors retained faith in me, but the proximity of the World Cup inevitably concentrated minds.

I wanted to complete my four-year cycle as one-day captain. After all, we became number one on my watch, and only a late-innings collapse in the 2013 Champions Trophy final against India at Edgbaston stopped us from winning England's first major final in five attempts. We had picked a team suited to fifty-over cricket that day, but rain reduced it to a twenty-over thrash.

Moores backed me publicly, as World Cup captain, just before Christmas. But, given the selection meeting was obviously going to focus on my position, I recognized a potential conflict of interest, and withdrew from it. Had I joined Peter Moores, James Whitaker, Mick Newell and Gus Fraser, I would have argued for stability, because wholesale changes in the build-up to previous major tournaments had been counter-productive.

I told Alice I intended to call Peter on the day of that meeting, to stress that I didn't want him to feel pressurized by his public show of faith. Above all, I wanted him to be honest. That might sound a bit naïve and unworldly, but I didn't want to sit there thinking he had backed me as one-day captain out of a misplaced sense of loyalty.

'I know there's a lot to talk about,' I told him. 'I still think I'm the right man to be captain, but be true to yourself. The form over the past twelve months has not been great. I appreciate that we've been plotting a path to this World Cup, and through to the Ashes next summer, but whatever decision is made I will not bear a grudge towards you.'

I had no interest in discovering the voting patterns, or whether, by making that assurance, I had inadvertently tipped the balance against me. When I took a call from Whitaker, asking if he could come to see me at home, it was obvious that the die had been cast. It was a big blow. I was back, deep in the bush.

There was only one person to blame, myself. I couldn't moan about being left out because I hadn't scored the runs, but it dented my pride and almost destroyed my spirit. To be brutally honest, for two or three days around Christmas I didn't really want to walk down the street. As ridiculous as it seems, I imagined strangers whispering, 'He's the bloke who's just got sacked.'

I rang Eoin Morgan on the day he was appointed as my

successor with the one-day team, to offer any help I could. I wished him well and assured him there were no hard feelings. He'd been given a hospital pass in many ways, because at that point in our development we were behind the curve in a limited-overs game that was changing so radically, so quickly.

Instead of measured, quantifiable preparation over the life cycle of a World Cup, we were like a student doing crash-course revision, trying to respond to the new realities of the game in a fifteen-match programme. Predictably, a young team uncertain of its identity failed to qualify for the knock-out phase in Australia and New Zealand.

I had three months at home before a tour of the West Indies from mid-April. I had been worn down by the KP saga, with its blizzard of unflattering headlines. Even my default position, grinding my way out of trouble, seemed dispiritingly inadequate. I pride myself on self-reliance, but I needed Alice to retain my sanity.

So much had happened in such a short space of time. I just unloaded on Alice, and her support was unwavering. I tried to see things from her perspective, as we were both coming to terms with the joys and responsibilities of the birth of our daughter, Elsie. Alice couldn't score my runs, chair my team meetings, reply to my detractors. She had to endure my hurt at the relentless negativity. She was on the outside looking in, and I was on the inside, cut to the quick. I had to hunker down and wait for my reward, because it was me against the world.

12. Redemption

The tranquillity of Sugar Ridge, a $50-million, 43-acre complex overlooking Jolly Harbour on Antigua's west coast, was deceptive. It might specialize in mindfulness and modern pampering, but over two long nights, locked in discussion with Peter Moores, it looked as if that was where my England Test captaincy would effectively come to an end.

Normally, the tougher the situation in which I find myself, the more resolute I become, but this was an extended cry for help, during a drawn Test match at a time of transition. The Gimp was working overtime on my shoulder, telling me that I didn't need the pressure. Until I poured my heart out to Peter, I was set on retiring at the end of the three-match series in the Caribbean.

Although, behind the scenes, moves were being made to appoint Andrew Strauss to the newly created role of England's director of cricket, the lessons of the previous fifteen months had not been heeded. I craved certainty, rather than well-meaning but damagingly casual interpretations of the situation regarding Kevin Pietersen.

The media, loving the ambiguities of the story, were disinclined to take no for an answer, and needed little encouragement from Colin Graves, the incoming chairman of the ECB. He had muddied the waters in an interview with the BBC in early March by suggesting that KP could only be considered for an England recall if he was consistently scoring runs in county cricket.

He doubled down on those comments in an interview with the *Daily Telegraph*, in which he observed, 'What happened in the past is history.' To be fair, he stressed he had no jurisdiction in matters of selection, but he urged readers to 'forget personalities. Selectors pick the best players in form, taking wickets and scoring runs. That is their job.'

Taken alongside a comment that, if KP scored really heavily, 'they can't ignore him, I would have thought', it gave Kevin his chance to shine. He was without a county at the time, having signed to play in the IPL and Caribbean Premier League, but within a couple of hours of the original interview he had told Sky TV he valued the potential opportunity.

He, too, doubled down in the *Telegraph*, where he was quoted as saying: 'Do I want to play for England again? Yes, of course I do. My time with England was cut short and I have always said I want to play again.' He promised to talk to Graves, a successful businessman who, in true Yorkshire tradition, evidently specialized in plain speaking.

That trait had already complicated my captaincy, since he described the West Indies as 'mediocre'. It was an unnecessarily provocative comment that led to the question 'Are we mediocre?' being plastered, in large letters, across their dressing-room wall. I had been looked after marvellously by the ECB for most of my career, but I didn't think an administrator of his stature should not have used such language.

I felt aggrieved that I was expected to suck it up and carry on regardless. Moores talked me round and, freed up mentally by the knowledge that my relationship with Strauss was about to be reinforced following the sacking of Paul

Downton, I scored my first Test century in just under two years, 105, in the first innings of the frenetic final Test in Barbados.

We lost, from a winning position, in three days and squandered the chance to take the series. That century had significance beyond its immediate inadequacy, because it was such a personal achievement, and I was distracted when asked in a post-match radio interview about the 'mediocre' comment. 'That's a Yorkshireman for you,' I said jokingly. 'They're quite happy to talk a good game.'

It's fair to say this didn't go down well with Geoffrey Boycott. I didn't know him that well but had huge respect for him as a defining voice of cricket, and one of the best batsmen of his era. We often discussed the intricacies of the game, and laughed easily at his favourite line, 'If I had a daughter, I'd let you marry her.'

His newspaper column the following day accused me of being 'so up his own arse, he thinks he is untouchable as captain'. For good measure, he added: 'Cook acts as if he is the best captain England have ever had. He is living in cloud-cuckoo land about his captaincy ability.' He described my relationship with Strauss as being too cosy.

We would make up, over time, but he was in no mood to toss white roses at my feet when we met, coincidentally, that day at the Lone Star restaurant on the west coast of Barbados. Since the match had ended early, I was out with Alice, Trotty and his wife Abi. Geoffrey was hosting a touring party of fifteen cricket lovers.

Given Dutch courage by a couple of lunchtime liveners, I wandered over and asked for a word, at his convenience. 'Let's do it now,' he said, excusing himself from his guests. I knew he was serious when he brought over his favourite cushion to sit with us. With a deep breath, and without using one of his trademark sticks of rhubarb, I opened the batting.

'Geoffrey,' I said, 'you and I have got on really well throughout my career. I've really appreciated you being a massive supporter of mine. I have absolutely no problem with you attacking how I bat, or with you criticizing my captaincy, because that is your job as a pundit. But to attack me personally in your column, as being arrogant, in a "who does he think he is?" sort of way, was wrong.'

Boycott fixed me with a gimlet eye. 'I think I've got the right to do that, because you slagged off a Yorkshireman in that radio interview,' he said. 'I was just defending him. You upset a Yorkshireman, so me being a Yorkshireman, I just went for you, no problem. What do Joe Root and Jonny Bairstow and all the Yorkshiremen in your team think of you now, then? You attacked one of us.'

His reasoning was distinctive, to say the least. We talked around the issues for about twenty minutes but Geoffrey, rather like his political heroine Margaret Thatcher, was not for turning. He was unapologetic, and not having my counter-argument, that my teammates were unconcerned by what they took as light-hearted comments at the end of a tour.

That storm in a Yorkshire teacup had blown itself out when I took a call from Strauss, who confided that he intended to sack Moores. I argued against it, from both a personal and professional point of view. I loved Peter as a bloke; he was a pillar of trust. He had been there for me in the Caribbean, when he'd understood the limits of my self-containment and I'd needed to blurt out some of my innermost feelings to someone who was deeply involved in my cricket.

I was genuinely upset. To get rid of him as head coach while he was in the process of embedding a new generation of England players was, in my view, an avoidable error of judgement. He was, for instance, helping Ben Stokes through that formative initial cycle of being good, bad and average. Straussy acknowledged my input as captain, but was adamant we needed a more hands-off coach, in the mould of Duncan Fletcher.

Moores deserved better than to be subjected to another PR disaster, when his departure was reported prematurely during a washed-out one-day international in Dublin, and not confirmed, along with the appointment of Strauss, until the following day. My sympathy for Peter was genuine, though I welcomed Andrew's replacement of Paul Downton.

Andrew was not coming in on mate's rates. He balanced our friendship with his authority, and I respected him as a leader who made, and stood by, difficult decisions. That's how a hierarchical system should work. He was brilliant for me, and I had no problem with him being firm in his demands of me.

KP was successfully reintegrating himself into county cricket with Surrey, but on the night before he completed an unbeaten innings of 355 against Leicestershire, Strauss told him his England career was over because of a 'massive trust issue'. Kevin spoke of 'deceit' following his invitation to the meeting by Tom Harrison, the new chief executive of the ECB.

To be brutally honest, when Strauss told me of his intentions, I went out and got drunk. Before that admission is taken out of context, I want to stress that this was not due to any personal animosity towards Kevin. We had both been dehumanized by the controversy, reduced to tokens of an argument staged, largely, by people who had never met us. I was relieved, released by the finality of the decision. It is no coincidence that, from that moment on, I found greater comfort in my batting.

It was a time to re-evaluate, and repair personal relationships. I thought back to Antigua and the gym at Sugar Ridge, where Michael Vaughan and I had studiously ignored one another over a couple of days as we had completed our respective workouts. He had been critical of me. He had also piled into Trotty without knowing the circumstances when he left the Ashes tour in 2014.

I put my wall up. I was prickly. The tension between us was obvious. Yet, on reflection, I realized that such sullen silence was wrong. As I said to Alice when I returned home, 'He's a bloke I batted with for England, a bloke I called Skipper. We can't let things get to this.'

Life isn't lived in a straight line. Everyone goes through blips, and I would go through one more, talking starkly and occasionally darkly about my future as England captain with Paul Farbrace before that summer's Ashes series. That's the nature of leadership. You teeter between necessary optimism and understandable pessimism.

Captaincy is rarely hunky dory. It just isn't like that. I had been taking the job home more often than I should. Though I'm usually pretty good at leaving cricket at the door, it is impossible, no matter what anyone says, to do that consistently. It is always there, at the back of your mind. You need to establish a balance before you tip yourself over the edge.

After speaking to Alice, I took the initiative, picked up

the phone to Vaughan, and got a few things off my chest. I reasoned that whatever happened, things could not go any worse than they had done over the previous year or so. We arranged lunch, and he talked animatedly, and insightfully, about the Australians, and the nature of the challenge that awaited.

I'd had a similar clear-the-air discussion with Shane Warne the previous year, telling him I found his criticism highly unfair. We had kept in touch, and the world hadn't fallen in. That, and the appointment of Farbrace as interim coach for the two-Test series against New Zealand, helped me move from being a closed book to a more receptive personality.

The mood was helped by the tenor of the opposition. The Kiwis, under Brendon McCullum, were a refreshingly open team. They reminded us it was possible to play Test cricket with spirit, and without a snarl. They were at ease. They had found themselves as a side. Losing didn't hurt them any less, but they had more of a smile on their faces. They didn't take themselves seriously.

They knew what they were meant to be. They had an underdog's mentality and chased the ball to the boundary as if their lives depended on it until the moment it hit the rope. As McCullum explained over a beer, 'We can't afford not to. We're not good enough to go, "Oh, well, someone else will just score those four runs . . ."'

I had played with Tim Southee, their right-arm fast-medium bowler, for Essex. He summed up their approach perfectly: 'I tried sledging. I tried being that tough macho man, but it just felt so awkward. It wasn't me. My way of playing is to give a little gyp, but not to be afraid of laughing at the funny moments. You have to be comfortable in yourself.'

That was the perfect message, at the perfect time, for an England team that had moved on from the more austere, methodical and introverted side that enjoyed such success under Andy Flower. We were less consistent, perhaps more naturally talented, and certainly more free-spirited. In psychological terms, we had more yellows and greens. I could be more relaxed with them as a leader.

It's funny. When your career is in the books, you forget the dark moments, and even some of the highs, but I'll remember that 124-run victory against the Kiwis in the first Test at Lord's in late May for a long, long time. The 100th match between the countries, it was sensational, one of the best I've played in. The old place was rocking, and the game ebbed and flowed marvellously; a record 1,610 runs were scored.

You don't often come from behind in the way we did, fighting back from 30–4 on the first morning, conceding a first-innings deficit of 134, and securing our fifth win in seven Tests with less than ten overs to spare. Ben Stokes was brilliant, following 92 in the first innings with an eighty-five-ball 100 in the second. He provided further momentum by taking the wickets of Kane Williamson and McCullum in successive deliveries.

My 162 in the second innings was one of my best, for several reasons. I batted instinctively, with freedom and fluency, despite admitting to Farby on the third day, when I was 32 not out overnight, that I was still struggling with the stress of captaincy. He revealed the essence of his coaching style, which involves a basic understanding of the human condition, by suggesting we talk over a beer.

He would revert to his role as assistant for the Ashes once

Trevor Bayliss had been confirmed as head coach, and had the perfect personality for a number two. Across sport, they tend to be the guy players unload upon, use almost as a conduit of emotion. Farby's easygoing nature was summed up in his team talk before the one-day series against the Kiwis: 'Fuck it. Let's just go and whack it.'

Trevor is very quiet, a lot cleverer than he lets on. His mask is to play the Aussie fool, the man in the floppy hat who sits at the corner of an outback bar, nursing a stubbie. When he does speak, his views are intelligent, well thought out and to the point. He was great for me because he wanted me to lead on my own initiative, rather than slavishly following a preordained plan.

That Ashes series would be my redemption. No one really gave us too much of a chance, but I sensed something stirring during a training camp in Spain. We didn't take cricket bats. We concentrated on slip catching for hours and spoke honestly to one another about our expectations. Scar tissue began to heal.

There was no point in hiding from the reality, that we had been humiliated the previous year. Mitchell Johnson was still being spoken of as a major threat. Yet Trevor, in his understated way, cut through recently formed reputations. He broke down the Australians both as players and as people, highlighting technical flaws and well-disguised fears.

Having destroyed the mystique, he then concentrated on our own outlook. We would follow the McCullum principle, and be open to both the public and, most pertinently, the opposition. We had nothing to hide and would have a lot to be proud of. Three days before the first Test we invited the Aussies into our dressing room after the game, win or lose.

Darren Lehmann, their coach, refused. We thought it strange, because there were no ulterior motives involved. Their reaction suggested they were just like us, human beings with inconsistencies and insecurities. We were at ease. We would play without fear and avoid the blame game if things went wrong. It was liberating, and, for the Aussies, disconcerting. I was encouraged to be unorthodox in my captaincy, and to embrace calculated risk.

Perhaps I overdid my bit for team morale by being hit in the balls, attempting to collect a sharply bouncing ricochet. Boy, did it hurt. Joe Root was in hysterics as the doctor came on to count them, for the first time since I was about thirteen. I forgave him, through the thinnest of smiles, because he had changed the complexion of a match played on a low, slow wicket.

The beauty of sport, and also its terror, is captured by two words, 'if only'. Things could have played out so differently had Rooty not been dropped, second ball, by Brad Haddin. We would have been 43–4 on the first morning and facing familiar demons. He scored 194 runs over the match, took two wickets with his occasional off-spin, and claimed the winning catch off Moeen Ali.

Funny old game.

As part of what was literally an open-door policy, I had resolved to invite former England greats into the dressing room to share our ambitions and understand our strategies. Beefy Botham had been with us that week; his role included the ceremonial awarding of the football trophy. The early morning kickabout had been banned by the ECB until Farby announced, in that languid way of his, 'I don't care. Let's play.'

The acid test of such new-found inclusivity and positivity was, of course, defeat. We were smashed in the next Test, at Lord's. Steve Smith got a double hundred and put on 284 for the second wicket with Chris Rogers, who made 173. I had my brain fade against Mitch Marsh at 96 in the first innings before we were bowled out for 103 in thirty-seven overs in the second, to lose by 405 runs.

Here we go again. Mitchell Johnson was hailed as a heavy-metal hero. Some sages missed the point by suggesting we were handicapped by playing on poor county pitches, but Mitchell took the pitch out of the equation: we don't often face bowling of that pace and quality in England. Our shot selection was poor. It was a pick-and-mix assortment of excuses and familiar complaints. 'The sun will come up in the morning,' Bayliss assured us. 'It's OK. We've just lost a game of cricket. We'll regroup.'

With that, he ushered us into two of the best weeks of our lives.

I hardly slept over that fortnight, a maximum of three hours each night. The difference was that my insomnia was due to excitement at the possibilities of a rapidly developing team, rather than dread of the consequences of individual or collective failure. The new mood was natural, rather than a shallow piece of public relations. Even the nerves had a different connotation. Everything felt right.

Jimmy Anderson, my best mate, blew the Edgbaston Test wide open by taking 6–47 in 14.4 overs before limping off with a side strain halfway through his ninth over in the second innings. Steve Finn, branded as 'unselectable' by Ashley Giles on the 2013–14 tour of Australia, had his moment of redemption, compensating by taking another six wickets.

We were way ahead of the game and needed only to chase down 121. I got out cheaply and when Adam Lyth was dismissed in the afternoon session on the third day, we were 51–2, and playing at run-a-ball pace. Great for the fans, but terrible for my blood pressure. I even asked Reg, our security man, for permission to run in a nearby park as Belly, who had found his form, led us to an eight-wicket win.

Suddenly, it was the Aussies' turn to be put in the stocks. Lehmann was forced to deny he had angered his players, and broken the spirit of their 'family first' policy, by not recalling Haddin after he missed the Lord's Test to be with his daughter Mia in a London hospital. Michael Clarke's captaincy was being picked apart. Batting coach Michael Di Venuto was urging the team to toughen up.

My priorities were revealingly different. 'Lads, we're in a situation probably no one thought we'd be in,' I told the team, in what was a messy dressing room. 'Don't go and finish yourself tonight. By all means enjoy the win, but please, please, please, don't go and get blind drunk.' Once they dispersed, I phoned Stokes, put him in charge of the night, and told him to decide when they had had enough.

He got them back to the hotel by midnight. They were on a promise. Win the Ashes by pressing home our advantage at Trent Bridge and I wouldn't care if they turned up legless at the Oval. As things turned out, the performance in Nottingham was 100 per cent proof. To be batting before lunch on the first day, after bowling Australia out for 60 on winning the toss, was intoxicating.

Stuart Broad's spell of 8–15 in nine and a half overs that morning was the most impactful I've ever seen. There's usually one partnership, to stem the bleeding. I don't think even he could believe it, especially since it's now safe to reveal that he wanted me to bat first. To do it on his home ground, knowing he shouldered primary responsibility in Jimmy's absence, was the mark of the man. No one delivers every day, but the best choose their moments.

The atmosphere in the changing room during the interval was dreamlike. Adam Lyth hit the last ball of the morning session for four, and no one seemed remotely interested in eating. It had the feel of Melbourne 2010, a sense of disbelief, tempered by the unspoken knowledge that if we batted properly, the Ashes would be ours.

Play long enough, and there is always something to bring you down to earth. I remembered, with a pang of regret and alarm, being in an Essex side that once lost to Yorkshire, after bowling them out for 50 in the first innings. Rooty, unbeaten on 124 at the end of a surreal first day, provided reassurance, pivoting the reply by sharing a fourth-wicket stand of 173 with Jonny Bairstow.

We weren't going to mess it up. We needed only twelve overs to wrap up a win, by an innings and seventy-eight, on the third morning. It was grey overhead, but the celebrations were colourful, almost karmic. Farby ensured that due deference was paid to Peter Moores. Lehmann, who had incited Australian crowds in 2013 by hoping Broady would be sent home 'crying', had to watch him pick up the most obvious man of the match award imaginable.

I was very emotional in a post-match interview with Michael Atherton and was in contemplative mood during a press conference staged in a claustrophobic, overheated squash court. I felt for Michael Clarke, whose captaincy had ended tearfully, in the same setting, but I also carried the spirit of those who had been alongside me over the previous two years.

Without being selfish, this felt like *my* team. The scenes, walking round the ground, signing autographs and posing for selfies three hours after the match, were the manifestation of a long-held idea. These guys had bought into the principle of reconnection. They were what I envisaged, when I spoke of us being England players, 24/7.

Changing an image is not a whim of administrators, or PR flim-flam merchants. It comes from the hearts of those who prove themselves under competitive pressure. We might have been loved as the world number one team, who beat all-comers during a heady spell, but it was cupboard love. The mood soon shifted when it was our turn to be hammered.

We weren't faultless, but on that day at Trent Bridge we illustrated a truth that had needed time to be taken on board. This was an accessible England team; we were bigger than the result, but not bigger than the game of cricket. We might not have played at our best consistently, but we played with gratitude. We were desperate to make our mark and didn't allow egos to get in the way.

The changing room was mobbed. Rooty conducted a TV interview sitting on a table, wearing a rubber Einstein face-mask, and doing Bob Willis impressions. People saw our human side. We were not robots, after all. We were genuine. I felt trusted as a leader, despite getting so many things wrong in the previous couple of years, and trusted the group in return. I looked around and saw individuals who had given something of themselves.

Stokesy had taken six wickets in the second innings. At his best, he is touched by genius. At his worst, he has had to grow up, fast. When I watch him now, I feel I played a small part in his development as a player and a person. He doesn't need me to hold his hand any more, but at certain times in his career he valued me being there, if he needed a second opinion.

I hope he learned a little from the way I went about things, when the scrutiny was intense and intermittently unfair. He has certainly changed radically after being cleared of affray following a street brawl outside a bar in Bristol in 2018. He knew he should not have been out on the town, in the middle of a series. It could so easily have been a horrible, defining moment.

He has learned his lesson. I see how he trains, how he prepares, how he cares about playing for England. The penny has dropped: he may be a maverick talent, but he will not be indulged. I needed the support of senior players, up to and including my spell as captain. People like Jimmy were there for me when I doubted myself.

I needed time to mature, to cultivate the humility to admit my shortcomings. I got a lot of things wrong, and learned that if you put your hand up, and admit your faults, it is possible to forgive and forget. You can't choose your teammates, and you are thrown together in an intense environment for up to four months, but if you love the game you will discover a set of values to live by.

Everyone has their individual priorities. International sport incorporates processes designed to manage pressure. Clashes are common because you are living on the edge. Conversely, it is also too easy to become lackadaisical. I respond if I see standards slipping, because if I do not do so the omission will grate on me. That doesn't mean to say, though, that I have a monopoly on wisdom.

This seems as good a time as any to apologize to a member of the England support staff on the 2018 tour of New Zealand. I won't mention him by name, on the assumption he knows who he is. We were awful for being bowled out for 58, and I criticized him for not being there on the first day because he was looking after his children due to his wife's illness.

'If this was an Ashes Test, you'd have been here,' I said, in a fit of pique and unworthy self-assurance. He denied it vehemently and, for forty-eight hours, we clashed massively. I have never shied away from stating uncomfortable truths as a captain, but on that occasion, I was completely wrong.

Family, you see, does come first.

13. Sanctuary

At first glance, anyone pausing in the lane to look across the adjoining field on a mild evening in early summer would have concluded the pressure of international cricket had finally got to me. There I was, walking in a circle, gesticulating wildly and shouting 'Baa' at a flock of around 200 sheep.

As hard as this is to believe, there was method in my apparent madness. Baa was a pet lamb that came running at the sound of its name. He slept in the house alongside Bonnie, the black Labrador, his companion on a daily basis around the house. Baa lived in the garden until he began to eat the flowers and was banished to the field.

I know, I couldn't get my head around it either.

Baa came with the territory when I first met Alice and stopped off in Bedfordshire on the way to training sessions in Loughborough, or to play squash with friends in the area. We had started seeing each other in my final year at school (Alice was in the year below), and we had kept in touch in our gap years, when she went travelling and I played grade cricket in Australia.

We began spending more time together, as she prepared to go to Reading University and my cricket career gathered momentum. The farm visits were just to see Alice as I didn't have much interest in agriculture at the time and had never had dogs at home in Essex, but I enjoyed the tranquillity of long country walks. It must have looked weird, a lamb trotting alongside a Labrador without a care in the world, but it represented a strange normality.

Matilda, the ewe, lived a similar life. Drunky Monkey is another pet lamb, a survivor of twins, Drunky and Monkey. They had a traumatic birth and acquired their names when they struggled to stand for twenty-four hours due to extreme dizziness. About a year later, one of them dropped dead. Since they were identical, no one knew how to distinguish the victim. The lucky one inherited both names.

That sort of practicality sums up farm life, which grew on me quickly. Pet lambs aside, the family lamb around 2,000 sheep with a further flock that do not lamb. It's a serious enterprise on the mixed farm and I learned to take things in my stride, especially during lambing season. The first ten days of life are the most critical, so prompt attention, however improvised, is important.

Like most sportsmen, I love my food. I walked into Alice's mum and dad's kitchen one Sunday evening and had my appetite whetted by the smell of pork, roasting in the top oven of the Aga. However, I then saw, to my great surprise, a lamb sitting in the warming oven, wrapped in a towel to keep it warm. I'd never seen anything like it, though for Alice's family it is second nature to do anything to keep a lamb alive.

It was suffering from hypothermia, one of the biggest dangers for new-born lambs, and to keep them warm is vital in those first few hours. Older sheep produce body heat from digesting their food and have thick wool. Lambs are vulnerable, since the so-called 'brown fat' they are born with will only keep them alive for a few hours. Common-sense care, especially on a Sunday with the roast dinner almost ready, is why that lamb was sitting in the Aga!

For five weekends during the lambing season the farm is open for families to come and see the farm in action. I always find it fascinating chatting to people who, like me, have had no farming experience and through these few days get to see the caring nature of farmers, which isn't often talked about.

Farming gives me perspective. It has helped to shape me and provides an antidote to the shallowness of celebrity and scrutiny that comes with top-class sport. Don't get me wrong: I'm grateful for the material rewards and personal satisfaction cricket has given me, but they need to be balanced with an awareness of the world that is around me.

I still joke with my father-in-law that I've never done a proper day's work in my life. I've farmed and played cricket. Though we both know that they are both incredibly hard work, I don't think they can count as a job when you enjoy them as much as I do. My favourite time of the farming year is lambing, when over the last few years I have probably been around the most.

Though the lambing season starts as early as December in some areas, our busiest period is between mid-February and mid-April. I usually volunteer for late-night sessions in the lambing shed. It is a silent, hypnotic place, in which sheep, many of whom are first-time mothers, spend the night in individual pens with their offspring. At the risk of sounding soppy, helping a ewe to give birth is magical, a special feeling.

The lamb emerges with a splutter, shakes its head instinctively and can need to be cajoled into breathing using a piece of straw to clear mucus from its nasal passage. You need to act fast, and also disinfect its navel to prevent potential infection. The mother licks it dry before it rises, on matchstick thin legs, and totters around in search of the teats.

These are perilous moments; the lamb must suckle to get life-giving colostrum milk. It is golden, packed with essential nutrients, proteins and antibodies. A lamb needs 100 millilitres in its first few hours.

Occasionally you will need to help with the process if the ewe is unable to give birth by herself. You try to let the process happen naturally, but sometimes a helping hand is important. You push your hand gently inside her, never entirely knowing what you will find. In an ideal situation you ensure the legs emerge before the head, in a movement like a swan dive. Once the head and shoulders pass through the pelvis, the lamb slithers out.

Nature, like international sport, can be simultaneously cruel and wonderful. There was one story last winter that illustrates this. I had just started the evening shift when I noticed a sheep struggling. You try to give the sheep more time, but I quickly realized that it would need some assistance. Unfortunately, the forward twin was entangled with its brother in the womb and had died, but, given the constricted space, I couldn't untangle them. I was gutted, as no matter what I tried for the next hour or so I couldn't help the other lamb.

According to the vet, there was nothing I could do, so I reluctantly went to bed around midnight fearing the worst. I left for training early next morning, and couldn't believe it when Alice called to tell me the ewe had lambed naturally and she and the lamb were fine.

It has been fascinating to learn the nuances of farm life over the past decade, and this has been imperative to keeping my brain from always thinking about cricket. The old shepherd's trick of bonding a lamb to a ewe whose lamb has died is to remove the skin of a dead lamb, and place it over the skin of an orphan lamb, in the hope it will be accepted by an adoptive mother. Instinct is powerful; a ewe will violently reject any lamb with an unfamiliar scent. If she allows it to suckle, you know you have had a successful adaption.

Another method is when the ewe's head is restrained for a short time, so that she cannot turn to see and smell which lamb is suckling. Her milk passes through the orphan, giving it her scent, and eight times out of ten she accepts it as her own. All the hard work, and consistent care, put in over the previous year is rewarded.

The breeding year begins in September, when the tup, the male, is put in with the females. His chest area is raddled, covered with an oil-based paint, which rubs off on the hindquarters of a receptive female. The paint colour is changed every two weeks, so that a timeframe of conception can be calculated and give a rough idea when she will give birth. A pregnant ewe will not accept a secondary attempt to mate. The ewe is then scanned ten weeks later, to see how many lambs she is carrying; the number is denoted by different-coloured dots.

The rearing process is surprisingly personal. You get to know the lambing shed, such as which ewes or lambs are vulnerable and need a careful eye over them for a few days. You begin to recognize lambs as distinctive individuals before they are turned out into a field. When it is very busy and 60–70 sheep are lambing every day for a few days, it's all hands to the pump. I once lambed for twenty-one consecutive nights when Alice wasn't feeling too great in the early stages of her pregnancy with Isobel. I was so tired. It made batting for ten hours in the Abu Dhabi heat seem fairly easy in comparison.

All this takes place on the family farm, about a mile from

where we live. We graze sheep at home, along with cows, one of which did some freelance landscaping when it broke into the front garden. That's Jimmy Anderson's worst nightmare. Quite frankly, he's terrified of cattle. For some reason, he didn't believe me when I told him they quite liked being stroked.

I must admit it took me time to trust horses. Perhaps that stems from Mum's childhood warning never to stand behind one. It could also have something to do with Norman, one of Alice's horses. He would gallop towards us as we entered his field to get him in for the evening. The first time I saw this, I turned and ran for my life and hurdled the five-bar gate like Colin Jackson, only to turn round and see Alice rolling about laughing at me!

I had learned to ride horses in Argentina, even though, like skiing and skydiving (which I tried in New Zealand in 2008), it was one of the pursuits forbidden by my ECB contract. It may have led to a questionable show of false confidence on tour in Sri Lanka. We were playing in Dambulla, in the dry Central Province. The stadium, built in 167 days overlooking a reservoir on ground leased from a local temple, held 30,000 but didn't have great training facilities. We staged an improvised shuttle session in a nearby field, and some of the lads were spooked by the sudden interest of several horses. 'Don't worry,' I said as they began to get skittish, 'they're only curious and having a bit of fun.'

Understandably, the session was swiftly abandoned. When I mentioned my calmness in such unfamiliar circumstances to Alice, I thought she would be impressed. 'I would have run away,' she said with a wry smile.

You obviously always have to be careful with farm animals,

but luckily enough I never had to report back to cricket with a farming injury, although once a pig somehow managed to butt Alice, splitting her nose and leaving her with two black eyes. You can imagine the comments when she turned up at the families' hospitality box the following day.

She was brought up on the family farm, where they farm sheep, free-range turkeys for Christmas and arable. Since university she has worked on the farm alongside looking after our three children. The farm gave her flexibility, in the form of the odd midweek day off in the early days of our relationship, and a month's grace in later years, when she had the scope to come out on cricket tours.

Visiting cricketers tend to be a reliable source of free help on the farm. Ryan ten Doeschate, my captain at Essex, was the latest cricketer to spend a day worming the sheep. I began by doing odd jobs and now feel as if I know what I'm doing around the farm. Alice still does a lot of work with the sheep, and I help through brute strength and gradually declining ignorance. Without wishing to sound sexist, I've got the muscle to catch a sheep and turn it over, to inspect its feet or check its teeth. It's easier for a bloke to do more of the physical element of the work.

I've always had a love of dogs, despite not having one as a child, and chose my boarding house at Bedford because it had one that I could walk before and after school. Farm work gives me a different element of identity, I suppose. In the early days, I played cricket, went to the gym, had a coffee and killed time. We all go through certain stages of life, don't we? There have been times when I've craved the release of going back to the farm. It has always given me a sense of peace.

Occasionally, the formalities of cricket get you down. My

pet hate as England captain was the group press conference. It was part and parcel of the job, a couple of times a week, before and after matches. I felt sorry for the journalists, to be honest. There were fifty or sixty of them in the room, and they knew you didn't really want to be there. You knew the topic they wanted to pursue, and the phrases or thoughts that would produce the headlines they required.

In that situation, usually near the end of the allotted time, questions tended to run into each other or, at best, be variations on a theme. It wasn't intimidating. It was more boring than anything. Of course, the game needs the media, which provides a platform from which to engage the public, but the process helps no one. My shield went up; from behind it I tossed out anodyne comments and plastic answers. One-to-one interviews, though rarer, were more satisfying since I was able to provide context and insight.

I relished the sanctuary of the farm, the absence of pressure to respond to specific agendas, but that sometimes involved an element of bluff and self-deception.

Alice and I both live a life of contrasts. Alice could, for example, spend a day in the lambing shed, wearing old clothes covered with all manner of muck, then be transformed into a dinner guest, in all her finery, at London's Landmark or Langham Hotel. We would laugh at the contrast and enjoy the variety of our lives.

I loved the fact that I wasn't consumed by cricket. I was obsessed with its mechanics and mental challenges, but it didn't completely define me. Though you don't reach the highest levels as an athlete without having the drive to run before dawn, or practise until your head and hands hurt, it helps to be able to forget your sport.

It is tempting to check the app, or even try to listen to *Test Match Special* on headphones when you're on the tractor, but switching off is not a sin. There were times when, not having been selected for a limited-overs international, I would spend a day in the fields not knowing how England were progressing. I was simply experiencing a different life.

I don't do that much tractor work due to the obvious summer months constraints, but I do enjoy the odd day driving carting grain if I get the chance. After cricket I'm sure I will spend a lot more time on the tractor, certainly volunteering for the work when *TMS* is on. I look after the sheep more because I'm usually available when they need looking after most, just before the domestic cricket season begins.

I understand what some folk mean when they talk about the timelessness of the land, and its link to our forebears. Rural communities are closer to that old cycle of birth, marriage and death in a small geographical area. They're more deeply rooted. I appreciate country traditions, and I've fully bought into the romanticism of the landscape and lifestyle. It can be really hard work, but there's something almost poetic in spending the day with the dogs, erecting electric fences in the pouring rain.

What it can give, however, is balance and solitude. I enjoy my own company, having that day on my own, working through a list of jobs. I don't have to think too deeply and would certainly never have the cheek to believe I had the experience to make critical decisions on the farm. There's a difference between knowing how to look after a thousand sheep on your own and running a business.

Ultimately, that's what a farm is, a business. I appreciate the reality will upset some people, and hope they will take my honesty into consideration, but, as a meat eater, I am quite comfortable with the contradiction of doing everything possible to keep an animal alive for five months in the knowledge that it will eventually end up as someone's dinner.

Farmers are not uncaring people at all. In fact, most are the total opposite, going above and beyond to care for their livestock. I relish their company, appreciate their outlook and feel privileged to have been introduced to their world. I understand the timeless logic of waiting for lambs to grow, before they are sold. We breed commercial rather than pedigree sheep, so most of our lambs will be sold for meat.

I would love to run my own farm. It will be difficult as cricket demands a similar time commitment, but it's not an impossible balance to strike. The week leading up to one of my milestone achievements, the 294 against India at Edgbaston in 2011, involved several successive sixteen-hour days, preparing for the Thame sheep fair, one of our most important sales of the year.

Since I had averaged 7.5 in the first two Tests, who needed nets? I worked in an open-air gym, sorting and handling animals rather than lifting dumbbells. I also associate farm duties with my becoming the youngest player to reach 10,000 Test runs, at the age of thirty-one years, five months and five days, on the fourth day of the second Test against Sri Lanka at Chester-le-Street in 2016.

I overhauled Sachin Tendulkar's record with a leg-side clip for four off Nuwan Pradeep, and had a good night after seeing England to a nine-wicket win with an unbeaten 47, because it was something special ticked off my bucket list. Alice's parents were there to see me, and we left early the following morning, with work to do.

When we got home, after a four-hour drive, it was

absolutely banging down with rain. The lambs needed to be weighed because there was a lorry booked in to take the lambs that made the desired weight to the abattoir the next day. Chris, Alice's dad, quite rightly didn't fancy going out, so it was left to me and the dog. The weather was horrendous; even the dog was nestling her nose beneath my coat as we took off, on a quad bike, to round up the 150 or so animals destined for market.

Once they were caught, we had to weigh them and load them on to the lorry. The process is automatic because of its familiarity, but I did wonder what the previous day's crowd, and the people watching on television, would have made of me there, soaked to the skin and caked in mud. So much for the halos and hurrahs reserved for the so-called cricket star.

Again, I respect the sensitivities involved, and trust my good faith will be recognized, but my love of both the countryside and the principles of its management has been deepened by my hobby – shooting. It has involved the development of a challenging new skill and is a pursuit that encourages the same sort of friendships and memories that can be found in more mainstream sports.

I am no George Digweed, who is Britain's best shot, having won, at the last count, a ridiculous 26 World Championships, 18 European Championships, 116 International Championships, 16 World Cups, 10 European Cups and 11 English and British Championships. *Wisden* also informs us he took eight wickets without conceding a run in five overs in a Sussex League Cup match. I promise I am not making this up, but he was playing for – who else? – Shooters Hill CC.

Shooting is rather like batting: the younger you begin, the

better chance you have of mastering its technicalities. It is not strictly dependent on hand–eye co-ordination; one of the most accurate shots I know is aged eighty-one. He's blind in his dominant eye, which forces him to lean over in the act of pulling the trigger. He struggles to walk. He has honed his skill since the age of fifteen.

I have been lucky over the last few years to spend some time with Beefy Botham, sharing our love for countryside sports near his home in North Yorkshire.

Similar interests, and shared experiences, can span the generations. I wasn't born when Beefy became a national hero during the 1981 Ashes, but, growing up, I became intrigued by his legend. He seemed such a compelling, devil-may-care character. My first real memory of him is from the 1992 World Cup, where he was a pinch-hitting opening bat as England lost to Pakistan in the final.

I know him as a very proud man, with a strong but thoughtful personality. He invited me to join him on a shoot about four years ago. We've had dinner together each summer and get on well socially. It is an extension of the dressing-room experience, where contrasting characters who might never have met without their sporting talent become unlikely friends.

He has mellowed slightly, but you can still see glimpses of the cricketer who transcended the game with his antics and achievements. We are bonded by our love of the countryside, but to make the connection with him I had to lose the insularity I'd developed as a player. I've learned that if you spread your wings, open yourself to new friendships and experiences, you can surprise yourself.

I don't have Beefy's aptitude for fishing, but I value his

cricketing insight and admire his philosophy towards life. He's interested in farming, and we discuss the changing nature of the countryside. Traffic is increasing, water tables are shifting. I look at a field differently from how I looked at one ten years ago.

I don't know as much about the arable side of farming, but I'm intrigued by what might be happening beneath the surface. I'll glance momentarily over hedges as I am driving, working out what the farmer is doing, and how he is managing the land. There is so much to see, so much to interpret; fifteen years ago, I wouldn't have had the slightest interest.

The farming community is extraordinary. It has its traditions, but it doesn't stand on ceremony. When I was growing up in Essex, our house received a thorough cleaning whenever a visitor was expected. Here, people just knock on the unlocked door unannounced and wander into my in-laws' farmhouse kitchen, where they will always be greeted with a cup of tea.

I would love to become a full-time farmer, but I also want to stay involved in cricket. I'm lucky that my options include commentary, corporate leadership work and even coaching, though to do that well in a team role requires an inordinate amount of time to be spent away from home and family. Since the countryside is such a draw, and I want to see my children grow up, I'm not sure how practical that would be.

I've been told that the key to a successful retirement is to focus on things you enjoy, and I've yet to work out what those will be. A part-time consultancy role in cricket might appeal. Performance sport and successful farming are hard, time-consuming occupations. Could I erect electric fences for sixty days straight? No, I couldn't. Could I do thirty days straight? Probably. Could I do thirty out of sixty? That might be the perfect compromise.

As I have spent more time in the local farming community, I have formed genuine friendships. I am a proud member of the Bastards, the Bedford Agricultural Study, Travel and Rural Development Society.

They made me chairman of the society's cricket club and put me in charge of organizing the Christmas dinner when I was sacked as England's one-day captain, because they reasoned that I had more time on my hands. There is also the Bedfordshire Farmers cricket team, which Tom Turner, a great friend from school and a neighbouring farmer in Great Brickhill, set up. We net on a Tuesday night in Tom's grain shed during the winter and play about fifteen fixtures a season. There is the obvious mid-season break for harvest, and most of the players 'seem' to be sponsored by Gray-Nicolls as my old kit gets a new home! My first game after my last Test match at the Oval was for the Farmers, and unbelievably I got my first ever hat-trick!

When you are done, you're done, aren't you? When I retire from the professional game, I think I'll only retrieve the bats from the attic to play for the Bedfordshire Farmers with my mates. Playing competitive club cricket won't interest me, though I hope to maintain close links with three cricket clubs: Maldon cricket club, where I grew up playing in Essex, Great Brickhill and Eversholt. Through them I have come to understand the role the game can play in strengthening the bonds of a community. Eversholt's setting is a combination of country and cricketing clichés. There is a small church, St John the Baptist, on the hill, dating back to Norman times. It was extended in 1230 and 1330; the first recorded baptism was in

1628. The village pub is opposite the graveyard, which has a memorial cross recording the sacrifice of two world wars.

The club operates from a small wooden pavilion and plays in a natural amphitheatre. Villagers watch from grassed banks while children play in an open-air swimming pool, built by a former duke of Bedford, apparently in return for the erection of a surrounding wall that enabled him to bathe naked in a nearby lake.

The first team is of a high standard and reached the final of the National Village Cup at Lord's in 2000. It has a thriving junior section; the outfield is full of youngsters on weekend mornings and weekday evenings.

It is imperative to try to help clubs and the values they can still represent. It is becoming harder to raise adult teams because family life isn't conducive to playing cricket all weekend. Children have greater opportunity, and modern life involves being here, there and everywhere.

It's a difficult dilemma to resolve. Cricket has given me everything. It has given me my life, really. I've travelled the world and had a vast range of experiences. Obviously, not everyone can go on to become an international, but the highs and lows of sport are educational. I wouldn't want our game to wither and die, because it would rob future generations of that type of opportunity.

It can still be a game of miracles and wonders. I sometimes think back fondly to the plastic sports radio Dad bought me when I was at St Paul's. I would listen to cricket in bed, through fragile headphones, under the covers. Test matches were broadcast on crackly Radio Four 198 long wave. You could vaguely hear Jonathan Agnew through the static; the rest was down to your imagination. It took you through time and space; games in New Zealand were being played tomorrow when it was still today.

How many of this generation of schoolboys will be lucky enough to be able to relate to my first cricket tour, to play in the Sir Garry Sobers forty-over tournament in Barbados? I was sixteen and accustomed to well-tended pitches. Here the wickets were rolled mud. Outfields were bare, dry and bumpy. I had an unprecedented duty to entertain.

The locals sat there, watching the world go by, and knew what they were looking for. 'Get on with it, Cook,' ordered one disembodied voice, with an unmistakable lilting accent, when I began studiously. 'Play some shots, man.' They loved Ramnaresh Sarwan, a Guyanese of Indian descent who would go on to captain the West Indies during a distinguished sixteen-year international career.

He scored a big hundred, but on the rare occasion he played a false shot the old boys on the boundary would be quick to give him strong advice. 'What are you doing, man?' they'd shout. 'You got to defend, you got to attack.' We were all too aware the final would be played at the Kensington Oval in Bridgetown, spiritual home of Sobers, Weekes, Hall, Griffith, Garner, Haynes and the rest.

Cricket is suffering in an impatient, time-poor society, but it still straddles boundaries of class and culture. It remains capable of surprising and engaging me, after all these years. Once, on holiday in the Maldives, I was persuaded to play by the hotel staff, who mainly hailed from India, Pakistan and Bangladesh.

The game was their release, on a solitary day off. They were fanatical about it and recognized me the instant I checked in with Alice. Of course I didn't deserve special treatment, but the waiters ensured speciality sushi was waiting on the lunch table each day. They were soon talking enthusiastically about the match they had planned. It proved to be the favourite day of our break.

It was serious stuff, island against island, played in shorts and bare feet. We took a boat to a nearby atoll, which was no more than fifty yards wide. It had two or three houses at one end, and as we set up the wicket, someone walked across the scrubby outfield with a freshly killed chicken, which was destined to be lunch.

I was worried about hitting the ball into the sea, so theatrically blocked my first few deliveries. The next bloke in just whacked it into the water; fielders dived in to retrieve the ball. It was a day of joy, laughter and perspective. I can't honestly remember the result of the match, but that's part of the attraction.

For once, I didn't have to win.

14. Spirit of Cricket

When things were getting tricky on that Ashes tour from hell in 2014, I went for a walk in one of Melbourne's central parks with Stuart Broad and Jimmy Anderson. We weren't logo-ed up, and wanted to be as inconspicuous as possible. To be honest, we didn't have much to shout about in any case.

We were sitting on a bench, minding our own business, when a guy wearing a 'Stuart Broad is a shit bloke' T-shirt headed purposefully in our direction. We exchanged glances. 'Here we go,' we thought. 'Cheating Poms, blah, blah, blah.' Broady's refusal to walk at Trent Bridge the previous summer had pursued him, and us, across the world.

'Mate,' the stranger said, addressing Australia's supposed public enemy number one. 'Any idea where the nearest coffee shop is?' When Broady confessed we weren't from around those parts, the guy said, 'No worries,' and walked on. He clearly hadn't recognized us. We fell about, but the 'shit bloke' didn't know whether to laugh or cry.

The incident just goes to show how impersonal and random criticism can be. It also raises deeper questions about the nature of the game. At the highest level it is played hard. Fairness is a relative term. Seeking an advantage is not a challenge to the conscience. Doing the right thing means different things to different people at different times.

So many grey areas emerge when you examine the issue in

any depth. Those who took offence at Broady refusing to walk in Nottingham after the Aussies had squandered their referrals were conspicuously silent when he walked after a much finer nick in the second innings.

Adam Gilchrist, whose insistence on walking famously upset his Australian teammates, was more concerned by the minute Stuart wasted tying a suspiciously loose shoelace when we were trying to disrupt the momentum of the match prior to regrouping during the lunch interval. We worked it out afterwards: thirteen people refused to walk during that Ashes series.

Of course, I am broadly sympathetic to the notion that cricket has a defining spirit, but when I'm asked about it, I find it hard to put into words what it means, beyond an unwritten commitment to a code of conduct drawn up in an era when it was regarded as a gentlemen's pastime. Professional sport is harsh; footballers dive to win penalties, tennis players manipulate injury breaks, rugby players operate on the fringe of the laws.

I'm one of those cricketers who won't walk.

It's an individual decision, formed by personal experience. In my case, the pivotal influence was Ronnie Irani, my first captain at Essex. Playing against Nottinghamshire, I clipped one to short leg off Mohammad Ali, a sharp left-arm bowler from Pakistan. There was an element of doubt about the catch, so I asked the fielder whether it was clean.

When he said it was, I took the bloke's word for it and walked off. That's what I had been brought up to do. When I got back to the dressing room, Ronnie was unhappy. 'The umpire has to make the decision,' he said. 'That's what he is paid to do.' When I asked him about walking, he replied, 'Never walk.'

His logic was that cricket was a game shaped by human error. As a batsman you are judged on statistics. There's not an asterisk against a certain score when you stand your ground, just as there isn't one when you are given out mistakenly. By walking, on a purely professional basis you are reducing your odds of being successful.

'Your job is to score runs, Cookie,' Ronnie said. 'If you're decreasing your odds, even by a small margin, you're making it harder for yourself.' That made perfect sense. He then added the caveat: 'If the umpire gives you a stinker, you can't kick the doors down. You can't moan about it because you've made your bed, and you have to accept it.'

There was a bit of pot and kettle in that, since Ronnie was mad, bad and dangerous to know when he was sawn off, but the advice about evening out the shockers has stayed with me. Of course, you get stick in the middle, all sorts of funny looks. They'll say, 'Fucking cheat . . . I can't believe you've not walked for that,' more out of habit than anything else.

What do you say when the umpire asks you whether you hit it? 'Not sure, mate.' Some might give you out for being cheeky, anyway. It's a matter of degrees of difference. If you smash it to the keeper and there are two DRS reviews left, you just walk off. If the umpire gives you a little nod, that tells you he knows what's happened, you're on your way. But if it is one you might get away with, an inside edge off the pad down the leg side, you keep schtum.

It works both ways. Bowlers and fielders appeal in an orchestrated fashion, even when they know the correct verdict is not out. That would suggest the 'spirit of cricket' is little more than a clever piece of marketing, or an optimistic form of nostalgia. There are limits, however, because I understand the principle of trying to protect the game from itself.

As a captain, for instance, I would never want my bowler to Mankad a batsman – run out the non-striker before delivering the ball. I'd call him back, warn him, and warn him again, if he persists in advancing down the wicket. The term comes from the first such dismissal in a Test match by Vinoo Mankad, an Indian who ran out Australia's Bill Brown during their 1947–48 winter tour.

That created an international incident, but, revealingly, Mankad was supported by Sir Donald Bradman. Referring to scandalized press coverage in his autobiography, he wrote: 'For the life of me, I can't understand why they questioned his sportsmanship . . . by backing up too far or too early, the non-striker is very obviously gaining an unfair advantage.'

The rules allow it, but, in my view, it is a low blow. That's not to say I don't appreciate the contradictions, complications and consequences. When Ravi Ashwin 'Mankaded' Jos Buttler in the IPL in March 2019 it came at a crucial juncture and enabled Ashwin's team, King's XI Punjab, to beat the Rajasthan Royals. In the bowler's unrelenting world, the move made sense, but I found it objectionable because it looked premeditated. Jos would not have been out of his crease if the bowler had made a natural movement, planting his back foot in the delivery stride. Instead, Ashwin paused, prompting the batsman to edge fractionally out of his ground.

Ashwin had form in that area, having done something similar to Sri Lankan batsman Lahiru Thirimanne after warning him in a group match in the Commonwealth Bank Series, held in Australia in 2012. In that case, his captain,

13. Celebrating my Test hundred with KP against the West Indies, at Bridgetown in 2009. I enjoyed batting with him as he took all the scoring pressure off. I could go about my business under the radar.

14. One of my favourite Test wins at Trent Bridge against Australia. Winning by just fourteen runs – you can see the euphoria and relief!

15. My last Test match as captain against India. Cricket is about the highs and the lows, and a tough tour was the final straw.

16. My first Test hundred for almost two years. It wasn't pretty but it was one I desperately needed.

17. One of my most satisfying innings, on my way to carrying my bat for 244 not out in the Boxing Day Test at the MCG in 2017.

18. The final champagne shower after my last Test match at the Oval. It was always a lot colder than it looked!

19. Graham Gooch, the childhood hero who became my mentor. He dispensed what he called 'The Knowledge', and stressed that as an opener, 'you have the opportunity to set the game up'.

20. Tour life, Jimmy, the girls and another airport.

21. Being knighted by the Queen is one of the most surreal and humbling experiences of my life. I don't think I will ever get used to being called Sir Alastair.

22. Sharing the winning feeling with Alice and Elsie after the Ashes in 2015, a very special moment.

23. We've been lucky enough to travel the world and see many places, but we've loved nowhere more than *Gavin and Stacey* inspired Barry Island!

24. Jack, who was due on the last day of my Test career, looking extremely pleased with himself here for standing up.

25. Elsie and Isobel helping me pack for going on tour.

Virender Sehwag, withdrew the appeal after consulting the umpires, Paul Reiffel and Billy Bowden.

Buttler was also the victim in 2014, when run out by Sri Lanka's Sachithra Senanayake in a decisive one-day international at Edgbaston. His captain, Angelo Mathews, reinforced the appeal because Jos had been warned about backing up in the previous over. We lost by six wickets with ten balls remaining. I top-scored with 56 out of 219, which didn't seem terribly important at the time.

Imposing ethical behaviour, or strengthening a sense of fair play, is a tricky element of captaincy. New Zealand's dressing-room door was slammed in the face of Paul Collingwood when he failed to withdraw England's appeal for Grant Elliott's run out after a mid-pitch collision with Ryan Sidebottom in the fourth one-day international at the Oval in 2008.

The Kiwis were incensed, arguing that Ryan had run directly at the batsman as he attempted a quick single. Daniel Vettori, their captain, later apologized for gesticulating and swearing from the balcony when his team won off the last ball of the match. They initially blanked Colly, who was contrite in an almost impossible situation. I wasn't playing, but it was an emotionally charged game. He was under pressure from the umpires and his own players.

At the very most, he had twenty seconds to make a decision that had unavoidable ramifications. What would I have done? Hopefully, I'd have asked for a dot ball, so that everyone went back to where they began. That's easy for me to say. Until you feel the heat of the moment, experience the pressure and transmit the tension of the situation – and I haven't, thankfully – you don't really know what you would do.

It was interesting that the MCC should make a point of publicly criticizing the Ashwin incident in this year's IPL as being against the spirit of the game. They stage an annual lecture, originally named in honour of Colin Cowdrey, in which characters as diverse as Desmond Tutu, Geoffrey Boycott, Beefy Botham, Kumar Sangakkara, Brendon McCullum and Brian Lara have outlined their thoughts and philosophies.

That is staged at Lord's, landing ground for the helicopter that ferried Allen Stanford, self-styled saviour of world cricket, and crates containing a supposed stash of $20 million in banknotes. He was welcomed gushingly by the ECB hierarchy, including Giles Clarke and David Collier, who sanctioned a winner-takes-all match against the so-called Stanford Superstars.

That was a West Indies team, selected by a panel overseen by Viv Richards. They prepared in Antigua under coaches Eldine Baptiste and Roger Harper. It was so disciplinarian that no-balls in the nets drew a fine. According to the late and legendary cricket writer Tony Cozier, one player, opening batsman Xavier Marshall, was dropped after failing a drugs test through his smoking marijuana.

I don't think performance-enhancing drugs are especially common in cricket, by the way, though the advantages of, say, a fast bowler building muscle mass are obvious. During the course of a year hair samples would be taken from the England team twice, as part of a programme to test for recreational drugs. Urine samples were taken randomly six or seven times a year to test for performance-enhancing drugs. You can always do more, I suppose, but that seemed adequate.

Going back to Stanford, some leading figures in West

Indian cricket, including Michael Holding, Clive Lloyd, Desmond Haynes and Ian Bishop, opted out, sensing it was too good to be true. Yet the fraudster's bluster and ambition swayed good judges like Mark Nicholas, who, according to Tony Cozier, observed that 'Stanford's calypso cricket revolution might just save the game's fall from grace'.

It was surreal, extraordinary. I wasn't at Lord's for his arrival, but watched on TV, as fascinated as the rest. It felt like a significant event, a little like the Packer breakaway must have felt in the seventies. Life-changing sums were being talked about, and it captured the spirit of the times as part of the advent of franchised cricket. The IPL was coming on stream, and players were starting to get itchy feet.

Obviously, Stanford's scheme was fundamentally flawed, given his subsequent conviction for orchestrating a $7 billion Ponzi scheme. He's serving a 110-year sentence in a federal penitentiary in Florida. We were called England but, as players, objected to the connotations of the title. Playing for your country is an honour, a special thing that should not be for sale. We had no say in it, and it didn't feel right.

The event itself was a circus, a shambles. We stumbled into the unknown. The match was staged next to Antigua airport, in a stadium Stanford named after himself when he funded renovations. It has now reverted to its original title, the Coolidge Cricket Ground, but is known locally as 'Sticky Wicket Stadium'.

That's appropriate, all things considered. Stanford was a bizarre figure who didn't endear himself by posing for photographs with Matty Prior's pregnant wife on his lap. My first impression of him was as someone who wanted fame as well as fortune.

It was sad, because it had the potential to splinter the squad. Each player on the winning side was due to earn £500,000. The ECB and West Indies Cricket Board took £3.5 million, with a further £1 million divided between the winning coach and the rest of the squad. That's obviously a lot of money for carrying drinks; as it turned out, Jimmy Anderson and I watched our innings from a swimming pool overlooking the ground, after training earlier in the day.

We didn't pick a specialist T20 squad and went with the one-day group that was due to go on to India. We made 99. Chris Gayle and Andre Fletcher, their opening pair, knocked off the runs in 12.4 overs. The local lads were beside themselves; they spoke of the cars and houses they would buy. The bubble burst quickly, but according to Tony Cozier, only one of them lost their money by ploughing it back into Stanford's crooked investment scheme.

Times have changed. Virat Kohli picked up £2 million for captaining Royal Challengers Bangalore in the 2019 IPL, while Ben Stokes was the highest paid foreign player, collecting £1.5 million for six weeks' work with Rajasthan Royals. Stanford's fleeting success owed a lot to his ability to play on the inferiority complex created by historic underpayment of cricket's best players.

Sportsmen who come from disadvantaged economic backgrounds are inevitably vulnerable to exploitation. Unfortunately, we see that, to an extent, in match fixing, especially on the subcontinent, where, by accepting as little as $100 from a corrupt bookmaker or gambler, a young player, very early in his career, can essentially sell his soul inadvertently. He is trapped, susceptible to blackmail, for the rest of his career.

The immediate motivation is understandable, since very few fledgling players make it. In a world without guarantees the chance of feeding the family for three months with that $100 is attractive. But if things go well, and his talent blossoms over two to four critical years of development into an international cricketer, he will feel the same individual or organization tapping him on the shoulder.

'You owe us a favour . . .'

Dressing-room gossip involves unsubstantiated stories, but I have never been approached to do anything illegal. I did, however, play in one of the most notorious Tests of all, at Lord's against Pakistan in 2010, the setting for the spot-fixing scandal that led to the banning and imprisonment of Salman Butt, Mohammad Asif and Mohammad Amir.

The sting, by undercover reporters from the *News of the World*, who secretly videotaped Mazhar Majeed, a corrupt sports agent, accepting money and promising deliberate no-balls on specific occasions, came at a time when, to be flippant, I couldn't buy a run. The deal was that the first ball of Amir's second over, the last delivery of Asif's fifth and the final ball of the first over in which Amir went around the wicket to a right-hander would be no-balls.

Amir's first one, to me, was so big that either he had completely messed up his run-in or something funny was going on. I thought Asif's was strange, to say the least, but didn't dwell on it, because it was marginal and, unlike the prodigy Amir, who had never overstepped the mark in first-class cricket, he had a history of problems in that area.

We were in a great position that Saturday night. I was caught behind for 10 off Amir on the Friday morning, after rain allowed only twelve overs on the first day. Jonathan

Trott's 184 and Broady's only Test century, 169, got us to 446 before we bowled them out for 74. Pakistan had lost four more wickets before the close, by which time, unbeknown to us, the ground was crawling with senior policemen.

The story broke, on an embargo, at 10 p.m. that evening. Suddenly my phone was alive with messages from friends, saying, 'Oh my God, are you watching TV?' I sat in bed, following events on Sky for hours with a sense of disbelief. It even crossed my mind that the match would be abandoned. The following day was one of my most surreal.

Andy Flower's team talk was direct and to the point. 'We've just got a job to do,' he said. 'Turn up, do it, and let everything else fall as it may. We've still got to play our cricket.' The Pakistanis arrived late; we had been in the players' dining room watching TV coverage of their team bus, still parked outside their hotel, wondering whether they would turn up.

We talk about the ultimate satisfaction of winning in Test cricket, but there was nothing remotely satisfying about that morning's play, when we wrapped up victory by an innings and 225 runs, with Graeme Swann taking five wickets. My abiding memory of it is the ICC's anti-corruption guy having a glass of red wine with his lunch. Though I suppose there was little left for him to do, it was as if nothing remotely odd had happened.

The affair left a sour taste, most notably because of the manipulation of the inexperienced Amir, who received his man-of-the-series award from a visibly disgusted Giles Clarke. For Butt, a captain, to apply such pressure is against everything the job is supposed to represent. Asif even accused him, in court, of abusing him to ensure he followed the plan. You have a responsibility to set the highest personal and professional standards.

Is there a problem with match- or spot-fixing in cricket? All but two of the major nations, Australia and England, have had prominent players banned because of it, so it is natural to worry about what goes on beneath the surface. Greed and human weakness are not specific to any one sport: just look at cycling or tennis to see the gradual erosion of trust.

As mentioned earlier in the book, I played with Mervyn Westfield for Essex. He was found to have conspired with Danish Kaneria, who, unforgivably, took six years to admit his guilt. Sport is, above all, meant to be a genuine contest. If I score 5 and 0, I want you to trust that those scores are a result of poor form, technique or decisions, or good bowling, rather than some preordained bookmakers' bingo.

I feel sorry for Pakistani cricketers, because they are paying the price for their nation's isolation, but as a Test team they have a history of turbulence. I played in the forfeited Test at the Oval in 2006, but was in the shower, having scored 83, when they were accused of ball tampering. Paul Collingwood and Ian Bell, who were at the crease, came in at tea and confirmed the ball had been changed because the umpires considered its condition had been altered.

Cue chaos. Our batsmen went back out into the middle to resume play, but the Pakistanis barricaded themselves in their changing room and refused to leave. By the time they emerged, under protest at being penalized five runs, the umpires had taken the bails off and awarded us the match, and the series, 3–0. We were ushered out of the ground, supposedly for our safety, and had to return in the morning to collect our kit. The match referee later acquitted the Pakistan captain Inzamam-al-Haq of ball tampering.

Ball tampering isn't black and white, because there are inconsistencies in interpretation. Though this is an area of current debate, you are not allowed to put an artificial substance on the ball, but you are permitted to spit on it, to assist the shine. You must not pick at the seam, but the ball cannot surely be said to be in a natural state if you are polishing one side of it.

That's legal, but when you put sugar on the surface, by eating a sweet and applying impregnated spit to the ball, that's a no-no. It certainly makes the ball shinier, but does it make it swing abnormally? The jury is out, though technically you are not allowed to take sweets on to the field. The residue from energy drinks, taken in the break? That's also in the grey area.

It can get a little silly. Faf du Plessis, South Africa's captain, was fined his entire match fee in a Test at Hobart in November 2016 for ball tampering when he was spotted on TV with a mint under his tongue. The Australian media pursued him like a convicted criminal in the build-up to the following Test, where I suspect I was not the only player silently hailing the strength of character that resulted in him scoring a century.

As he explained afterwards: 'As a player, I was always taught when you're trying to get the ball to swing you've got to put something on the ball. So for me, that was a normal day at the office. I wasn't trying to do something different. My technique was bad: the sweet was out on my tongue, and the camera could see it. Obviously now I know that you can't be that obvious about it.'

I've eaten sweets and shined the ball without directly using sugary spit. Many players chew gum. There's something delightfully old-fashioned about the memory of the Aussies being upset when Marcus Trescothick was caught in possession of a Murray Mint in the 2005 Ashes. Australian teams of that vintage were hardly blushing innocents.

When I first faced them, in 2006, they played tough. A little like Stephen Hendry or Ronnie O'Sullivan in snooker, they occasionally won on reputation. I thought them fine; they chirped a bit, but never sought to bully me, as a new kid on the block. I won four out of seven series against them; we usually gave as good as we got. It was almost a badge of honour when Brad Haddin called us bad winners.

Of course, they sledged when they got on top of you. That's fine, providing it doesn't degenerate into personal abuse. That doesn't happen too often, though I once had a ding-dong with South African wicketkeeper Mark Boucher, who accused me of being a 'silver spoon', among other things, when we fell out over the position of the sightscreen.

'Why don't you just let the umpires umpire?' I observed, with the brashness of youth. 'Why don't you just fucking bat?' Boucher replied, before launching into a volley that would have made a docker blush. As he went on the attack, I learned an important lesson. To get involved in that sort of stuff you have to enjoy confrontation and be quick-witted. I was neither.

If you chirped KP, it fired him up. Sometimes he needed indignation and aggression to get him going. When I came on to the international circuit, I heard plenty of tales about the supreme stupidity of goading Steve Waugh or Brian Lara. They tended to prove their point through weight of runs, rather than the acidity of their words.

My job with Jimmy Anderson was to keep him operating

on that edge, above nice but below horrible. If he was too friendly, he didn't have that snap in his bowling. It was a sign he was not concentrating. If his head had gone, he was never going to be clinical enough to use his skills. I used to act as his barometer, fielding and shining the ball at mid-off. The idea was to get him in his red zone, where aggression was balanced by analysis. The number of wickets he took while in that perfect state of mind was remarkable; in later years he has found the knack of winding himself up without outside help, and of calming down when required. He has discovered his optimal level of performance.

There is a lot of verbal testing of players, especially when they are fresh on the scene. You could take a gamble with David Warner by having a go at him. He would always want the last laugh, the last word, and that could distract him. But there was never any certainty that it wouldn't backfire. I prefer the term 'managing the situation' to 'sledging'.

Sometimes, it is the hot spot of the game. It's tense, the bowler and batsman are both ticking, and it flares up. I think it is brilliant, because it shows this is a game played by human beings. The phrase 'don't cross the line' is a horrible expression, but it has a certain truth to it. I love watching sport, though, when there is an edge to it.

That could be a full-blooded local derby in football, where tackles are engineered to be fractionally late and deceptively painful. As a rugby fan, I mourn the fact a forward can't get his retaliation in first by delivering a sly punch. I don't mind seeing a bit of anger and angst. It is all part of the mix, and there is no accounting for taste.

It's odd what gets people worked up. Jelly-beangate, at Trent Bridge in 2007, was weird. A mountain was made out of a molehill when Indian tail-ender Zaheer Khan walked in after the drinks break to find jelly beans in front of his stumps. He thought there were just two, which he swept away with a flourish and a good-natured laugh. In fact, he didn't notice a third one, beige, in his footmarks.

When he saw it, after the following delivery, he began waving his bat around as though it was a toothpick. He accused KP of throwing the sweet at him while he was batting, something that Kevin theatrically denied. My mugshot was on the back page of the *Sun* the next morning, along with those of Ian Bell and Matty Prior, those closest to the scene of the alleged crime.

'Who did it?' screamed the headline. I was at short leg and named in the *Telegraph* as 'suspect number one' in some sort of Agatha Christie parody. You couldn't make it up. Now that the statute of limitations has expired, I can dob in Belly with a clear conscience. It's always the quiet ones: he thought it would be a laugh to share some of the jelly beans we had eaten during the break in play.

Shahid Afridi bit the ball repeatedly while captaining Pakistan against Australia in Perth. Bottle tops have been surreptitiously used to damage the ball for years. Michael Atherton, England's answer to Alan Titchmarsh, was caught with dirt in his pocket. I have to say, though, it was a new one on me when Australian opener Cameron Bancroft tried to hide sandpaper down his trousers.

While we're on the subject of newspaper headlines, a former Aussie Rules player wrote an all-time classic in the Darwin newspaper, the *Northern Territory News*. It featured a full-length front-page photo of Bancroft staring balefully down the front of his pants, accompanied by the headline

'Why I've Got Some Sticky Near My Dicky'. Apparently, an earlier version was 'Balls on the Line'.

When I first saw the reports, from the third Test against South Africa in Cape Town in March 2018, I knew they were in trouble. We were in New Zealand at the time and, as the story unravelled, the suspicions aroused during the preceding Ashes series in Australia seemed justified. They seemed to have got what was coming to them.

Steve Smith took the responsibility as captain and was banned, along with Warner and Bancroft, after sponsors and politicians weighed in, but there seemed more to it than that. That series against us had a strange emotional intensity. When Nathan Lyon, a genuinely nice guy, spoke about being prepared to 'headbutt the line', it wasn't healthy.

Darren Lehmann, as coach, stood down in a tacit admission that the culture he had helped to create had soured. The Cape Town incident itself, in which TV pictures captured Bancroft hurriedly stuffing the yellow sandpaper down his pants, was comically inept. I suppose it shows what happens when you're under pressure and don't think clearly.

Our suspicions had been aroused in Perth, when they managed to get the ball reversing an inordinate amount when the outfield was still wet, following three hours' rain. When the series was complete, and we had lost 4–0, the teams shared a beer in the dressing rooms at the SCG. Warner, a couple of beers into his celebration at the time, mentioned to a group of England players that he had used substances attached to the strapping on his hand to accelerate the deterioration of the ball during a first-class match.

I looked at Steve Smith, who shot a glance that said, 'Ooh, you shouldn't have said that,' but I'm the type to let bygones be bygones. I felt for Smith when he was booed early in the 2019 tour of England, in which the Ashes was the main course after the World Cup hors d'oeuvre. He, and the other two, had accepted their punishment, served their time and deserved a clean slate.

Have there been times on the field when I've thought 'you cheating bastards'? Of course, but you simply get on with the game. That's how it is, how it was, and how it will probably always be in professional sport. People push the laws, and their luck, to the limit.

15. Passing the Torch

Joe Root might look like a cherub, fresh-faced and innocent, but appearances can be deceptive. He left an indelible impression on me, in more ways than one, when he made his Yorkshire debut, against Essex, in a meaningless forty-over match at Headingley on the last day of the 2009 season.

We were a little hungover, after celebrating promotion from Division Two, but this small blond-haired kid cut through the fog. He later admitted to being 'petrified', and initially struggled to hit the ball off the square, but scored 63, as an opener, in a manner that suggested we had stumbled across a serious talent.

The great ones announce themselves. They make you sit up and take notice. The crispness of his ball striking, once he found his rhythm, made the same impact, in a completely different way, as the first time I saw Jos Buttler in a one-day innings. Joe's black county kit looked loose, a little too big for him, but he had a presence, an authenticity. He had obviously been coached well; his technique was assured for a teenager. There was a correctness and precision about his batting. His style was reminiscent of Michael Vaughan, another England captain produced by the same club, Sheffield Collegiate. They followed the same pathway from Yorkshire Boys, and even used the same brand of bat and boots.

Joe also had the hard heart of a pro. He caught me at mid-off, dropped the ball, and still claimed it. I wasn't particularly bothered about being given out, because there was nothing on the game. He eventually confessed, much to his embarrassment, nine years later, in the dressing room at the Oval at the end of my final Test. I naturally gave him grief, but had to admit I had no idea of what he had done. The catch was a sitter; he might have had to dive for it, but when it slipped, he just scooped it off the ground. It was cheeky, but showed strength of mind, and confidence beyond his years. He was only sixteen, remember. A more seasoned pro would have probably obeyed convention, said, 'I dropped that,' and thrown it in, but Rooty showed the sort of spikiness I quickly recognized in Jimmy Anderson.

He was a winner.

Our paths crossed occasionally before he was picked for his first senior tour, in India in 2012. He was obviously very comfortable in an elite environment. He wasn't a gym junkie, had a little bit of puppy fat, which he has yet to lose, but he looked like he belonged.

International cricket didn't faze him. He wasn't scared by the challenge. He waited patiently for his chance and looked ready to play when we picked him for the final Test at Nagpur. Batting at six, as opposed to his normal position as opener, his 73 in our first-innings 330 made him joint top-scorer with Kevin Pietersen.

First tours are usually dangerous affairs, because they represent a step into the unknown, but the way Rooty walked to the middle, a massive smile shining out from under the England cap that had been presented by Paul Collingwood, was reassuring. The bloke could play spin, having perfected his technique with the Lions in Bangladesh and Sri Lanka, and he relaxed into the moment. He's now at the stage of his career where perspective is possible. To me, he is the most complete English batsman I've seen. More intriguingly, I wonder if, in different circumstances, he could have made KP an even better player.

Rooty has proved it is possible to average more than 50 in both Test and one-day cricket. His consistency of performance is phenomenal. The last time I saw his limited-over stats he was averaging 58 over the past four years, with a strike rate in excess of 90. He is almost redefining the boundaries of the modern game, in tandem with Jos Buttler.

Kevin set the same pioneering standard in terms of power and improvisation but had his moments when his form dipped slightly. Rooty can't match the magical nature of some of his innings but has huge impact on a regular basis. I suspect KP would have responded to the metronomic brilliance of the younger man's batting; they could have formed a devastating partnership for England.

Realistically, though, international teams are in a constant state of transition. Ian Bell called, just after 9 p.m. on the night before we collected the Ashes at the Oval in 2015 and asked for a chat over a beer in the bar. I was surprised by the timing of the request, but Belly had, in his understated way, struggled in that series. I had seen signs of internal turmoil and was planning to speak to him after the celebrations in any case. The biggest giveaway involved him making a conscious change to his daily routine, by getting to the ground ridiculously early. That hinted at a deeper sense of unease, because he was a quiet guy who internalized things. If Belly needed help in any way, I would be there for him. He had been one of the pillars of my captaincy, a selfless individual, who had put his heart and soul into the game. He simply delivered.

We spoke for an hour that evening, starting with small talk about his beloved Aston Villa before getting down to the nitty gritty. He told me he was thinking about retirement and valued my insight. I argued against making a snap decision. It wouldn't be irreversible, but it would set in chain a series of events. 'I don't see a bloke who is ready to retire,' I told him. 'I see a bloke who is tired. I see a bloke who needs a break from international cricket. I don't see a bloke who is gone.'

His talent had been spotted early, and mined relentlessly, for nigh on sixteen years. Like many of us, he had dealt with his own insecurities while balancing a heavy workload and a growing family. That journey, through England's Under-19s, A team and senior side, is a marathon, and it is not uncommon to hit the wall along the way. You get to know people pretty well as a captain, or at least you think you do. Belly spoke about having had his fill, but I sensed that, deep down, he suspected he wasn't done with the game. As we sat together, chatting quietly, it became clear he didn't want to be seen to be taking the easy option. He wasn't keen on a sabbatical, because it is a big thing to give away your place without the finality of retirement. He agreed he should carry on.

That three-Test trip, against Pakistan in the United Arab Emirates in October and November, didn't break him, but it justified his unease. It was fiendishly hot, a grind, and I felt compelled to administer a rare bollocking to the entire group, when I sensed standards slipping. This wasn't international cricket as grand theatre, on the big stage. It was hard yakka in near-empty grounds.

I shared a partnership of 165 with Belly in the first Test, during my 836-minute trudge to 263 in the Sheikh Zayed Cricket Stadium in Abu Dhabi. He contributed 63 and had two more scores in the forties as we lost a series we really should have drawn, but when I looked in his eyes towards the end, I knew he was struggling.

The tank was empty. He was running on fumes. I should have pushed for him to take a measured break, when given the chance, because when the game hits you, it hits you hard. I hated that his Test career should end with a six-ball 0, but when we convened the selection meeting for the subsequent tour against South Africa, from mid-December, I argued that we should not take him. That stance wasn't taken lightly, because it had ramifications beyond the numbers. Any team sacrificing a player with 118 caps and 7,727 Test runs is taking a calculated gamble. Discarding such accumulated wisdom was doubly difficult, since it involved someone for whom I had the greatest respect, as a player and person.

As is sometimes the way of things, I tried, and failed, to get through to him on the phone to explain his omission before it became public knowledge. He was obviously the most conspicuous of the five changes we made after that Pakistan series. When we did speak, he was hurt, and disappointed. He told the press he was 'absolutely gutted'.

He hasn't lost his love of cricket. He is far from finished with the game. He will use his experiences, good and bad, to inform his coaching. I appreciate this is no consolation for the way things played out, but the episode made me consider how I would wish to depart when the time came. It was the start of the thought process that ended with that apologetic return to the dressing room at the Oval in 2018.

The immediate challenge was daunting, but not without encouragement. South Africa were a fabulous team, regarded as the best in the world at the time, but showing signs of wear and tear. They had lost three of their four previous Tests going into the series, and were being hunted down in the rankings by India.

Of all the teams we compete against, the South Africans are probably the most similar in terms of temperament. Their ethos is to play cricket hard and have a beer at the end of the game. When we clashed, we did so because we had so much in common. To coin one of Stuart Broad's favourite phrases, this series would be one to look back on, over a bottle of red, in ten years' time. I had never beaten them but had come to admire them as opponents, and men, as eras shifted. I took a few lumps facing Graeme Smith's team, which featured the likes of Jacques Kallis, my mate Mark Boucher, Makhaya Ntini, Dale Steyn and Vernon Philander. Shaun Pollock has an awesome record in both forms of the game, as bowler and catcher, yet is one of the most underrated modern cricketers.

Morne Morkel, a really nice guy, caused me a lot of grief down the years. He was probably at his peak as a bowler when he retired from international cricket in the spring of 2018. Tall and quick without being an absolute rocket, his natural shape, angling it in, was awkward for left-handers. He had tended to bowl half a yard too short, but once he picked up the knack of finding the perfect length for challenging the top of the off stumps, he was hard, hard work.

Graeme Smith assumed the captaincy early in his career, at the age of twenty-two, and played with edge and acceptable arrogance until his retirement in 2014. He failed to walk when Ryan Sidebottom claimed for caught behind, following Smith's huge drive in the fourth Test at the Wanderers in January 2010. There was an obvious noise; if that happens when the batsman is playing well away from his body, he has almost certainly hit it.

On-field umpire Tony Hill disagreed. Since we were playing without the Hotspot technical aid, and operating an early version of DRS, Andrew Strauss immediately referred it to Daryl Harper, the third umpire, who upheld the decision. Smith, unbeaten on 15, went on to make 105. South Africa won the match by an innings and squared the series. We were convinced Harper's monitor hadn't had the sound turned on.

When we flew home the following evening the British Airways pilot, a member of the Barmy Army, woke us as we were preparing for descent into London. After the usual preamble, hoping we had enjoyed the overnight flight, he added, 'You'll be pleased to know that Daryl Harper's ejector seat worked perfectly over the equator.' Predawn laughter echoed down the plane.

Seven months later, after an investigation into three complaints by the ECB, Harper was cleared by the ICC of failing 'to make proper use of new technology'. The sound feed provided by the host broadcaster SABC was deemed to have failed. In other words, a minion hadn't put the plug in. Smithy was laughing all the way to the run bank.

Leadership has a wider social significance in South African sport, so the job is never easy. Hashim Amla considered giving up the captaincy when we won the first Test in Durban by 241 runs and stepped down after batting for 707 minutes in scoring 201 in the drawn second Test at Newlands in Cape Town, which is one of my favourite places to play cricket.

He was succeeded by AB de Villiers, whom I had known

since we were kids, making our way in the Under-19s. I even got him out once, with a speciality delivery that rolled along the floor and hit him on the toe. We kept in touch as our careers progressed. He gave up wicketkeeping on becoming Test captain and could probably have done without us winning in Johannesburg, to take the series, in his first match.

Broady was a force of nature in their second innings, taking five wickets while conceding a solitary run in thirty-one deliveries as we bowled them out for 83. James Taylor, at short leg, took two miraculous catches, but attention was rightly seized by a definitive personal performance, a showcase for one man's skill, physical fortitude and sheer bloody-mindedness.

There was a lot of talk at the time about rationalizing the workload of bowlers like Broady and Jimmy. They were doing huge mileage and placing great strain on their bodies. At first, I simply could not believe the statistics. If we spent a long time in the field, they could be doing up to thirty kilometres a day, running in on unyielding ground, in temperatures of 35 degrees. Something like four times their bodyweight would go through their knees and ankles, six times in relatively quick succession, on a regular basis. Little wonder that, given the application of such forces, Jimmy had his back issues. The hardest thing about dealing with Broady was trying to change his mind. He took advice as if he was being asked to drink curdled milk.

I obviously played an awful lot of cricket with them both. The mind games worked out evenly. As captain, I had to balance their comfort zones with my wider views and responsibilities. Ultimately, as the ones delivering the ball, they knew what they wanted to do. Occasionally, that didn't involve factoring in what I wanted them to do.

The captain has the final say when a bowler asks for a field change but must calculate the degree of dissatisfaction disagreement will cause. Broady, for instance, always wanted an extra cover with far greater enthusiasm than I could muster. Having one stubborn man telling another stubborn man what to do is not the recipe for an easy life. Our stand-offs on the pitch usually involved an agitated form of semaphore. Broady would be waving his arms this way and that, demanding positional changes. I love bowlers who know their own minds, but there are limits. Whereas others would be a bit more malleable, he didn't like taking no for an answer.

I had to strike that balance between being a dictator, a diplomat and a disciple. I knew that if I gave in to him consistently, there would be murmurings about my authority. Equally, I couldn't risk alienating him, or suggesting to the others that I was inflexible. Ultimately, I loved him. Whisper it, I still do. Anyone who gives so much deserves a certain latitude.

The South Africans restored a modicum of pride by winning the final Test at Centurion. Morkel got me out in both innings – for 76 and 5, respectively. Kagiso Rabada, aged only twenty, took thirteen wickets in the match. We were obviously disappointed, but it meant that, to a degree, everyone had something to celebrate when the teams congregated in the home changing room afterwards.

This was a session with a difference, because it featured a fines meeting. It was a bit like a rugby players' court and operated on the principle that anyone could impose a punishment, on teammate or opponent. The explanation didn't have to be particularly plausible, but it carried consequences if it wasn't deemed impressive. We enjoyed each other's company and were happy to share the stick.

As captains, AB and I were nailed early, and often. I fined Quinton de Kock, because he missed the Wanderers Test after twisting his knee falling over, supposedly walking his two Jack Russells the previous afternoon. Dane Vilas, his replacement, arrived an hour after the match started, despite a police escort, at the end of a comical 1,000-kilometre dash to Johannesburg by plane and train from Port Elizabeth.

Their media officers had tried to hush it up, but Dean Elgar, the South African opener, obviously hadn't been briefed on the cover story, and blurted out the tale of two little dogs. I slaughtered Quinton, light-heartedly suggesting that was the worst excuse I'd heard for getting pissed on duty. Rabada chimed in, fining Nick Compton for batting with only one eye open, like a drunk trying to find his way home. It was a great couple of hours, harmless fun, sporting banter as it should be.

I'm often asked to summarize the basic attraction of being a professional cricketer. That's hard to put into words, but it has something to do with shared experience. I've literally travelled the world with the likes of Jimmy and Broady. We've laughed a helluva lot, cried occasionally, celebrated and commiserated together. We've even posed naked together, helping to raise awareness of testicular cancer as part of the Everyman Campaign. You don't become family, but you do become extremely close friends. Cricket holds you close, grips you tighter than is sometimes comfortable, because it is a game of emotional contrasts that lasts a long time. I understand the primeval satisfaction of walking off a rugby pitch, battered and bruised, after eighty-odd minutes in the trenches with your mates, but that's an entirely different feeling from sharing a close, hard-fought Test match with a bunch of blokes who are continually on edge.

You feel absolutely drained. I'm mates with Dylan Hartley, the England rugby captain, and he gives me some tap about being in a sport that involves following the sun. To someone involved in brutal, personalized combat, in near-perpetual winter, that seems an attractive alternative. Try batting beneath a helmet for six hours in intense heat. Try putting yourself through a modern bowler's workload. Even fielding for long spells, relatively static but switching concentration on and off, takes it out of you.

The punishment was self-inflicted, but I have never seen someone play through the pain Ben Stokes endured from a succession of ill-fitting boots in Perth during the 2013–14 series. They fell to bits, and he was basically sandpapering his toes. He got through two pairs of protective socks in each session and was scraping his flesh on rock-hard ground during his follow-through. At the end of the day you could almost see bone beneath flayed skin. Obviously, it was excruciating, but you'd have never known it by Stokesy's demeanour. He just got on with it. Having hand-made, specially measured boots, like most internationals, didn't occur to him early in his career. He was the roughest of diamonds, raw and impulsive, biffing the ball all over the place in practice and playing with an almost reckless abandon.

That 2016 series in South Africa was, for him, a landmark of sorts. His 258 off 198 balls in Durban was extraordinary. It was the second-fastest double century in Test history, off 163 balls, and the fastest 250 in history. No England batsman had hit more sixes in one Test innings – eleven. He shared a record-breaking stand of 399 with Jonny Bairstow, whose unbeaten 150 was also a powerful statement of intent.

As strange as it seems, such startling statistics throw us off the scent. Stokesy is driven by the team, rather than obsessed by individual recognition. I genuinely don't think he cares about himself, so long as England are winning. That selflessness has turned him into the hardest-working England player in recent years, irrespective of the mistakes he has made growing up in public.

I wasn't in the West Indies in 2014 when he infamously broke his wrist punching a locker after getting out for 0 in the third one-day international in Antigua, but wasn't particularly surprised. His wildcat approach always had an element of self-reproach, and he impulsively abandoned a promising rugby-league career as a teenager.

Everyone tends to forget he played two T20 internationals on that tour, with his hand in bits. Peter Moores did the groundwork, helping him to channel his aggression positively, but lasting change comes from within. Lesser characters would have been intimidated by his implosion in the 2016 T20 World Cup final, when he conceded four successive sixes to give the West Indies an unlikely win, but he continued to front up.

Any team in an office, classroom or building site, works on human chemistry. The DNA of the team I eventually handed over to Joe Root in the spring of 2017 was unique, since no side is identical, but it contained a familiar balance of personalities. Moeen Ali, and to a slightly lesser extent Jos Buttler, emphasized its chilled, more free-spirited nature. They didn't want to win with any less fervour, but they were more relaxed about the process. Mo is particularly placid. I don't think I've ever seen him angry, except when Liverpool lose. The closest I've got to winding him up is by questioning his football pedigree and allegiance. He bites, gently, when you suggest he seems such a butterfly he was probably a Manchester United fan in his youth. When pressed, he will point you to a YouTube clip of him and Jimmy being given a tour of Anfield by Jürgen Klopp.

His cricket is a serious business. It runs through his family and radiates through his community. He is such an important figure as a man of faith and perspective. He has a fatalistic attitude that things are written. If he gets 0 today, it could be his destiny to score a century tomorrow. Succeeding does matter to him, profoundly, but he gives the impression it doesn't. His attitude that, 'Look, it's just a game of cricket,' has rubbed off on a few people around him. He still cares, of course, and in a purely playing sense I feel sympathetic towards him, because he has been here, there and everywhere in the batting order. He is cricket's answer to a Post-it note, a utility player who can be stuck anywhere on the scorecard. He doesn't make a fuss.

It has been a tough gig. He came in, under Moores, as a batsman who could bowl a bit of spin. When Graeme Swann retired, and Monty Panesar waned, he was thrown into the breach. He worked incredibly hard, with Mushtaq Ahmed's help, to become a very, very good off-spinner. They shared a cultural link, a respect for seniority that has, in turn, been passed on to Adil Rashid. Someday, someone is going to make a buddy movie called *Mo'n'Rash*. Their families lived about fifteen miles apart in northern Pakistan, and they played against each other in their early teens. As they have grown older, they have derived stability and guidance from their religion. They are inseparable.

Rash has taken time to bed in at the highest level, but as a leg-spinner he is an integral member of England's white-ball team. In broader terms, Mo suggests that English cricket's failure to make the most of the talent pool containing second and third generation Asian immigrants is a complicated issue that will work itself out, with time. Together they represent powerful proof that international sport can be a multicultural, unifying force.

It also has a certain impatience, reflected in the attitude of some of those on the fringes. I was pulled up short at the end of that 2016 tour of South Africa when a radio reporter asked me whether, having won two Ashes series, and won in India and South Africa, I was considering stepping down. 'You've achieved everything as a captain,' he said. 'Are you going to stop?'

On the one hand, that sort of question to a professional sportsman is abrupt to the point of being offensive. On the other, I knew what he was getting at. He wasn't quite reading my mind, but I was nibbling at the fringes of the issue with increasing interest. Losing the last four Tests in India in the run-up to Christmas that year took me to a tipping point.

To be fair to everyone concerned, I had to signal my intention to continue as captain through the following winter's Ashes series in Australia. I ignored the background noise of pundits like Geoffrey Boycott calling for me to stand down and concentrated on the inner voice that occasionally speaks sense. I'd had a record run of fifty-nine Tests in charge. The time was right to return to the ranks. Rooty was ready to lead. We both had the maturity, and mutual respect, to make things work. I had just exceeded 11,000 runs in Test cricket and felt confident of adding more. It meant a lot when Andrew Strauss, my old opening partner, spoke about my determination, conviction and pride.

Joe had had his moments. I don't know what went on in that Walkabout bar in Birmingham back in 2013, when he was supposedly punched by David Warner. I'd left by then and, frankly, didn't bother to find out because I couldn't have cared less. It was blown out of proportion and as relatively sensible adults they made up.

He retained the cheekiness that made him claim that catch against me on his debut. He could still be mischievous, and push people to the limits by teasing them unmercifully, but as soon as he took the captaincy, he understood the responsibilities of the role. All of us learn on the job, to a greater or lesser degree.

He came to me for a chat before his first series, against South Africa. It might seem the most natural thing in the world to do, but it was also one of the most difficult, because of what others might read into it. I lived up to my immediate promise, that I would be there as a sounding board, if required, and I would do nothing to tread on his toes. It had to be his team, in his image. He said certain things in certain team meetings, particularly about our batting, that I would not have said. It's not wrong that we should hold diametrically opposed views on something we knew so well; there are two sides to every argument. I didn't air my side because I didn't want him to feel I was putting him under any pressure.

We spoke about general principles, but he had to find his own way. It took between two and three years for me to feel truly comfortable in the job, which is roughly where he is now. That initial spell takes a lot out of you, particularly mentally. You almost wish you could programme the lessons, reset and go again.

We live and learn. We stumble, fall and rise again. We separate the myths and cherish the realities. We discover what is important, and what is an indulgence. I have never forgotten

Andy Flower's observation when he told me I was the new England captain in that meeting room in Southampton: 'Just because you've got the armband, it doesn't mean you know everything.'

You know what? He was right.

16. Names and Numbers

'After twenty-five years in cricket I've decided to move on. Cricket has given me everything I have. Thank you for being a part of this journey. This game taught me how to fight, how to fall, to dust off, to get up again and move forward. It has been a lovely journey. See you on the other side.'

With that message to his 4,650,000 Twitter followers, Yuvraj Singh announced his retirement from international cricket in early June 2019. In a flourish of which Bollywood would be proud, it was accompanied by a twenty-three-second, slow-motion video in which he turned his back to the camera, stroked the shoulder of his blue India shirt, number 12, and walked off, out of shot.

The greats of the Indian game, led by Virat Kohli, paid tribute. Yuvraj earned his immortality in 2011 by helping Sachin Tendulkar win his World Cup. He accumulated 362 runs in the tournament at an average of 90.50, took fifteen wickets and was named man of the match four times. That was the year he was diagnosed with lung cancer; his survival spawned a charity that has done untold good.

How should any of us be remembered? Yuvraj was a player of his time, a powerful left-handed middle-order batsman and left-arm spinner who excelled in white-ball cricket. Stuart Broad will probably not thank me for reminding you that Yuvraj hit him for six sixes in an over at the 2007 World T20, which India won. He played forty Tests, 304 one-day internationals and fifty-eight T20s.

Good numbers. I did not know him that well, but one line in his retirement speech – 'it's been a love–hate relationship with the sport in retrospect' – will have resonated with many cricketers. It reminded me of a conversation we had, playing together for MCC in a T20 tournament in Dubai in March 2015. He congratulated me for having recently passed 10,000 Test runs.

'You're going to go down in the record books as a legend of cricket,' he told me, out of the blue.

It's difficult to know what to say to that. Half-jokingly, I replied, 'You're laughing all the way to the bank.'

His response was instant: 'I'll swap it all, to have your Test career.'

The finality of the statement took me back. He didn't qualify it by saying he would swap an awful lot to have my set of numbers. He was all in. His comment wasn't really about me. It was a reflection on the status of the most traditional form of the game, by a player whose wealth and reputation were formed during the IPL revolution.

Yuvraj won the IPL twice. His final achievement was to help Mumbai Indians become champions in 2019. I've never played in that tournament, never experienced its fireworks and fervour, though I have an inkling what it would feel like, because of the amazing atmosphere generated in India by one-day internationals.

Call me short sighted, but I didn't immediately recognize the importance of the IPL. I didn't see it transforming cricket, in micro time, as it has. I was wrong. I may look back and wonder whether I could have changed my game to fit the franchise format, but it is not a matter of enduring regret. Test cricket was ingrained in me from childhood.

The skill factor in modern T20 cricket is extraordinary. Barriers have been broken down. Things that were once considered impossible are now commonplace. The game has changed beyond recognition. In the land of the high-stakes shootout, the gambler is king. The contrast to the early days of one-day cricket is like comparing a Model-T Ford with a Bugatti Veyron.

When the sixty-over World Cup was brought in (the number of overs was reduced to fifty in 1987), there seemed little point in chasing 260 to win. That sort of challenge intimidated teams, who would have a glorified net in reply. As the game evolved, we were taught to hit pockets. Graham Gooch was a pioneer. Mark Ramprakash mastered the shot over extra cover for two or four. It required skill and nerve, but there was a decent margin for error.

It was not the done thing to take on the man on the boundary. It was deemed too risky to attempt to hit the ball over the head of the fielder at deep mid-on. Far better to advance down the wicket to fashion a chip shot, like a golfer, over extra cover and into the gap for a couple. It was essentially cautious batting for relatively limited reward. Coaches were insurance salesmen. Now they're circus ringmasters. If you're caught in the deep, you're expected to shrug your shoulders, admit you mishit it and try again next time. Nowadays the big shot is perfected in the nets, like a booming drive on a golf range. The odds are overwhelmingly in its favour.

As emerging players at Essex, we would never have thought of standing in the middle of the square at Chelmsford and bombing the ball into the river. If you hit a boundary, you followed Goochy's edict, took a single next ball and got off strike. Perceptions have changed. In Jos's eyes a sequence of 6, 4, 6, 1 is better cricket. The white-ball cricket is about transference of power and freedom of spirit.

Modern bats are bigger in profile, with an inviting sweet spot, but less heavy because the wood is drier. They tend not to last as long, and break more easily, so equipment isn't a major factor in the revolution. I used my best bat, a lovely thin yellow-handled thing, in 2005. It was so responsive I lent it to Ravi Bopara. Legend has it that Albert Trott, who played Test cricket for both Australia and England, hit a ball over the Lord's pavilion in 1899, so that can't have been a bad bit of timber.

A glance in the gym would offer a better indication of change. It used to be a no-go area for batsmen. Now every player has a tailored strength-and-conditioning programme. I'm no bio-mechanist, but it stands to reason that if you have a lot of muscle behind a well-timed shot, the ball will disappear into the distance.

Mentally, though, it is a different proposition. I shared a net with Alex Hales in my last one-day series. He had the ability to run down the wicket and hit the net-spinners for six at will, off every delivery. His Gimp was obviously telling him, 'Don't worry, you can do it,' but he didn't quite get it right at game time and was caught at deep mid-off a couple of times.

I said to him, 'It must be really hard being you.' By that I meant it was understandable that he should listen to the inner voice telling him he could clear the rope by seventy yards. That sort of self-knowledge can be dangerous since it leads to a subconscious assumption it is possible to hit every ball, any delivery, for six. If you know you can do it, when do you choose to do it?

That highlights one of batting's most intriguing factors, its individualism. I've never had Alex's problem of succumbing to temptation, because I don't have his extraordinary power. I have three or four reliable elements of influence: if I can't cut, chip or pull the ball, I leave it, or defend.

Someone like Ravi Bopara, who has shared my journey from Maldon to the MCG, has, perversely, had it harder than me because his technique and dexterity allow him more potentially profitable areas on which to concentrate. Those extra options mean he has to make a lot more decisions under pressure than I do.

Handling that distraction, the dilemma of trying to balance pop with prudence, must be a hard thing to deal with. I've noticed that the modern-day generation of fifty-over batsmen tend to kill you one day and go quietly the next. Of them all, Joe Root, a player grounded in old-school techniques, probably emerges as the most consistent.

Cricket isn't losing anything. It is still in a transitional phase, where there is an absolute need to have someone of Rooty's sureness. He is not a natural power hitter, but he is England's pivotal batsman. Add that to the inventiveness of shots that look improvised but are meticulously rehearsed, and you have a proper team.

The Dil Scoop, introduced by Tillakaratne Dilshan at the 2009 World Cup, was a game changer. It was a product of street cricket, played with a tennis ball, in Sri Lanka, where there was little room either side of the wicket. He went down on one knee, leaned into the ball, and swept it over the wicketkeeper's head. Jos Buttler tried it, felt he couldn't do it the Dilshan way, but found his own method, after hour upon hour of painstaking practice. He is of the generation that grew up with T20, which started in 2003. It had an obvious influence, just as I was inspired by Test and four-day county cricket. The modern player must be far more adaptable; the old-school player approached one-day cricket identically to the longer form, apart from self-consciously having a whack in the last fifteen overs.

To be the complete cricketer is very hard, because that demands a very broad skillset. Joe Root, Steve Smith and David Warner are among the very few players who can relate to all forms of the game. Some excel in two, across twenty or fifty overs. Others, like me, are good in the longer forms, but struggle to make an impact in T20.

As for me playing in The Hundred, the ECB's marketing-driven competition aimed at a new audience for cricket, which is scheduled to start in July 2020? I don't think so. Being in one of eight city-based franchise teams, playing a shortened hundred-ball form of the game, is a step too far. An old dog can only learn so many new tricks.

Innovation is no bad thing per se. Cricket has always had room for the experimental. Mushtaq Mohammad of Pakistan first tried out the switch-hit shot playing for Northamptonshire in the mid-seventies. Mike Gatting infamously attempted an impetuous reverse sweep in the 1987 World Cup final against Australia in Kolkata, deflecting Alan Border's first ball to wicketkeeper Greg Dyer in a key phase of a run chase that ended seven short.

Sometimes fortune favours the brave, or at least excuses the misguided. MS Dhoni, a law unto himself on a cricket field, will be forever associated with the helicopter shot, a fusion of timing and instinct. It involves a strong, quick-wristed flick off a fuller length ball, towards the leg side, and ends with the bat being twirled above the head.

Tekkers, as I think they say in football.

For me, the greatest advance was Kevin Pietersen's switched-hand reverse sweep, with which he deposited Scott Styris over the extra-cover boundary at the Riverside in June 2008. Just imagine, for a moment, how strange it would feel if you hit a shot with your wrong hand. It is such an unnatural act. Yet Kevin's shot also incorporated remarkably quick feet, an amazingly sharp brain and flexibility of position that would have put most of us in traction. For good measure, he repeated the trick against a slower ball, a sequence that involved waiting in his reversed position and hitting it virtually straight over long off. No wonder Styris gawped with amazement before joining in the applause. Kevin had toyed with the shot in T20, but this was new territory, even for a batsman who had announced himself two years earlier with a reverse slog sweep off Muttiah Muralitharan into the Eric Hollies Stand at Edgbaston.

Some of the responses to the destruction he wrought in Durham were way over the top. MCC, guardian of the game's laws, announced it would be considering the shot's merits at a previously scheduled meeting. There was some frankly daft talk about bowlers changing from right to left arm in stride, and not making the decision whether to bowl around or over the wicket until the last possible moment.

Shock and awe. KP was made for the IPL and he knew it.

I marvel at such skill and audacity. I played my first scoop against Chris Jordan, having never practised it in my life. I was 80-odd not out, calculated he was going to bowl a yorker and used beginner's luck to paddle it. Bowlers learn quickly, however. The slower ball, out of the back of the hand, is old hat these days. It's now delivered even slower, from deeper in the hand.

Batsmen have to cope with slower-ball bouncers, knuckle balls adapted from baseball. Some of the balls wobble like freshly set jelly. They are no longer inclined to submit to the yorker and are primed to create or make the most of fractional errors in length. Bowlers are trying to get their retaliation in first, before they are brutalized by batsmen like Buttler, who hit eleven consecutive boundaries against the West Indies in February 2019 and needed only thirty-two deliveries to go from 50 to 150.

Glorious, but ridiculous. I dare you not to love it.

Watching Buttler or Chris Gayle in full flow is like playing *Brian Lara Cricket* on the PC when we were kids. They are the Superman Cheat, which lets you hit every ball for four or six, in human form. I was in the Essex dressing room, watching TV, when England just missed out on 500 at Trent Bridge, and someone said, 'They're playing a game which is just not real . . .'

It looked so easy. I was in awe of what those guys were doing, even though I had played alongside them in different forms of the game. I haven't got their type of talent, their free-form creativity, our equivalent of a cross between jazz and heavy metal. Could they bat for eleven hours in 40-degree heat on a ground so silent you can hear nesting birds in the roof of the stand? Possibly not, though Ben Stokes wouldn't need to hang around that long, in any case, to brush up on his ornithology.

It's different strokes for different folks in its most literal sense, but there are unifying factors. Jos Buttler is the poster boy for this new form of cricket, but Shane Warne, his mentor in the IPL with Rajasthan Royals, gave him the confidence to transfer his skills into the Test arena. It took time for him to come to terms with red-ball cricket, but he admits: 'I'm desperate to reach my potential.' His versatility is deeply impressive, made to measure. He opens with violent intent in T20. In the fifty-over game he's the finisher, held back for the big push. He keeps wicket to the white ball but concentrates on his batting in Test matches. His character is trusted by the men he serves as vice-captain, Eoin Morgan and Joe Root.

There are parallels with young players emerging in English football. They are unafraid of self-expression and take great pride in the extravagant skills they developed playing cage football as kids. They are quick-witted, and ready to try new tricks on the biggest stage. They will not sacrifice their enthusiasm because they are not scared of failure.

Buttler is a kindred spirit in that respect. His response when a photographer noticed that he had written 'Fuck it' on his bat handle was revealing. 'It puts cricket in perspective,' he explained. 'When you nick off, does it really matter?' In the great scheme of things, no. To a captain or coach craving stability and security, perhaps yes.

Jos had played thirty-one Tests over five years until the summer of 2019, averaging nearly 36 and scoring a single century, 106 against India in 2018. It hasn't been an easy ride, with Geoffrey Boycott characteristically suggesting 'a seven-year-old schoolboy would have played better' in the 2015 Ashes, but his determination to excel is admirable.

He speaks about having 'fun' learning new strokes. His

favourite is the ramp shot, over the wicketkeeper. Confidence is a transferable item; he understands he can't play those shots with such freedom in Test cricket and wouldn't do so indiscriminately, but he reserves the right to employ an element of surprise. Bowlers think they know what they are dealing with, and plan accordingly, but can be knocked out of their stride.

They also appreciate the allure of the five-day game, even when they make their name, and their fortune, in four-over bursts in franchise cricket. Jofra Archer, Buttler's teammate with Rajasthan Royals, seized the imagination when he qualified for England and was selected for the 2019 World Cup. His ability to bowl with speed and accuracy, to deliver smoothly at 95 mph, is applicable across the game.

Look into his background, and you will find the examples of commitment above and beyond the call of duty that are common among successful athletes. He remodelled his action following back problems after being discovered playing club cricket by Sussex, and even rolled his own mud wicket so he could practise at home in Barbados.

I have no problem with Archer shifting allegiance to England. We live in an age where nationalities are becoming blurred across all sports. At the last count, twenty-nine cricketers have represented two different countries at international level; fifteen have done so in Test cricket. Eoin Morgan, Boyd Rankin and Ed Joyce have all been on the conveyer belt between Irish and English cricket.

I never had to deal with the issue of circumstances curtailing my ability to fulfil my potential as a cricketer. I was lucky the opportunity to play cricket for England was my birthright. I have been brought up to support anyone who represents my nation. Without wishing to sound jingoistic, I'm English through and through.

I don't have the right to judge those who have done what they thought best for themselves. Morgan was a fantastic cricketer, denied his chance to play for Ireland beyond the odd one-day game – twenty-three, to be precise, between 2006 and 2009. He may not have lost his broad Irish accent and he may retain family roots in the land of his birth, but his life is in England. His heroes, principally Graham Thorpe, were English. The idea of playing for England began to take shape when he studied at Dulwich College in South London from the age of thirteen. He brought with him an intriguingly different set of skills. He played hurling as a schoolboy, growing up in Dublin. The grip for the two-sided bat, or hurley, is the same as the one used in cricket's reverse sweep.

The modern England team is, as we have discussed, a cultural and ethnic mix. Jonathan Trott, for instance, played Under-19 cricket for South Africa, but has had a British passport since birth, because his dad is English. He's had to take light-hearted stick as an adopted Brummie but feels very English. His children have been brought up here. He belongs.

Others will inevitably follow a similar path. Simon Harmer, a world-class off-break bowler who has had such an impact with us at Essex over the past couple of years that he now captains our T20 team, has extended his county contract until 2021. By then, although he played five Tests for South Africa in 2015, he will be eligible for England.

Kyle Abbott, who played eleven Tests, and Rilee Rossouw, who was being developed as understudy to AB de Villiers, caused controversy in South Africa in early 2017 by standing down from international cricket to sign long-term county deals with Hampshire. They argued that they were seeking greater financial security; I don't blame anyone for taking up opportunities as they occur in life.

The nature of the professional cricketer is changing. The T20 generation are global players, who are not necessary identified with one team. Jonny Bairstow is as Yorkshire as they come but reached a new constituency in his debut season in the IPL, where he averaged 55.62 at a strike rate of 157.24 for Sunrisers Hyderabad. He had barely got off the plane from India before he was into a World Cup training camp and scoring 126 in a one-day international against Pakistan.

The modern hybrid player has so more many opportunities to play; Buttler, for instance, represents Sydney Thunder in the Big Bash, while remaining grounded in county cricket for Lancashire. He played for Comilla Victorians in the Bangladesh Premier League. Dawid Malan took a pay cut, from playing T20 cricket in Bangladesh, to represent England in the Ashes in 2017, where he scored his maiden Test hundred at the WACA. Players shouldn't really have to make such a choice, but the economics of the game have changed as radically as their professional lifestyle.

Franchise cricket operates as a satellite system and answers a constant need for TV content. Malan, for instance, captains Middlesex but spent last winter playing for Cape Town Blitz in South Africa's Mzansi Super League, for Peshawar Zalmi in the Pakistan Super League, and for Khulna Titans in the Bangladesh Premier League.

Every sport wants to maximize its income and enhance its exposure, but sometimes you can have too much of a good thing. Crowds were down in the last edition of the Big Bash in Australia; they have been uniformly poor in the Caribbean Super League. It is easy to say the calendar should be rationalized, but professional principles apply.

Like other athletes in other sports facing identical issues, we play too much. That might not be as physically destructive in cricket as in, say, rugby, but there is a logical erosion of impact. Everyone needs a rest, but what happens when you are two weeks into a month off, and your agent calls with news that a franchise is offering £50,000 for three matches? The temptation to accept is enormous.

I've never been on that circuit. I missed the boat in one sense. I played a solitary season of T20 for Essex, and even scored an unbeaten 100 against Surrey in front of 17,000 at the Oval, but didn't have the desire to devise an effective method. I was set on becoming the best Test player I could be for England.

Is Test cricket as close to administrators' hearts as they say it is? Possibly not. The five-day game is declining in one sense, because it is not making money in many countries. It is a difficult discussion, due to the emotions it evokes, but my thinking was refined by a conversation with Ryan ten Doeschate, my captain at Essex, whom I get on really well with.

Tendo is a fascinating bloke, whose approach to life is summarized by his Twitter bio, which contains only the quote: 'Take the risk of thinking for yourself, much more happiness, truth, beauty, and wisdom will come to you that way.' He's South African-born, is aged thirty-nine, and one of the best players to represent a non-Test playing nation, the Netherlands. His career is best described as esoteric. An Essex cricketer since 2003, after being spotted in South

Africa by Graham Gooch, he has played for the following teams since 2010: Mashonaland Eagles, Canterbury, Tasmania, Kolkata Knight Riders, Impi, Otago, Chittagong Kings (now Vikings), Gazi Tank Cricketers, Adelaide Strikers, Dhaka Dynamites, Karachi Kings, Comilla Victorians, Rajshahi Kings and Lahore Qalandars.

He helped Balkh Legends win the inaugural Afghanistan Premier League in Sharjah in late October 2018, and ended the year playing for Bhairahawa Gladiators in the Everest Premier League, a six-team tournament in Nepal that stages all matches on three wickets at the Tribhuvan University ground in Kirtipur, just outside Kathmandu.

Despite that CV, he had dedicated his sporting life to Essex. He struggled badly on arrival; his bowling, which had been spectacularly successful because of his mastery of the yorker, went to pot for a while. I once saw him, head in hands, after being hit to all parts by Scott Styris in a match against Middlesex and wondered whether he would survive. He went out and won us that game with the bat and has never looked back. He is a fantastic leader of men, as comfortable discussing the past with county legends such as Goochy, Keith Fletcher and Doug Insole as he is playing cards on the bus or in the dressing room with an up-and-coming teenager. He has that knack of being able to relate to people on a variety of levels.

His wider views, then, carry weight. As an England player, I argued that there was a need to protect Test cricket proactively by redirecting some of the marketing budgets used to promote the white-ball form of the game. Tendo disagreed, on the principle that Test cricket is a business, like any other. It is impossible to protect a business from market forces.

Shield it artificially for ten years, and the money men will still be cynical about its prospects. They will act accordingly. Unless Test cricket is willing to fight back, and reproduce itself as a marketable product, it will die a death. To do so, it needs help from the authorities, who must utilize the well-funded promotional expertise that is being employed in other forms of the game.

Perhaps it is time to embrace the thought that less can be more. A more strategic approach to Test cricket, with fewer, better-promoted matches, would restore a sense of occasion and reduce pressures on players who are having to shoehorn in commitments to other, more lucrative forms of the game. Test cricket is changing, in any case.

It is not necessarily a bad thing that very few matches last the full five days, because longevity gives it authenticity, but run rates are higher, and games are moving along quicker. The skill of defensive batting, which once produced days in which teams plodded to 220–2, has been replaced by greater attacking intent, which results in being 350–6 at the close. It is more exciting to watch.

I've nothing against franchise cricket, but I wonder whether it fulfils a sportsman's basic instinct, to leave something behind. Another team, another game, another town. It all seems a bit ephemeral. Does it create the same sense of satisfaction? Yet, to argue against myself, I appreciate how much work goes into it. You cannot approach it half-heartedly, because it will eat you up.

Yuvraj concentrated my mind in a similar fashion to Tendo, by hinting at the importance of history, despite my natural scepticism. It still seems unreal to consider that I'm the fifth highest scorer of all time. No England player has more Test runs, more hundreds, more catches, more consecutive matches, more games as captain.

What's in a name? What's in a number?

Comparing players across generations is one of my biggest bugbears, because I question its relevance. Cricket is a game that encourages romanticism and nostalgia, but looking back and thinking 'it was better in my day' is self-delusory because, rather like Formula 1, it is now a different sport, tailored to a different time. Making judgement calls between Juan Manuel Fangio, Ayrton Senna and Lewis Hamilton is as futile as adjudicating between Denis Compton, Viv Richards and Joe Root.

Modern life has been accelerated out of all recognition. Life stories are told in minutes on social media. My hunch is that, in thirty years' time, the pioneers of T20, like KP and Gayle, AB de Villiers and Buttler, will be treated with the reverence my generation reserves for such Test greats as Hobbs, Sutcliffe and Bradman.

For me to be linked to them, through the record books, is deeply affecting, and in my more reflective moments a little embarrassing. It's scarcely believable to be spoken of in the same breath as such players. It means I can look back at what I have achieved with a lot of fondness, but I'm obliged to ask myself whether I am worthy of such associations. It risks offending the cricketing gods.

It's slightly easier now that I've retired, and don't have to back it up in international cricket any more, but I'm aware that I might still have to take one for the Oval, just to keep me in my place.

17. Not Found Wanting

It was Saturday, 8 December 2018, the thirty-eighth anniversary of John Lennon's murder. Chelsea ended Manchester City's unbeaten run in the Premier League. Northampton Saints, my rugby team, defeated the Dragons 48–14 at Franklin's Gardens in the European Challenge Cup. I had a pleasant off-season lunch, with about twenty friends, and got the surprise of my life.

I'm not one of those obsessives who feel the need to check my phone every nanosecond, but for some reason I let it rest between my legs, on my chair. It was set to silent, but when it began to vibrate incessantly, I thought I'd better check to see if anything untoward had happened to my family, or the farm. It was a text from Mike Martin, my agent:

'You need to check your emails urgently . . . and by the way, I am not calling you Sir.'

So many thoughts rush through your mind at such a moment: 'Whatever you do, don't react, Alastair. If this is what you think it is – and it can't be anything else, can it? – it is highly confidential. Play it cool. Just finish your dessert, excuse yourself, and go outside to tell Alice she is about to become a Lady.'

You never consider yourself worthy of such an honour, but I thought I had missed out, because recipients tend to be told of their good fortune about six weeks before an official announcement, which, in this case, would come on New Year's Eve.

I was aware a knighthood had been the subject of idle chatter around the time of my retirement from the England team. Theresa May, a cricket fan as well as prime minister, gave a rather flattering interview about her impressions of my career. In late October, Lord Tyrie submitted a written question, number HL10964, to the House of Lords 'To ask Her Majesty's Government what consideration they have given to recommending Alastair Cook for knighthood'.

Lord Young of Cookham, the Government's spokesman, played an immaculate forward defensive: 'The Government does not comment on individual honours nominations. Due to the confidential nature of the honours system, discretion regarding individual cases is considered important to safeguard [its] confidentiality and integrity . . .'

Recommendations are made by ten independent committees. I was unaware of the fact that confirmation of my honour was delayed because it had been posted to the wrong address. The letter from the Palace was redirected later, after Mike had been contacted. I would like to take the opportunity to apologize to my namesake, whoever he is, for the shock and ultimate disappointment he must have felt on receiving it in the first place.

The news broke, slightly prematurely, in *The Times*, where Michael Atherton wrote about me as a kindred spirit: 'All openers know that the scoreboard reads 0–0 when they walk out to bat; the bowlers are at their freshest and most eager; the ball is shiny, hard and new and the seam at its most proud; and the fielders are full of optimism, and mouthy with it. Nowhere is easy to bat in international cricket but coming in occasionally at 200 for two allows the mind some respite and a reprieve. Openers never get that.'

Remember, though. That's what we are talking about here – a cricketer. I'm not a life-saving hero, a cancer-curing scientist. I've been fortunate to play a game I love for so long, and I must say I do feel a little young to be a knight of the realm. It's very strange to walk into a room and be announced as 'Sir Alastair Cook'. I don't think I'll ever get used to that, as long as I live.

People don't call me 'Sir Alastair' when I'm in the Red Lion or the Green Man, my closest village pubs. There are no airs and graces when I am worming the sheep. It will always be plain old Beefy and Cookie when we are together. As for my Essex teammates, they predictably came up with a new nickname, with fourth-form connotations. I am now known to all and sundry as 'Sac' . . .

I didn't realize that I was the first active English cricketer to be knighted, but, as mentioned in the previous chapter, identification with icons is daunting. It took Alec Bedser forty years to be so honoured. The other players – Hobbs, Hutton, Cowdrey and Botham – are part of a bloodline that some see as sacred. That's hard to get your head round.

As a sportsman you become accustomed to excessive praise and unwarranted criticism from perfect strangers. That's part of the job. This was my chance to share my good fortune with friends and family. Alice used a special WhatsApp group to organize open house on New Year's Day. It was a special celebration, one of those memories that will last a lifetime.

By then the knighthood was public knowledge. We made an appreciable dent in the thirty-three specially labelled bottles of champagne, one for each Test hundred, presented to me by the England boys. The investiture itself, on 26

February, was surreal. Everyone has a quiet terror at offending protocol. I knelt, head bowed, with my right knee on a crimson silk-velvet stool, as the sword, which belonged to George VI, lightly touched my right and then my left shoulder.

Sorry to shatter any illusions, but Her Majesty does not say 'Arise, Sir Alastair . . .'

The Queen was serene, and impeccably informed. She congratulated me before commenting on the excellence of the West Indies bowlers in the recent Test series and asked how lambing was going on the farm. I appreciate people have differing views on the validity of the honours system, but for me it was a deeply affecting moment.

Following afternoon tea at the Ritz, the extended family returned to reality. It was a time of personal reflection, since I found myself at an intersection of my life. I still had cricket, in the form of a three-year contract with Essex, but the emphasis had shifted.

Another paragraph from Athers's article struck a chord: 'In time, he will surely recognize that his greatest achievement was not the gift from some mandarin at Whitehall, but the knowledge that when tested time and again he was not found wanting. The rest is an adornment. That day in September, when the ground stood and drowned him in wave after wave of adulation, will give him a more lasting inner glow than will any reflection from a shiny bauble. That memory will last a lifetime.'

We all have moments when we wonder who we are, and where we are going. The privilege of recognition, in all its forms, gives you the gift of reflection. A series of questions began to take shape: What were the fundamental lessons I had learned along the way? How would I use them? Would I be capable of living my life at a different pace?

One of my earliest lessons in cricket was also one of the most important: you can't do things on your own, but ultimately you will be defined as an individual, despite it being a team sport. I owe an enormous debt of gratitude to Graham Gooch, a constant presence for most of my career, but had to do things my way. I was the one who walked out there to bat. There was no one holding my hand when I did so.

I accept I was entrenched in my ideas. I am notoriously stubborn. Logically, if that approach had worked for me as a player, why would it not work for me as a captain? Going back to that conversation with Andy Flower, I knew I didn't know everything, but was so scared of wandering off, listening to too many people and becoming a victim of muddied thinking that I was too reserved.

It was only as I became more comfortable in my skin as a captain that I realized I had to be more collaborative. Talking to people who see things from a different angle is rejuvenating. It gives you additional ideas, shares and lessens the burden. Self-imposed pressure eases, because you are not preoccupied with keeping things close to your chest.

I wish I had done so earlier, but how would I have known, straight away, that was the right thing to do? We are who we are. Given the multifaceted nature of the job of England captain, there has to be an element of trial and error. It is a very different challenge, even if your leadership style is seasoned in county cricket.

It's a dissimilar situation, a different job but an amazing job. There's no doubt it brought out my natural resilience.

Living through the KP affair proved to me that if I have something in which I believe I will keep ploughing on. I've always been fascinated by the psychology of personal achievement, especially when there is a physical element to the challenge.

I've read a lot about the SAS, and the quiet fortitude of their guys. They don't show out. They never strut around. They step back, analyse and act. I would love to spend time with them, to discover the true meaning of mental strength. Everyone says I have it, but it is also my comfort blanket. Do I take it for granted, or can I develop it into other areas?

When I announced my retirement a lot of people, including Athers, suggested I should have taken a sabbatical. Sports massage therapist Mark Saxby, a constant feature of my England career, and a valued source of personal support, came to me at the Oval and said: 'I've got to ask you this. Why are you retiring? You're only thirty-three years old. You've got your whole life, a whole world of cricket, ahead of you. You didn't need to retire. You should have just taken the winter off.'

I did think about it, for about five minutes. But, as I told Mark, I was in a good place. This wasn't a decision taken out of desperation, when I was deep in the bush. No one around me really needed the uncertainty of me marking time in what is often a horrible halfway house. You might not be there, in the dressing room or out in the middle, but the story will still be all about you.

When will he come back? Who will be under threat when he does so? How will his teammates feel? Was that fair, in my own mind? How would I feel as it all played out? Everyone might be looking at me as if I was mad to walk away, but was hanging on a realistic option? Was it really what I needed at this time in my life?

So many questions, but only one answer. I was done.

Obviously, I can't say this with any great certainty, but on balance I don't think six months off would have refreshed me. Knowing myself, and recognizing my inherent intransigence, I had reached a point of no return. Any selfishness on my part, because of some romantic notion that I would be transformed into a fresher, ageless version of me, would have been counter-productive.

I'd had my time. I didn't want to be the elephant in the room. I didn't want someone like Rory Burns to wonder if he was merely keeping my place warm. He has a position to secure, a career to forge. It is his turn to see if he can handle everything that comes with opening the batting for England.

Despite the speculation, no one came asking me to reconsider before this summer's Ashes. In any case, I had moved on. Even taking the emotional power of memory into account, eight months or so on from that perfectly scripted farewell at the Oval, I am not missing playing for England.

Playing for England was all I ever wanted to do, and my life was structured around fulfilling that ambition. The transitional period is tricky, because one of my identities, that of international cricketer, has been taken away. It was always going to happen at some stage, and it is inevitably a hold-your-breath moment. It takes a while to rebalance your life.

There are differences, though my life with Alice has always been slightly disorganized, in being here, there and everywhere. I still bounce between cricket and the farm, the kids and cricket, and sometimes wonder where I am going to land. I'm around for odd days, but I'm still dancing to the rhythms of a cricket season.

Playing for Essex is distinctive, because you are in performance mode the whole time. That's unlike playing for England, where you are in preparation mode for most of the time. Test cricket has a different cadence. You might have a month off after a tour, have a couple of games for your county to start ticking over, and then go into the rituals of another series. You become used to the routine of a five-day Test match being sandwiched between separate bursts of two to three days' preparation. You must deal with the intensity of competition, chill out briefly, and build yourself up to do it all again. It is a life of structured highs and lows. Compared to that, in county cricket you are flatlining.

That's taken a while to get used to, because I found the intensity in the international game surprisingly energizing. I'm not demeaning or disrespecting playing for Essex, because it is demanding in a different way. I'm still coming up against very good, extremely dedicated, consistently skilful players. The level is high, but not as severe.

This is the first time, since the age of twenty-one, that I am playing with the security of something other than a one-year deal. I have a three-year contract, so I'm no longer obliged to endure the 'what if?' scenario, which usually looms two or three months into a professional cricketer's summer. Even when I appeared settled with England, I went through the annual process of review and renewal. I no longer deal with the strategic uncertainty of living from tour to tour, central contract to central contract.

There can never be true stability at the highest level. The

world may seem bigger when you step into the England team, but there are still obstacles to overcome, boundaries to be breached. A better pay structure carries the threat of complacency, but the more far-sighted player realizes that, by playing twenty-five Tests or fifty one-day internationals he can earn the sort of money that can substantially change his life.

Inevitably, exposure brings pressure. Your profile is higher, so more people want a piece of you. You must learn to read character, find a way of working out who and what you can trust. If you are lucky, as you progress in your work you will have a young family to consider. You must rationalize their demands while never losing sight of the need to score enough runs or take enough wickets to keep the carousel turning.

Abu Dhabi, in April 2019, was the start of the transition to the final phase of my career. The stadium was deserted, apart from a small tour group escaping the English winter to watch Essex's low-key pre-season friendly with Somerset. When our bus pulled into the stadium forecourt, feral cats retreated out of the sun and watched intently from underneath parked cars.

Workmen painted the lobby and put up plasterboard partitions without energy or urgency. The dressing rooms were musty and carried veiled warnings to which we have become accustomed in an age of suspicion. 'Mobile Phones prohibited' read one sign. 'No internet access'. The number of a confidential whistleblowers' hotline was on a poster in the corridor outside.

Sitting behind clear plastic in the players' section of the stand, after scoring 50-odd, gave me the chance to weigh up the dynamics of a different dressing room. An England dressing room is a ruthless place, in which the preoccupation of highly motivated individuals is survival. A county team contains players in different phases of their careers, with contrasting motivations.

There's the eighteen-year-old kid, straight from the Academy. There's the twenty-two-year-old who has been around a bit, and has his eye on a county cap. There's the twenty-four-year-old who is privately fretting, thinking, 'This is my last chance.' There's the twenty-seven-year-old breakout player, desperate to be selected for England, and there's the thirty-seven-year-old who is still enjoying his cricket and wants to stick around for another couple of years.

I asked myself what my value would be to such a diverse group. I needed something other than the selfish pursuit of making big runs to quell the scary thought that there was a pointlessness to my presence. I got it when Maggs – Anthony McGrath, our second-year head coach – asked me to be a sounding board for anyone who needed the release of an alternative viewpoint.

He felt that people would pick up little things from me. I'm not the oracle. I've never pretended to know it all, but I suppose I'm not quite so self-contained as I once was. I designed a method to give me success and longevity; if I can share practical examples with a young player who wants to learn, without the hierarchical formalities of being a coach, I'm more than happy to do so.

Basic guidelines, beyond the complexities of technique? Never over complicate. Don't make a simple game very hard. Apply yourself, ingrain what you believe to be the best of you. With clarity comes consistency, but always remember that sport can be contradictory. Stuff just happens. There's nothing you can do about the saddest fact of a cricketer's life, that you wish you knew, at twenty-one, what you know at thirty-five.

I'm not quite at the stage where I'm sitting in front of the fire in fond reminiscence of the old days and the old ways, but I am seeing the game through a different lens. As England captain I consciously refused to talk up an opposition player, or team, beyond the bland niceties of a press conference that no one takes the slightest notice of.

I was desperate not to fail. I wanted to score more runs than anyone else. If that meant keeping my true thoughts to myself, then so be it. Now, though, I have the freedom to be frank. Instead of viewing someone like Virat Kohli as a rival, I see him for what he is, a master of his trade. He no longer represents a danger, a point of potentially unflattering comparison.

I recognize the resilience it took for him to overcome his early struggles in England. I am in awe of his ability to compartmentalize a life that is not his own. But most of all, I can enjoy the beauty of his batting, the extraordinary way in which he responds to the evolving demands of a run chase in one-day cricket. The placement of his shots, and the consistency of his technique, are stunning. I hadn't realized until now how good he is.

I've never been one for quantifying a player purely on the evidence of the record books. That doesn't mean I have any less respect or admiration for those bygone heroes who had occasionally to make their runs on uncovered wickets, or on imperfect pitches without the insurance of a protective helmet. I simply prefer to make my judgements through personal experience. On that basis, and with apologies for omitting

Morne Morkel and Ishant Sharma, the bowlers who probably caused me the most difficulty, I consider Ricky Ponting, Jacques Kallis and Brian Lara to be the three standout players of my generation.

Rod Marsh, who took charge of the England Academy for four years, up to 2005, used to tell a story about Ponting and the 'bouncer sessions' he starred in at the indoor centre at the Adelaide Oval when he did the same job for the Australians. Aussie coaches would feed tennis balls, encased in leather, into a bowling machine set to aim at the head at 100 mph.

Those sessions were brutal and drew blood. Only Ricky seemed immune to punishment; he was never hit and swiped away deliveries in front of square leg. To me, as a twenty-one-year-old breaking into the England team, he was different gravy. He seemed to have so much time to hook and pull the ball, getting his foot down the pitch early. He struck it so crisply and cleanly.

His 196 against us in the Brisbane Test in 2006 stays with me as the perfect example of his willpower, skill and defiance. He batted for more than seven and a half hours, across two days, before Matthew Hoggard trapped him leg before. He reached 100 in 136 balls, retrenched and survived another 186 deliveries before he left, visibly angry, swishing his bat across the turf at his perceived casualness.

He thirsted for more, having blotted out all the pre-match noise. He was measured in defence, barely played a false stroke and used his feet brilliantly. The local press, in typical trampoline fashion, compared him to Bradman a couple of days after questioning his capacity to lead his country. I saw someone operating at a higher level, batting on a different planet from the rest of us.

Kallis was a complete cricketer, capable of catching pigeons at slip and amassing 292 Test wickets. His batting, ruthless and serene, enabled him to accumulate 13,289 Test runs at an average in excess of 55. His technique had such simplicity and repeatability. His temperament ensured he never looked flustered. He could control matches single-handedly.

I played against Lara only once, for MCC at Arundel in July 2004. He was recovering from a two-day bout of flu, and laced his 113, from 105 balls, with eighteen fours and two sixes. We probably got off lightly, since his four previous first-class innings were 400 not out, 53, 120 and another 113. He retired ill, complaining about his physical fragility and the strength of our team.

He took Min Patel, a wily slow left-arm spin bowler who was good enough to make two Test appearances for England eight years earlier, to the cleaners on a turning wicket. I had just been named England's Under-19 captain, and so wouldn't have been on Lara's radar, and was in danger of succumbing to a bout of hero worship.

The way Lara moved fields around, and played in-to-out shots from the rough against the spin, was touched by genius. Plenty of observers said nice things about me, as a certainty to play for the senior England team, after I scored 89 in a twenty-nine-run defeat, but watching him made me realize how far I had to go.

Of the current crop, Jos Buttler has Lara's ability to make you watch and wonder how he manages it. He radiates positivity in everything he does, a state of mind that transfers easily across to his batting. There is never a hint of indecision; he plays with an unforced confidence that tells bowlers, of the highest quality, that they are in trouble.

Speaking of quality bowlers, Jimmy Anderson is the most skilful I have seen. He is not one of those who can blast a tail out. He doesn't generate a fear factor, though he reaches 90 mph, and rarely picks up easy wickets. People think of him as a seam bowler, a deliverer of good old-fashioned line and length, but he is more, much more, than that. He might not be able to bat, but he is possibly the best cricketer England has ever produced.

His versatility, diligence and accuracy, aligned to his game intelligence, have enabled him to evolve as a player while remaining effective at the highest level. He can swing it and reverse it, and has mastered the art of wobble seam, initiated by Australia's Stuart Clark, who took twenty-six wickets at an average of 17 in his debut Ashes series, in 2006–07.

Clark could make the ball dart about on the most insipid pitch, by releasing it so that the seam wavered from side to side, rather than slicing through the air in an upright fashion. It involved widening the fingers on the grip, and aiming the ball so that it pitched on the edge of the seam. The subsequent movement was unpredictable and often deadly.

As so often, the difference between recognizing potential for improvement and actually realizing it is sheer hard work. Jimmy practised wobble-seam constantly, over a couple of years, until it became second nature. He saw how Mohammad Asif of Pakistan profited from a similar technique before his downfall in 2010, and had the open mind needed to make small, subtle alterations.

On overseas tours, for the past six or seven years, he has consistently worn down batsmen with an uncanny ability never to miss his length. That might not generate immediate reward, but his precision tests patience, erodes mental discipline. It is not untypical for Jimmy to pick up three wickets in his third spell, having entered it with miserly figures of, say, 0–22.

We do different jobs, but share the same attitudes. We should never have become best mates, since we appear to be polar opposites in many ways, but mutual respect has allowed us to develop one of those close friendships that rarely flourish in something as intense and insecure as international sport.

There are not many people, in any walk of life, with whom you can speak honestly, to the point of baring your soul. Our relationship is underpinned by that sort of trust. We are also so comfortable in one another's presence that we can spend an evening together, ordering room service and doing our own thing, barely exchanging a word.

On the field, Jimmy used me as a sounding board. I helped him to control his emotions, but knew he had to reach a certain level of agitation to get the best out of himself. To go back to those psychological profiles, I was the assassin, trying to keep the warrior in check. I'd watch for the warning signs, of him walking back to his mark too quickly, for example, and steaming back in without really thinking about what he intended to do.

I think he, in turn, recognized and respected my single-mindedness and my resistance to pressure. He knew I wasn't imposing my authority as captain on him when I told him he was bowling half a yard too short, or too full. He understood I was thinking with him, rather than for him, when I suggested he should try to swing the ball rather than wobble it.

A captain's sensitivity to the mood of his bowlers is vital. On a day when we had the opportunity to bat long and deep he was full of the joys of spring. On a bowling day, he wouldn't say a word on the bus on the way to the ground. He was absorbed by the nature of the forthcoming challenge; he knew it would be hard, even though he makes bowling look easy. An unguarded comment at the wrong time and there would have been hell to pay.

Jimmy needed to be half-wired, and I had to be strong enough to ride out the response if I said or did something he didn't like. There have been times when I've had to tell him, 'You're gone,' and taken him out of the attack. He would flare up, go into a strop for a couple of overs, and then sulk for a bit. He would never want to stew in his own juices out at long on, though. I knew keeping him closer to the action at mid-off would accelerate the process of getting his head back in the game.

Jimmy and I are probably wired a little differently from 90 per cent of people. That doesn't make us better, merely better suited to our work. We can be prickly, but our success is linked to our bloody-mindedness. At the time, I didn't realize Jimmy cried at my final England game. I had to have a little giggle to myself, because that blunt Northern exterior hides a shy, reserved man.

He was there for me when he thought I needed quiet reassurance. He had my back when he believed it was unprotected. When I wanted to chat through a tactic or a problem, we would do so quietly, in the privacy of a hotel room. I wanted him by my side because I knew his intensity, like Stuart Broad's, reflected his singular purpose, winning games of cricket for England.

Everyone at that level is, to a greater or lesser degree, aware of their so-called brand, but Jimmy's authenticity as a bloke is unchallengeable. His honesty may be brutal, and his humour can be deadpan, but players who come into the England set-up having judged him prematurely on false assumptions are quickly converted to his cause. You see a different side to him as a teammate rather than an opponent.

Hesitant though I am to turn Test cricket into a travelogue, there is no doubt that climate plays its part in a player's development. Australia's outdoor lifestyle offers natural advantages. The hard, quick wickets in South Africa are educational. It is as difficult to think of a manic New Zealander as it is to envision a quiet day on tour in India.

Cricket acts as a release from the drudgery of everyday life across the subcontinent, but is not immune from economic influence. The lineage of the game in Sri Lanka, a small nation capable of producing great players like Kumar Sangakkara or Mahela Jayawardene, is being threatened by financial pressures that prompt promising players to play semi-pro club cricket in England or Australia rather than developing in the domestic system.

I've been fortunate in having responsive dressing rooms, so I am not known as a shouter, or a teacup thrower. I was at my most strident in Abu Dhabi in 2015, where it was as hot, and as humid, as Sri Lanka at its worst. That requires a three-day acclimatization period, but when training becomes a shambles because of the heat you have to act.

I got everyone in and let rip: 'All I've heard is how hot it is. It's unseasonably hot. What do you want me to do, turn the fucking sun down? That's what we've got to deal with. That's what we're playing in. It's going to be the same for the other side. Stop fucking moaning. Support staff, sort your shit out. I want ice towels done before we get here. I want to hear us and see us practising like an England team should.' It worked, possibly because of the novelty factor of me piling into them. Everyone responded.

The human chemistry of any dressing room is delicate. There is a natural divide between bowlers and batsmen that lends itself to piss-taking. Bowlers will say, 'I wish I could bowl at you lot,' and batsmen will inform them of the pleasure they would take smashing them into the next county. I hate the word banter, but internal rivalry usually goes little further than that.

Bowlers tend to talk to one another on the field, especially when they are operating in tandem, since the era in which they were routinely hidden at fine leg between overs has gone. They are now usually found at mid-on or mid-off, close enough to share observations and strategies. Obviously, they will be unhappy if their own batsmen fail to give them the opportunity to rest by losing wickets quickly, but as long as criticism doesn't become personal, it is manageable.

Social instability is invariably magnified by sport's prominence. One of my trickiest situations as England captain came in Bangladesh in 2016. Reg Dickason, our security expert, said it was safe to tour, despite terrorist activity. I addressed a team meeting, told the lads I trusted his judgement and said we should fulfil our obligations.

There is no right and wrong in such situations. The players on the Test leg of the tour opted to follow my lead. Eoin Morgan preferred not to travel. There was no resentment at such an acutely personal choice, because, as a tightly knit group, we operated on the principle of mutual respect. Security concerns sit differently with different individuals, because external factors vary. We all have family members to consider.

My situation was complicated by Alice being in the last stages of pregnancy with our daughter Isobel. I couldn't miss a Test match, because of the strength of the views I had expressed, but flew back to England at the tail end of the one-day series. Alice was induced on 13 October, and I spent fourteen hours with Isobelle before making the return journey.

As you can imagine, I was in bits. The emotional intensity of birth stirred the most powerful of feelings, and I was lucky that I had the moral support of a friend, who coincidentally shared a connecting flight to Oman. I felt I was letting my wife and my family down. The justification, that I was chasing my dreams, was wearing a bit thin.

I was no different from a globetrotting businessman or a foreign correspondent. My job meant I had to spend long periods away from home. I had rationalized that with Alice early on in our relationship. I wasn't the normal, run-of-the-mill boyfriend, not because I was somehow special, but because that was how I made my living.

The one huge change in my life since the Oval has been the birth of our son Jack, who could have caused all sorts of havoc by turning up, as predicted, on the day of that 147. He was less than two hours old when I was given an insight into his future, as the son of a former England captain. 'Has he got his first cricket bat yet?' asked the midwife.

Give him a chance. It might be that he absolutely loves driving tractors, just as Elsie or Isobel might fancy themselves as the new Charlotte Edwards. You never know, do you? That is part of life's beautiful uncertainty. Like all fathers, all I pray for is that they will be healthy and happy. If that involves sport, then great.

There's a cool photograph of me, with Jimmy, on the cover of the 2019 edition of *Wisden*. The skeletal frame of the Oval gas holder is in the background. That'll be something to look back on when we are in our sixties, and our families will be glad to get us out of the house. I don't want to sound like a human fortune cookie, or one of those centenarians who are asked for the secrets of long life when the Queen's telegram arrives, but I can sum up cricket's most important life lesson in four words.

Don't be found wanting.

Epilogue: One Moment in Time

I was batting at Chelmsford, helping to set up the win against Warwickshire that took Essex to the top of the County Championship. It was a surreal, semi-detached experience. Like almost everyone in the ground on that Sunday afternoon, I had half an eye on the historic drama unfolding forty-five miles away, at Lord's.

Every couple of overs, the umpires quietly updated us on England's run chase in the World Cup final. Both teams were second guessing the significance of murmurs and exclamations from spectators. Attention wandered occasionally, to indistinct figures on a half-hidden TV screen in a hospitality area on the boundary. From the middle, I could not quite make out the score.

Once play had been completed for the day, with me unbeaten on 34 and Matt Quinn, our Kiwi night watchman, yet to get off the mark, we jostled for position in front of the set in the home dressing room. Ben Stokes and Jos Buttler were yet to reach their half centuries; even amongst experienced pros, the tension was palpable.

The sense of anticipation was so gripping I did not take my pads off until the super over was confirmed. The changing area was alive with conjecture; the tenor of texts grew in intensity as the countdown entered a critical phase. As I reflected, in a message to Michael, my collaborator on this book, 'Only sport can do this.'

At its best, sport sucks people in. It has a strange gravitational pull. I was not quite on the outside looking in, since I was watching friends and former teammates put everything on the line in the sort of pressurized situation we all live for as international sportsmen, but distance gave me a different perspective.

I had never seen Lord's so energized; it had the feel of Edgbaston on a particularly mad day. Chris, my father-in-law, was there with his son Henry. The couple in front of them walked out with four overs remaining because they could not bear to see England lose. The sense of disbelief spread to our dressing room, where someone announced: 'If Stokesy pulls this off it will be the best finish ever.'

As future schoolboys will hopefully be able to recount, England – well, Ben Stokes – needed 15 to win in the final regulation over. The truth of Andy Flower's phrase, about teams or individuals revealing themselves, was reinforced when Stokesy refused to take a single from the first two balls of the over. He was effectively taking responsibility for four years' work, and precise performance planning.

He looked spent, but was sending out the message, 'I will do this.' That took incredible nerve and confidence. Earlier in his career he would not have had the mental discipline, strength and courage to take it so deep. I usually hesitate about using such a word in a sporting context, but it was heroic. It made me so proud of him.

I do not wish to claim credit for any aspect of his career, but he came into our England side as a very rough diamond. He – no one else, despite those around him – has turned himself into the world-class cricketer we saw that day. He delivered when it mattered most, which, to reiterate another eternal truth, is the essence of mental strength.

We've subsequently seen many scenes of people cheering the freakish deflection off his bat as he dived to make his ground, which reduced England's target to three off the final two deliveries. The Essex team (Quinny apart, for obvious reasons) were no different. I jokingly exclaimed through the din, 'I never get overthrows like that.'

We had the luxury of losing our minds. Stokesy was thinking clearly. He changed his approach and even went against a fundamental aspect of his character, by refusing to take the risk of the 'hero' shot over the top. He preferred to concentrate on getting bat on ball, and ensuring that, at worst, England would have that super over.

He succeeded, despite Trent Boult's comparable brilliance, in having the calmness to complete run outs of Adil Rashid and Mark Wood from those two final deliveries. Could Boult play the Stokes role for New Zealand, and haul his team over the line, almost single-handedly? The jury was still out when he conceded 15 runs in his super over.

Though Chris Woakes was a viable alternative, Jofra Archer was the most obvious choice to bear the burden. It was another reminder of how professional cricket has changed during the course of my career. When I started, it was all about Test cricket. Jofra has learned his skill primarily in the shorter form of the game. He has made himself a world-class death bowler, under the contrasting pressure of being a high-profile franchise player.

No matter the colour of the ball, margins are extremely fine at the highest level. I didn't think the offside wide should have been called from Archer's opening delivery, but he refused to be flustered even when Jimmy Neesham hit him over midwicket, in the general direction of Regent's Park, for six. Two to win off the final ball, and everything was in slow motion.

Martin Guptill hit the ball to midwicket. Jason Roy swooped, collected and threw. Buttler broke the stumps with a split-second to spare. The bubble burst and suddenly there were bodies everywhere. It was only later that evening that I felt able to reflect on the bigger picture, and my hope that an aspiring professional cricketer would be out there thinking, 'I'll have some of that. I want to test myself. I will work harder.'

This was a team's moment in time. It is quite possible that that winning eleven will never play together again. Sport moves on, advances at pace. I was in the privileged position of knowing what it meant to the individuals involved. Though the triumph was collective, examples of personal achievement were compelling.

Liam Plunkett made his Test debut in Pakistan in 2005, when I was a prospect, in the squad, accumulating experience. He had his problems, leaving Durham for Yorkshire, and totally reinvented himself, from an aggressive seamer who sprayed it a bit, to a must-pick middle-over bowler, capable of consistent accuracy under pressure.

Aware that his place in the squad was being challenged, he evolved again in the build-up to the tournament. He developed versatility and subtlety, working on the slower, back-of-a-length delivery and the slower ball bouncer. By redefining himself, he proved himself as a player and person. Professional sport can be a cold place, but when such a genuinely good guy does well it is a cause for celebration.

Eoin Morgan, together with Andrew Strauss and Trevor Bayliss, should take all credit for the transformation of England's one-day team. To be honest, he was given a hospital pass when he took the squad into the 2015 World Cup. That didn't end well; I will always remember Straussy promising, 'These next four years will be different.'

It took someone with his foresight to make the decision to change, and force England to take white-ball cricket more seriously. Eoin's team consciously tried to be trendsetters, to play aggressively and aspire to scoring 400 from their fifty overs. He had the confidence to trust his players, even when they were occasionally questioned for failing to bat out their allocation.

The leadership he showed, in facing up to the criticism, and suggesting he'd prefer the positivity of making a total of, say, 330 from forty-three overs, was exceptional. Watching from afar, his captaincy was authentic. He possessed the talent and presence of mind to back up his fearless philosophy. Sometimes, arriving at the crease with England on 20–2, he would take the brave option and immediately walk down the wicket, knowing he would be slaughtered if it went wrong.

Ironically the final, tied on 241, was old school. If ever there was anyone you'd have cried out for as a captain, to see us home with 80 from 100 balls, it was Jonathan Trott. That's ironic, but it is no coincidence that the one consistent factor between the heroes of 2019 and our team, which became world number one in 2011, was Andrew Strauss.

He's a special bloke, the most rounded person, in my experience, ever to come out of cricket. He is one of those great leaders who excel in different roles and environments. As my captain, he had vision and drive. As my boss, as

England's director of cricket, he demonstrated decisiveness and insight. As my friend, he showed kindness and empathy.

He took me, as a young opening batsman, under his wing. His wife Ruth acted similarly with Alice, guiding her through the balancing act between sport and family. They were our guiding lights. Ruth's loss, to cancer, was tragic. It shook us, as a couple. It impacted on the entire cricket community. Her goodness will endure, through the charitable foundation established in her name.

I met Andrew a couple of days after the World Cup final, at the premiere of *The Edge*, a film about our number one team. He had undergone a traumatic year, but I could see in his eyes the quiet satisfaction of a job well done. There were no airs, no graces, no grand gestures. He has never shown out much. That's probably why we get on so well; we are similar in character.

It was a poignant occasion, on a number of levels. About a dozen of us were there; it was the first time in several years we had got together. Watching the film reminded us of the amazing experiences we had shared. Every player has his own story, but we all felt the power of the question, posed to Trotty in a subsequent question-and-answer session:

'Would you do it all again?'

'In a heartbeat.'

He broke down attempting to explain how he missed batting with the likes of Straussy, me and KP, but those three words summed everything up. We were so privileged to play for England. We were blessed to share such highs and lows. Life isn't perfect, but time lends perspective. We were united by more than what separated us.

Professional sport can take a forbidding toll. I would ask

any fan, tempted to condemn a player who has failed as being 'useless' to watch a sequence in the film, in which Trotty is explaining his inner thoughts on getting out in Brisbane, where I'd seen him weeping in the dressing room. He was caught at deep square leg and the commentator was criticizing him for 'dumb cricket'.

Trotty had batted with tears in his eyes. He had a searing headache. His system had shut down. His mind was blown. He was not conscious of walking back towards the pavilion. His testimony was deeply personal, but relevant to us all. We are not robots. Other elements can creep into our game. The mental health of any performer is precious.

Years pass, careers come and go, but the team is a stake in the ground. It anchors us to our achievements, reconnects us with who we were, and why we were able to enjoy our moment in time. I was lucky to play with so many exceptional cricketers, but, ultimately, runs and wickets are not of paramount importance.

I've learned to go beyond the present, and cherish memories that will be a golden thread, running through the rest of our lives.

Appendix: A Career in Numbers

Compiled by Max Wadsworth

Overview

SIR ALASTAIR NATHAN COOK

Born: 25 December 1984 (Gloucester)

Teams: England, Bedfordshire, England Lions, England Under-19s, Essex, Marylebone Cricket Club

Nickname: Cookie, Chef

Playing role: Opening batsman

Batting style: Left-hand bat

Bowling style: Right-arm slow

Height: 6ft 2in

First test v India, Nagpur, 1–5 March 2006

Last test v India, the Oval, 7–11 September 2018

Batting and Fielding Statistics

	Matches	Innings	Not Out	Runs	Highest score	Average	Balls faced	Strike rate	100s	50s	4s	6s	Ducks	Catches
Tests	161	291	16	12472	294	45.35	26562	46.95	33	57	1442	11	9	175
One-day Internationals	92	92	4	3204	137	36.40	4154	77.13	5	19	363	10	7	36
T20 Internationals	4	4	0	61	26	15.25	54	112.96	0	0	10	0	0	1
First class*	297	526	39	23253	294	47.74	45711	50.86	65	110				315
List A*	168	166	11	6055	137	39.06	7571	79.97	12	35				68
T20s*	32	30	2	892	100*	31.85	699	127.61	1	5	95	15		13

*Statistics correct at time of print

Bowling Statistics

	Matches	Innings	Balls	Runs	Wickets	Best innings	Best match	Average	Economy	Strike rate
Tests	161	2	18	7	1	1/6	1/6	7.00	2.33	18.00
One-day Internationals	92	-	-	-	-	-	-	-	-	-
T20 Internationals	4	-	-	-	-	-	-	-	-	-
First class*	297		282	211	7	3/13		30.14	4.48	40.20
List A*	168		18	10	0	-	-	-	3.33	-
T20s*	32	-	-	-	-	-	-	-	-	-

*Statistics correct at time of print

Test Matches

All Test Innings

Year	Country	Venue	Runs
2006	India	Nagpur	60
2006	India	Nagpur	104
2006	India	Mohali	17
2006	India	Mohali	2
2006	Sri Lanka	Lord's	89
2006	Sri Lanka	Edgbaston	23
2006	Sri Lanka	Edgbaston	34
2006	Sri Lanka	Trent Bridge	24
2006	Sri Lanka	Trent Bridge	5
2006	Pakistan	Lord's	105
2006	Pakistan	Lord's	4
2006	Pakistan	Old Trafford	127
2006	Pakistan	Headingley	23
2006	Pakistan	Headingley	21
2006	Pakistan	The Oval	40
2006	Pakistan	The Oval	83
2006	Australia	Brisbane	11
2006	Australia	Brisbane	43
2006	Australia	Adelaide	27
2006	Australia	Adelaide	9
2006	Australia	Perth	15
2006	Australia	Perth	116
2006	Australia	Melbourne	11
2006	Australia	Melbourne	20
2007	Australia	Sydney	20
2007	Australia	Sydney	4
2007	West Indies	Lord's	105
2007	West Indies	Lord's	65
2007	West Indies	Headingley	42
2007	West Indies	Old Trafford	60
2007	West Indies	Old Trafford	106
2007	West Indies	Chester-le-Street	13
2007	West Indies	Chester-le-Street	7
2007	India	Lord's	36
2007	India	Lord's	17
2007	India	Trent Bridge	43
2007	India	Trent Bridge	23
2007	India	The Oval	61
2007	India	The Oval	43
2007	Sri Lanka	Kandy	0
2007	Sri Lanka	Kandy	4
2007	Sri Lanka	Colombo (SSC)	81
2007	Sri Lanka	Colombo (SSC)	62
2007	Sri Lanka	Galle	13
2007	Sri Lanka	Galle	118
2008	New Zealand	Hamilton	38
2008	New Zealand	Hamilton	13
2008	New Zealand	Wellington	44
2008	New Zealand	Wellington	60
2008	New Zealand	Napier	2
2008	New Zealand	Napier	37
2008	New Zealand	Lord's	61
2008	New Zealand	Old Trafford	19
2008	New Zealand	Old Trafford	28
2008	New Zealand	Trent Bridge	6
2008	South Africa	Lord's	60
2008	South Africa	Headingley	18
2008	South Africa	Headingley	60

Continued

Year	Country	Venue	Runs
2008	South Africa	Edgbaston	76
2008	South Africa	Edgbaston	9
2008	South Africa	The Oval	39
2008	South Africa	The Oval	67
2008	India	Chennai	52
2008	India	Chennai	9
2008	India	Mohali	50
2008	India	Mohali	10
2009	West Indies	Kingston	4
2009	West Indies	Kingston	0
2009	West Indies	North Sound	1*
2009	West Indies	St John's	52
2009	West Indies	St John's	58
2009	West Indies	Bridgetown	94
2009	West Indies	Bridgetown	139
2009	West Indies	Port of Spain	12
2009	West Indies	Port of Spain	24
2009	West Indies	Lord's	35
2009	West Indies	Lord's	14
2009	West Indies	Chester-le-Street	160
2009	Australia	Cardiff	10
2009	Australia	Cardiff	6
2009	Australia	Lord's	95
2009	Australia	Lord's	32
2009	Australia	Edgbaston	0
2009	Australia	Headingley	30
2009	Australia	Headingley	30
2009	Australia	The Oval	10
2009	Australia	The Oval	9
2009	South Africa	Centurion	15
2009	South Africa	Centurion	12
2009	South Africa	Durban	118
2010	South Africa	Cape Town	65
2010	South Africa	Cape Town	55
2010	South Africa	Johannesburg	21
2010	South Africa	Johannesburg	1
2010	Bangladesh	Chattogram	173
2010	Bangladesh	Chattogram	39
2010	Bangladesh	Dhaka	21
2010	Bangladesh	Dhaka	109
2010	Bangladesh	Lord's	7
2010	Bangladesh	Lord's	23
2010	Bangladesh	Old Trafford	29
2010	Pakistan	Trent Bridge	8
2010	Pakistan	Trent Bridge	12
2010	Pakistan	Edgbaston	17
2010	Pakistan	Edgbaston	4
2010	Pakistan	The Oval	6
2010	Pakistan	The Oval	110
2010	Pakistan	Lord's	10
2010	Australia	Brisbane	67
2010	Australia	Brisbane	235
2010	Australia	Adelaide	148
2010	Australia	Perth	32
2010	Australia	Perth	13
2010	Australia	Melbourne	82
2011	Australia	Sydney	189
2011	Sri Lanka	Cardiff	133
2011	Sri Lanka	Lord's	96
2011	Sri Lanka	Lord's	106
2011	Sri Lanka	Southampton	55
2011	India	Lord's	12
2011	India	Lord's	1
2011	India	Trent Bridge	2
2011	India	Trent Bridge	5
2011	India	Edgbaston	294
2011	India	The Oval	34
2012	Pakistan	Dubai (DSC)	3

Year	Country	Venue	Runs
2012	Pakistan	Dubai (DSC)	5
2012	Pakistan	Abu Dhabi	94
2012	Pakistan	Abu Dhabi	7
2012	Pakistan	Dubai (DSC)	1
2012	Pakistan	Dubai (DSC)	49
2012	Sri Lanka	Galle	0
2012	Sri Lanka	Galle	14
2012	Sri Lanka	Colombo (PSS)	94
2012	Sri Lanka	Colombo (PSS)	49
2012	West Indies	Lord's	26
2012	West Indies	Lord's	79
2012	West Indies	Trent Bridge	24
2012	West Indies	Trent Bridge	43
2012	West Indies	Edgbaston	4
2012	South Africa	The Oval	115
2012	South Africa	The Oval	0
2012	South Africa	Headingley	24
2012	South Africa	Headingley	46
2012	South Africa	Lord's	7
2012	South Africa	Lord's	3
2012	India	Ahmedabad	41
2012	India	Ahmedabad	176
2012	India	Mumbai	122
2012	India	Mumbai	18
2012	India	Kolkata	190
2012	India	Kolkata	1
2012	India	Nagpur	1
2012	India	Nagpur	13
2013	New Zealand	Dunedin	10
2013	New Zealand	Dunedin	116
2013	New Zealand	Wellington	17
2013	New Zealand	Auckland	4
2013	New Zealand	Auckland	43
2013	New Zealand	Lord's	32
2013	New Zealand	Lord's	21
2013	New Zealand	Headingley	34
2013	New Zealand	Headingley	130
2013	Australia	Trent Bridge	13
2013	Australia	Trent Bridge	50
2013	Australia	Lord's	12
2013	Australia	Lord's	8
2013	Australia	Old Trafford	62
2013	Australia	Old Trafford	0
2013	Australia	Chester-le-Street	51
2013	Australia	Chester-le-Street	22
2013	Australia	The Oval	25
2013	Australia	The Oval	34
2013	Australia	Brisbane	13
2013	Australia	Brisbane	65
2013	Australia	Adelaide	3
2013	Australia	Adelaide	1
2013	Australia	Perth	72
2013	Australia	Perth	0
2013	Australia	Melbourne	27
2013	Australia	Melbourne	51
2014	Australia	Sydney	7
2014	Australia	Sydney	7
2014	Sri Lanka	Lord's	17
2014	Sri Lanka	Lord's	28
2014	Sri Lanka	Headingley	17
2014	Sri Lanka	Headingley	16
2014	India	Trent Bridge	5
2014	India	Lord's	10
2014	India	Lord's	22
2014	India	Southampton	95
2014	India	Southampton	70
2014	India	Old Trafford	17
2014	India	The Oval	79

Continued

Year	Country	Venue	Runs
2015	West Indies	North Sound	11
2015	West Indies	North Sound	13
2015	West Indies	St George's	76
2015	West Indies	St George's	59
2015	West Indies	Bridgetown	105
2015	West Indies	Bridgetown	4
2015	New Zealand	Lord's	16
2015	New Zealand	Lord's	162
2015	New Zealand	Headingley	75
2015	New Zealand	Headingley	56
2015	Australia	Cardiff	20
2015	Australia	Cardiff	12
2015	Australia	Lord's	96
2015	Australia	Lord's	11
2015	Australia	Edgbaston	34
2015	Australia	Edgbaston	7
2015	Australia	Trent Bridge	43
2015	Australia	The Oval	22
2015	Australia	The Oval	85
2015	Pakistan	Abu Dhabi	263
2015	Pakistan	Abu Dhabi	DNB
2015	Pakistan	Dubai (DSC)	65
2015	Pakistan	Dubai (DSC)	10
2015	Pakistan	Sharjah	49
2015	Pakistan	Sharjah	63
2015	South Africa	Durban	0
2015	South Africa	Durban	7
2016	South Africa	Cape Town	27
2016	South Africa	Cape Town	8
2016	South Africa	Johannesburg	18
2016	South Africa	Johannesburg	43
2016	South Africa	Centurion	76
2016	South Africa	Centurion	5
2016	Sri Lanka	Headingley	16

Year	Country	Venue	Runs
2016	Sri Lanka	Chester-le-Street	15
2016	Sri Lanka	Chester-le-Street	47
2016	Sri Lanka	Lord's	85
2016	Sri Lanka	Lord's	49
2016	Pakistan	Lord's	81
2016	Pakistan	Lord's	8
2016	Pakistan	Old Trafford	105
2016	Pakistan	Old Trafford	76
2016	Pakistan	Edgbaston	45
2016	Pakistan	Edgbaston	66
2016	Pakistan	The Oval	35
2016	Pakistan	The Oval	7
2016	Bangladesh	Chattogram	4
2016	Bangladesh	Chattogram	12
2016	Bangladesh	Dhaka	14
2016	Bangladesh	Dhaka	59
2016	India	Rajkot	21
2016	India	Rajkot	130
2016	India	Visakhapatnam	2
2016	India	Visakhapatnam	54
2016	India	Mohali	27
2016	India	Mohali	12
2016	India	Mumbai	46
2016	India	Mumbai	18
2016	India	Chennai	10
2016	India	Chennai	49
2017	South Africa	Lord's	3
2017	South Africa	Lord's	69
2017	South Africa	Trent Bridge	3
2017	South Africa	Trent Bridge	42
2017	South Africa	The Oval	88
2017	South Africa	The Oval	7
2017	South Africa	Old Trafford	46
2017	South Africa	Old Trafford	10

Year	Country	Venue	Runs
2017	West Indies	Edgbaston	243
2017	West Indies	Headingley	11
2017	West Indies	Headingley	23
2017	West Indies	Lord's	10
2017	West Indies	Lord's	17
2017	Australia	Brisbane	2
2017	Australia	Brisbane	7
2017	Australia	Adelaide	37
2017	Australia	Adelaide	16
2017	Australia	Perth	7
2017	Australia	Perth	14
2017	Australia	Melbourne	244
2018	Australia	Sydney	39
2018	Australia	Sydney	10
2018	New Zealand	Auckland	5
2018	New Zealand	Auckland	2
2018	New Zealand	Christchurch	2
2018	New Zealand	Christchurch	14
2018	Pakistan	Lord's	70
2018	Pakistan	Lord's	1
2018	Pakistan	Headingley	46
2018	India	Edgbaston	13
2018	India	Edgbaston	0
2018	India	Lord's	21
2018	India	Trent Bridge	29
2018	India	Trent Bridge	17
2018	India	Southampton	17
2018	India	Southampton	12
2018	India	The Oval	71
2018	India	The Oval	147

All Test Matches

Year	Country	Venue	Result
2006	India	Nagpur	Drawn
2006	India	Mohali	Lost
2006	Sri Lanka	Lord's	Drawn
2006	Sri Lanka	Birmingham	Won
2006	Sri Lanka	Nottingham	Lost
2006	Pakistan	Lord's	Drawn
2006	Pakistan	Manchester	Won
2006	Pakistan	Leeds	Won
2006	Pakistan	The Oval	Won
2006	Australia	Brisbane	Lost
2006	Australia	Adelaide	Lost
2006	Australia	Perth	Lost
2006	Australia	Melbourne	Lost
2007	Australia	Sydney	Lost
2007	West Indies	Lord's	Drawn
2007	West Indies	Leeds	Won
2007	West Indies	Manchester	Won
2007	West Indies	Chester-le-Street	Won
2007	India	Lord's	Drawn
2007	India	Nottingham	Lost
2007	India	The Oval	Drawn
2007	Sri Lanka	Kandy	Lost
2007	Sri Lanka	Colombo (SSC)	Drawn
2007	Sri Lanka	Galle	Drawn
2008	New Zealand	Hamilton	Lost
2008	New Zealand	Wellington	Won
2008	New Zealand	Napier	Won
2008	New Zealand	Lord's	Drawn

Continued

Year	Country	Venue	Result
2008	New Zealand	Manchester	Won
2008	New Zealand	Nottingham	Won
2008	South Africa	Lord's	Drawn
2008	South Africa	Leeds	Lost
2008	South Africa	Birmingham	Lost
2008	South Africa	The Oval	Won
2008	India	Chennai	Lost
2008	India	Mohali	Drawn
2009	West Indies	Kingston	Lost
2009	West Indies	North Sound	Drawn
2009	West Indies	St John's	Drawn
2009	West Indies	Bridgetown	Drawn
2009	West Indies	Port of Spain	Drawn
2009	West Indies	Lord's	Won
2009	West Indies	Chester-le-Street	Won
2009	Australia	Cardiff	Drawn
2009	Australia	Lord's	Won
2009	Australia	Birmingham	Drawn
2009	Australia	Leeds	Lost
2009	Australia	The Oval	Won
2009	South Africa	Centurion	Drawn
2009	South Africa	Durban	Won
2010	South Africa	Cape Town	Drawn
2010	South Africa	Johannesburg	Lost
2010	**Bangladesh**	**Chattogram**	**Won**
2010	**Bangladesh**	**Dhaka**	**Won**
2010	Bangladesh	Lord's	Won
2010	Bangladesh	Manchester	Won
2010	Pakistan	Nottingham	Won
2010	Pakistan	Birmingham	Won
2010	Pakistan	The Oval	Lost
2010	Pakistan	Lord's	Won
2010	Australia	Brisbane	Drawn
2010	Australia	Adelaide	Won
2010	Australia	Perth	Lost
2010	Australia	Melbourne	Won
2011	Australia	Sydney	Won
2011	Sri Lanka	Cardiff	Won
2011	Sri Lanka	Lord's	Drawn
2011	Sri Lanka	Southampton	Drawn
2011	India	Lord's	Won
2011	India	Nottingham	Won
2011	India	Birmingham	Won
2011	India	The Oval	Won
2012	Pakistan	Dubai (DSC)	Lost
2012	Pakistan	Abu Dhabi	Lost
2012	Pakistan	Dubai (DSC)	Lost
2012	Sri Lanka	Galle	Lost
2012	Sri Lanka	Colombo (PSS)	Won
2012	West Indies	Lord's	Won
2012	West Indies	Nottingham	Won
2012	West Indies	Birmingham	Drawn
2012	South Africa	The Oval	Lost
2012	South Africa	Leeds	Drawn
2012	South Africa	Lord's	Lost
2012	**India**	**Ahmedabad**	**Lost**
2012	**India**	**Mumbai**	**Won**
2012	**India**	**Kolkata**	**Won**
2012	**India**	**Nagpur**	**Drawn**
2013	**New Zealand**	**Dunedin**	**Drawn**
2013	**New Zealand**	**Wellington**	**Drawn**
2013	**New Zealand**	**Auckland**	**Drawn**
2013	**New Zealand**	**Lord's**	**Won**
2013	**New Zealand**	**Leeds**	**Won**
2013	**Australia**	**Nottingham**	**Won**
2013	**Australia**	**Lord's**	**Won**
2013	**Australia**	**Manchester**	**Drawn**
2013	**Australia**	**Chester-le-Street**	**Won**

APPENDIX: A CAREER IN NUMBERS

Year	Country	Venue	Result
2013	**Australia**	**The Oval**	**Drawn**
2013	**Australia**	**Brisbane**	**Lost**
2013	**Australia**	**Adelaide**	**Lost**
2013	**Australia**	**Perth**	**Lost**
2013	**Australia**	**Melbourne**	**Lost**
2014	**Australia**	**Sydney**	**Lost**
2014	**Sri Lanka**	**Lord's**	**Drawn**
2014	**Sri Lanka**	**Leeds**	**Lost**
2014	**India**	**Nottingham**	**Drawn**
2014	**India**	**Lord's**	**Lost**
2014	**India**	**Southampton**	**Won**
2014	**India**	**Manchester**	**Won**
2014	**India**	**The Oval**	**Won**
2015	**West Indies**	**North Sound**	**Drawn**
2015	**West Indies**	**St George's**	**Won**
2015	**West Indies**	**Bridgetown**	**Lost**
2015	**New Zealand**	**Lord's**	**Won**
2015	**New Zealand**	**Leeds**	**Lost**
2015	**Australia**	**Cardiff**	**Won**
2015	**Australia**	**Lord's**	**Lost**
2015	**Australia**	**Birmingham**	**Won**
2015	**Australia**	**Nottingham**	**Won**
2015	**Australia**	**The Oval**	**Lost**
2015	**Pakistan**	**Abu Dhabi**	**Drawn**
2015	**Pakistan**	**Dubai (DSC)**	**Lost**
2015	**Pakistan**	**Sharjah**	**Lost**
2015	**South Africa**	**Durban**	**Won**
2016	**South Africa**	**Cape Town**	**Drawn**
2016	**South Africa**	**Johannesburg**	**Won**
2016	**South Africa**	**Centurion**	**Lost**
2016	**Sri Lanka**	**Leeds**	**Won**
2016	**Sri Lanka**	**Chester-le-Street**	**Won**
2016	**Sri Lanka**	**Lord's**	**Drawn**

Year	Country	Venue	Result
2016	**Pakistan**	**Lord's**	**Lost**
2016	**Pakistan**	**Manchester**	**Won**
2016	**Pakistan**	**Birmingham**	**Won**
2016	**Pakistan**	**The Oval**	**Lost**
2016	**Bangladesh**	**Chattogram**	**Won**
2016	**Bangladesh**	**Dhaka**	**Lost**
2016	**India**	**Rajkot**	**Drawn**
2016	**India**	**Visakhapatnam**	**Lost**
2016	**India**	**Mohali**	**Lost**
2016	**India**	**Mumbai**	**Lost**
2016	**India**	**Chennai**	**Lost**
2017	South Africa	Lord's	Won
2017	South Africa	Nottingham	Lost
2017	South Africa	The Oval	Won
2017	South Africa	Manchester	Won
2017	West Indies	Birmingham	Won
2017	West Indies	Leeds	Lost
2017	West Indies	Lord's	Won
2017	Australia	Brisbane	Lost
2017	Australia	Adelaide	Lost
2017	Australia	Perth	Lost
2017	Australia	Melbourne	Drawn
2018	Australia	Sydney	Lost
2018	New Zealand	Auckland	Lost
2018	New Zealand	Christchurch	Drawn
2018	Pakistan	Lord's	Lost
2018	Pakistan	Leeds	Won
2018	India	Birmingham	Won
2018	India	Lord's	Won
2018	India	Nottingham	Lost
2018	India	Southampton	Won
2018	India	The Oval	Won

Bold (as captain)

All Test Series

Year	Country	Venue	Result
2006	India	Away	Lost
2006	Sri Lanka	Home	Drawn
2006	Pakistan	Home	Won
2006	Australia	Away	Lost
2007	West Indies	Home	Won
2007	India	Home	Lost
2007	Sri Lanka	Away	Lost
2008	New Zealand	Away	Won
2008	New Zealand	Home	Won
2008	South Africa	Home	Drawn
2008	India	Away	Lost
2009	West Indies	Away	Lost
2009	West Indies	Home	Won
2009	Australia	Home	Won
2009	South Africa	Away	Drawn
2010	**Bangladesh**	**Away**	**Won**
2010	Bangladesh	Home	Won
2010	Pakistan	Home	Won
2010	Australia	Away	Won
2011	Sri Lanka	Home	Won
2011	India	Home	Won
2012	Pakistan	Neutral	Lost
2012	Sri Lanka	Away	Drawn
2012	West Indies	Home	Won
2012	South Africa	Home	Lost
2012	**India**	**Away**	**Won**
2013	**New Zealand**	**Away**	**Drawn**
2013	**New Zealand**	**Home**	**Won**
2013	**Australia**	**Home**	**Won**
2013	**Australia**	**Away**	**Lost**
2014	**Sri Lanka**	**Home**	**Lost**
2014	**India**	**Home**	**Won**
2015	**West Indies**	**Away**	**Drawn**
2015	**New Zealand**	**Home**	**Drawn**
2015	**Australia**	**Home**	**Won**
2015	**Pakistan**	**Neutral**	**Lost**
2015	**South Africa**	**Away**	**Won**
2016	**Sri Lanka**	**Home**	**Won**
2016	**Pakistan**	**Home**	**Drawn**
2016	**Bangladesh**	**Away**	**Drawn**
2016	**India**	**Away**	**Lost**
2017	South Africa	Home	Won
2017	West Indies	Home	Won
2017	Australia	Away	Lost
2018	New Zealand	Away	Lost
2018	Pakistan	Home	Drawn
2018	India	Home	Won

Bold (as captain)

Test-Match Record v Countries

Country	Tests	Won	Lost	Drawn	Win%
AUSTRALIA					
Home	15	8	3	4	53%
Away	20	3	15	2	15%
Total	**35**	**11**	**18**	**6**	**31%**
BANGLADESH					
Home	2	2	0	0	100%
Away	4	3	1	0	75%
Total	**6**	**5**	**1**	**0**	**83%**
INDIA					
Home	17	11	3	3	65%
Away	13	2	7	4	15%
Total	**30**	**13**	**10**	**7**	**43%**
NEW ZEALAND					
Home	7	5	1	1	71%
Away	8	2	2	4	25%
Total	**15**	**7**	**3**	**5**	**47%**
PAKISTAN					
Home	14	9	4	1	64%
Neutral	6	0	5	1	0%
Total	**20**	**9**	**9**	**2**	**45%**
SOUTH AFRICA					
Home	11	4	5	2	36%
Away	8	3	2	3	38%
Total	**19**	**7**	**7**	**5**	**37%**
SRI LANKA					
Home	11	4	2	5	36%
Away	5	1	2	2	20%
Total	**16**	**5**	**4**	**7**	**31%**

Continued

Country	Tests	Won	Lost	Drawn	Win%
WEST INDIES					
Home	12	9	1	2	75%
Away	8	1	2	5	13%
Total	**20**	**10**	**3**	**7**	**50%**

Total	Tests	Won	Lost	Drawn	Win%
Home	89	52	19	18	58%
Away	66	15	31	20	23%
Neutral	6	0	5	1	0%
TOTAL	**161**	**67**	**55**	**39**	**42%**

Test-Series Record v Countries

Country	Series	Won	Lost	Drawn	Win%
AUSTRALIA					
Home	3	3	0	0	100%
Away	4	1	3	0	25%
Total	**7**	**4**	**3**	**0**	**57%**
BANGLADESH					
Home	1	1	0	0	100%
Away	2	1	0	1	50%
Total	**3**	**2**	**0**	**1**	**67%**
INDIA					
Home	4	3	1	0	75%
Away	4	1	3	0	25%
Total	**8**	**4**	**4**	**0**	**50%**
NEW ZEALAND					
Home	3	2	0	1	67%
Away	3	1	1	1	33%
Total	**6**	**3**	**1**	**2**	**50%**

Country	Tests	Won	Lost	Drawn	Win%
PAKISTAN					
Home	4	2	0	2	50%
Neutral	2	0	2	0	0%
Total	**6**	**2**	**2**	**2**	**33%**
SOUTH AFRICA					
Home	4	2	1	1	50%
Away	1	0	0	1	0%
Total	**5**	**2**	**1**	**2**	**40%**
SRI LANKA					
Home	4	2	1	1	50%
Away	2	0	1	1	0%
Total	**6**	**2**	**2**	**2**	**33%**
WEST INDIES					
Home	4	4	0	0	100%
Away	2	0	1	1	0%
Total	**6**	**4**	**1**	**1**	**67%**

Total	Series	Won	Lost	Drawn	Win%
Home	27	19	3	5	70%
Away	18	4	9	5	22%
Neutral	2	0	2	0	0%
TOTAL	**47**	**23**	**14**	**10**	**49%**

Tests v Country

Country	Tests	Innings	Not out	Runs	Highest score	Average	Balls faced	Strike rate	100s	50s	Ducks	4s	6s
Australia	35	64	2	2493	244	40.20	5288	47.14	5	11	3	283	1
Bangladesh	6	11	1	490	173	49.00	829	59.10	2	1	0	51	2
India	30	54	3	2431	294	47.66	5374	45.23	7	9	1	283	3
New Zealand	15	27	0	1047	162	38.77	2357	44.42	3	4	0	127	1
Pakistan	20	36	1	1719	263	49.11	3505	49.04	5	8	0	205	0
South Africa	19	36	0	1263	118	35.08	2873	43.96	2	9	2	158	2
Sri Lanka	16	28	4	1290	133	53.75	2808	45.94	3	7	2	140	1
West Indies	20	35	5	1739	243	57.96	3528	49.29	6	8	1	195	1

Tests in Country

Country	Tests	Innings	Not out	Runs	Highest score	Average	Balls faced	Strike rate	100s	50s	Ducks	4s	6s
in Australia	20	36	2	1664	244	48.94	3369	49.39	5	5	1	171	1
in Bangladesh	4	8	1	431	173	61.57	718	60.02	2	1	0	42	2
in England	89	155	7	6568	294	44.37	13675	48.02	15	32	4	816	3
in India	13	26	2	1235	190	51.45	2818	43.82	5	4	0	141	3
in New Zealand	8	15	0	407	116	27.13	982	41.44	1	1	0	50	1
in South Africa	8	15	0	471	118	31.40	1049	44.89	1	3	1	56	0
in Sri Lanka	5	10	1	435	118	48.33	1054	41.27	1	3	2	47	0
in UAE	6	11	0	609	263	55.36	1463	41.62	1	3	0	50	0
in West Indies	8	15	3	652	139*	54.33	1434	45.46	2	5	1	69	1

Venue	Tests	Innings	Not out	Runs	Highest score	Average	Balls faced	Strike rate	100s	50s	Ducks	4s	6s
Home	89	155	7	6568	294	44.37	13675	48.02	15	32	4	816	3
Away	66	125	9	5295	244	45.64	11424	46.34	17	22	5	576	8
Neutral	6	11	0	609	263	55.36	1463	41.62	1	3	0	50	0

Tests by Year

Year	Tests	Innings	Not out	Runs	Highest score	Average	Balls faced	Strike rate	100s	50s	Ducks	4s	6s
2006	13	24	2	1013	127	46.04	2290	44.23	4	3	0	112	0
2007	11	21	0	923	118	43.95	1907	48.40	3	5	1	107	0
2008	12	21	0	758	76	36.09	1593	47.58	0	8	0	103	1
2009	14	24	3	960	160	45.71	1984	48.38	3	4	2	110	1
2010	14	24	2	1287	235	58.50	2350	54.76	5	4	0	148	3
2011	8	11	0	927	294	84.27	1835	50.51	4	2	0	97	0
2012	15	29	3	1249	190	48.03	2981	41.89	4	3	2	138	5
2013	14	27	0	916	130	33.92	2153	42.54	2	6	2	106	0
2014	8	13	1	390	95	32.50	897	43.47	0	3	0	45	0
2015	14	26	1	1364	263	54.56	3123	43.67	3	8	1	150	0
2016	17	33	3	1270	130	42.33	2447	51.90	2	7	0	151	1
2017	11	20	1	899	244	47.31	1831	49.09	2	2	0	110	0
2018	10	18	0	516	147	28.66	1171	44.06	1	2	1	65	0

Types of Test Dismissal

Caught in field	102
Caught by wicketkeeper	79
LBW	54
Bowled	35
Stumped	4
Run out	1
Total	**275**

Time at Crease in Test Matches

622 hours and 11 minutes
or
25 days, 22 hours and 11 minutes

Test Dismissals by Bowler's Arm

	Dismissals	**Bowled**	**Caught in field**	**Caught by wicketkeeper**	**Stumped**	**LBW**	**Run out**	**Average**	**Ducks**
Right-arm bowler	207	25	82	60	2	38	0	40.67	8
Left-arm bowler	67	10	20	19	2	16	0	38.37	1
Unknown arm	1	0	0	0	0	0	1	190.00	0

Test Dismissals by Speed of Bowler

	Dismissals	**Bowled**	**Caught in field**	**Caught by wicketkeeper**	**Stumped**	**LBW**	**Run out**	**Average**	**Ducks**
Pace bowler	197	28	66	66	0	37	0	34.62	8
Spin bowler	77	7	36	13	4	17	0	54.14	1
Unknown	1	0	0	0	0	0	1	190.00	0

Test Dismissals by Arm and Speed of Bowler

	Dismissals	Bowled	Caught in field	Caught by wicketkeeper	Stumped	LBW	Run out	Average	Ducks
Right-arm pace	150	20	55	51	0	24	0	35.14	7
Right-arm spin	57	5	27	9	2	14	0	55.22	1
Left-arm pace	47	8	11	15	0	13	0	32.97	1
Left-arm spin	20	2	9	4	2	3	0	51.05	0
Unknown	1	0	0	0	0	0	1	190.00	0

Test Dismissals by Batting Order

	Dismissals	Bowled	Caught in field	Caught by wicketkeeper	Stumped	LBW	Run out	Average	Ducks
1st position	136	22	49	39	2	23	1	42.97	5
2nd position	128	11	50	39	2	26	0	46.88	4
3rd position	11	2	3	1	0	5	0	52.54	0

Test Record (Grounds in Britain)

Ground	Tests	Innings	Not out	Runs	Highest score	Average	Balls faced	Strike rate	100s	50s	Ducks	4s	6s
Sophia Gardens, Cardiff	3	5	0	181	133	36.20	377	48.01	1	0	0	15	0
Riverside Ground, Chester-le-Street	4	7	1	315	160	52.50	675	46.66	1	1	0	36	0
Edgbaston, Birmingham	10	16	1	869	294	57.93	1540	56.42	2	2	2	113	0
Headingley, Leeds	11	19	0	718	130	37.78	1618	44.37	1	3	0	87	1
Lord's, London	26	47	2	1937	162	43.04	4045	47.88	4	12	0	248	1
Old Trafford, Manchester	8	13	1	685	127	57.08	1348	50.81	3	3	1	88	0
The Rose Bowl, Southampton	3	5	1	249	95	62.25	541	46.02	0	3	0	27	0
The Oval, London	13	24	0	1217	147	50.70	2590	46.98	3	7	1	154	1
Trent Bridge, Nottingham	11	19	1	397	50	22.05	941	42.18	0	1	0	48	0
Total	**89**	**155**	**7**	**6568**	**294**	**44.37**	**13675**	**48.02**	**15**	**32**	**4**	**816**	**3**

Most Tests

Ground	Tests
Lord's, London	26
The Oval, London	13
Headingley, Leeds	11
Trent Bridge, Nottingham	11

Most Runs

Ground	Runs
Lord's, London	1937
The Oval, London	1217
Edgbaston, Birmingham	869

Best Batting Average

Ground	Average
The Rose Bowl, Southampton	62.25
Edgbaston, Birmingham	57.93
Old Trafford, Manchester	57.08
Riverside Ground, Chester-le-Street	52.50

Test Record (Grounds Abroad)

AUSTRALIA

Ground	Tests	Innings	Not out	Runs	Highest score	Average	Balls faced	Strike rate	100s	50s	Ducks	4s	6s
Adelaide Oval, Adelaide	4	7	0	241	148	34.42	535	45.04	1	0	0	26	0
Brisbane Cricket Ground, Brisbane	4	8	1	443	235	63.28	953	46.48	1	2	0	43	0
Melbourne Cricket Ground,Melbourne	4	6	1	435	244	87.00	755	57.61	1	2	0	50	0
WACA Ground, Perth	4	8	0	269	116	33.62	574	46.86	1	1	1	28	1
Sydney Cricket Ground, Sydney	4	7	0	276	189	39.42	552	50.00	1	0	0	24	0
Total	**20**	**36**	**2**	**1664**	**244**	**48.94**	**3369**	**49.39**	**5**	**5**	**1**	**171**	**1**

BANGLADESH

Ground	Tests	Innings	Not out	Runs	Highest score	Average	Balls faced	Strike rate	100s	50s	Ducks	4s	6s
Zahur Ahmed Chowdhury Stadium, Chattogram	2	4	0	228	173	57.00	387	58.91	1	0	0	20	2
Shere Bangla National Stadium, Mirpur, Dhaka	2	4	1	203	109	67.66	331	61.32	1	1	0	22	0
Total	**4**	**8**	**1**	**431**	**173**	**61.57**	**718**	**60.02**	**2**	**1**	**0**	**42**	**2**

INDIA

Ground	Tests	Innings	Not out	Runs	Highest score	Average	Balls faced	Strike rate	100s	50s	Ducks	4s	6s
Sardar Patel Stadium, Motera, Ahmedabad	1	2	0	217	176	108.50	483	44.92	1	0	0	28	0
Punjab Cricket Association Bindra Stadium, Mohali, Chandigarh	3	6	0	118	50	19.66	235	50.21	0	1	0	18	0
MA Chidambaram Stadium, Chepauk, Chennai	2	4	0	120	52	30.00	318	37.73	0	1	0	11	0
Vidarbha Cricket Association Stadium, Jamtha, Nagpur	1	2	0	14	13	7.00	121	11.57	0	0	0	1	0
Eden Gardens, Kolkata	1	2	0	191	190	95.50	381	50.13	1	0	0	23	2
Vidarbha CA Ground, Nagpur	1	2	1	164	104	164.00	403	40.69	1	1	0	19	0
Wankhede Stadium, Mumbai	2	4	1	204	122	68.00	388	52.57	1	0	0	22	1
Saurashtra Cricket Association Stadium, Rajkot	1	2	0	151	130	75.50	290	52.06	1	0	0	15	0
Dr Y. S. Rajasekhara ACA-VDCA Cricket Stadium, Visakhapatnam	1	2	0	56	54	28.00	199	28.14	0	1	0	4	0
Total	**13**	**26**	**2**	**1235**	**190**	**51.45**	**2818**	**43.82**	**5**	**4**	**0**	**141**	**3**

NEW ZEALAND

Ground	Tests	Innings	Not out	Runs	Highest score	Average	Balls faced	Strike rate	100s	50s	Ducks	4s	6s
Eden Park, Auckland	2	4	0	54	43	13.50	184	29.34	0	0	0	5	0
Hagley Oval, Christchurch	1	2	0	16	14	8.00	33	48.48	0	0	0	2	0
University Oval, Dunedin	1	2	0	126	116	63.00	284	44.36	1	0	0	16	0
Seddon Park, Hamilton	1	2	0	51	38	25.50	132	38.63	0	0	0	7	0
McLean Park, Napier	1	2	0	39	37	19.50	90	43.33	0	0	0	7	0
Basin Reserve, Wellington	2	3	0	121	60	40.33	259	46.71	0	1	0	13	1
Total	**8**	**15**	**0**	**407**	**116**	**27.13**	**982**	**41.44**	**1**	**1**	**0**	**50**	**1**

SOUTH AFRICA

Ground	Tests	Innings	Not out	Runs	Highest score	Average	Balls faced	Strike rate	100s	50s	Ducks	4s	6s
Newlands, Cape Town	2	4	0	155	65	38.75	328	47.25	0	2	0	19	0
SuperSport Park, Centurion	2	4	0	108	76	27.00	286	37.76	0	1	0	16	0
Kingsmead, Durban	2	3	0	125	118	41.66	301	41.52	1	0	1	12	0
The Wanderers Stadium, Johannesburg	2	4	0	83	43	20.75	134	61.94	0	0	0	9	0
Total	**8**	**15**	**0**	**471**	**118**	**31.40**	**1049**	**44.89**	**1**	**3**	**1**	**56**	**0**

SRI LANKA

Ground	Tests	Innings	Not out	Runs	Highest score	Average	Balls faced	Strike rate	100s	50s	Ducks	4s	6s
Asgiriya Stadium, Kandy	1	2	0	4	4	2	7	57.14	0	0	1	1	0
Galle International Stadium	2	4	0	145	118	36.25	342	42.39	1	0	1	18	0
P. Sara Oval, Colombo	1	2	1	143	94	143	347	41.21	0	1	0	15	0
Sinhalese Sports Club Ground, Colombo	1	2	0	143	81	71.5	358	39.94	0	2	0	13	0
Total	**5**	**10**	**1**	**435**	**118**	**48.33**	**1054**	**41.27**	**1**	**3**	**2**	**47**	**0**

UAE (v PAKISTAN)

Ground	Tests	Innings	Not out	Runs	Highest score	Average	Balls faced	Strike rate	100s	50s	Ducks	4s	6s
Dubai International Cricket Stadium	3	6	0	133	65	22.16	392	33.92	0	1	0	14	0
Sharjah Cricket Stadium	1	2	0	112	63	56	283	39.57	0	1	0	8	0
Sheikh Zayed Stadium, Abu Dhabi	2	3	0	364	263	121.33	788	46.19	1	1	0	28	0
Total	**6**	**11**	**0**	**609**	**263**	**55.36**	**1463**	**41.62**	**1**	**3**	**0**	**50**	**0**

WEST INDIES

Ground	Tests	Innings	Not out	Runs	Highest score	Average	Balls faced	Strike rate	100s	50s	Ducks	4s	6s
Antigua Recreation Ground, St John's, Antigua	1	2	0	110	58	55	237	46.41	0	2	0	12	0
Kensington Oval, Bridgetown, Barbados	2	4	1	342	139	114	725	47.17	2	1	0	36	1
National Cricket Stadium, St George's, Grenada	1	2	1	135	76	135	332	40.66	0	2	0	16	0
Queen's Park Oval, Port of Spain, Trinidad	1	2	0	36	24	18	62	58.06	0	0	0	2	0
Sabina Park, Kingston, Jamaica	1	2	0	4	4	2	26	15.38	0	0	1	0	0
Sir Vivian Richards Stadium, North Sound, Antigua	2	3	1	25	13	12.5	52	48.07	0	0	0	3	0
Total	**8**	**15**	**3**	**652**	**139**	**54.33**	**1434**	**45.46**	**2**	**5**	**1**	**69**	**1**

Most Test-Match Runs Scored in Partnerships

Player	Innings	Runs
Andrew Strauss	132	5253
Kevin Pietersen	58	3558
Jonathan Trott	51	2711
Joe Root	52	2513
Ian Bell	54	1859
Paul Collingwood	22	1107
Nick Compton	23	1061
Michael Vaughan	22	904
Gary Ballance	22	881
Alex Hales	21	766

Best Test-Match Partnerships

Runs	Player	v Country	Venue	Year
329	Jonathan Trott	Australia	Brisbane Cricket Ground, Brisbane	2010
259	Joe Root	India	Kennington Oval, London	2018
251	Jonathan Trott	Sri Lanka	Sophia Gardens, Cardiff	2011
248	Joe Root	West Indies	Edgbaston, Birmingham	2017
233	Paul Collingwood	Pakistan	Lord's, London	2006
231	Nick Compton	New Zealand	University Oval, Dunedin	2013
229	Andrew Strauss	West Indies	Kensington Oval, Bridge-town, Barbados	2009
222	Eoin Morgan	India	Edgbaston, Birmingham	2011
213	Ravi Bopara	West Indies	Riverside Ground, Chester-le-Street	2009
206	Kevin Pietersen	India	Wankhede Stadium, Mumbai	2012

TEST RECORD	CAPTAIN	%	NOT CAPTAIN	%
Won	24	41%	43	42%
Lost	22	37%	33	32%
Drawn	13	22%	26	26%
Total	**59**	**41%**	**102**	**42%**

Toin Coss in Tests

Won	28
Lost	31
Chose to bat	19
Chose to bowl	9

Test-Match Batting Record

	Tests	Innings	Not out	Runs	Highest score	Average	Balls faced	Strike rate	100s	50s	Ducks	4s	6s
Captain	59	111	7	4844	263	46.57	10445	46.37	12	24	3	551	6
Not captain	102	180	9	7628	294	44.60	16117	47.32	21	33	6	891	5

Most Test Matches as England Captain

Player	Matches	Won	Lost	Drawn	Win%
Alastair Cook	**59**	**24**	**22**	**13**	**41**
Michael Atherton	54	13	21	20	24
Michael Vaughan	51	26	11	14	51
Andrew Strauss	50	24	11	15	48
Nasser Hussain	45	17	15	13	38

Test-Match Series Record v Countries (As Captain)

Country	Series	Won	Lost	Drawn	Win%
AUSTRALIA					
Home	2	2	0	0	100%
Away	1	0	1	0	0%
Total	**3**	**2**	**1**	**0**	**67%**
BANGLADESH					
Away	2	1	0	1	50%
Total	**2**	**1**	**0**	**1**	**50%**
INDIA					
Home	1	1	0	0	100%
Away	2	1	1	0	50%
Total	**3**	**2**	**1**	**0**	**67%**
NEW ZEALAND					
Home	2	1	0	1	50%
Away	1	0	0	1	0%
Total	**3**	**1**	**0**	**2**	**33%**
PAKISTAN					
Home	1	0	0	1	0%
Neutral	1	0	1	0	0%
Total	**2**	**0**	**1**	**1**	**0%**

Continued

Country	Series	Won	Lost	Drawn	Win%
SOUTH AFRICA					
Away	1	1	0	0	100%
Total	**1**	**1**	**0**	**0**	**100%**
SRI LANKA					
Home	2	1	1	0	50%
Total	**2**	**1**	**1**	**0**	**50%**
WEST INDIES					
Away	1	0	0	1	0%
Total	**1**	**0**	**0**	**1**	**0%**
TOTAL	**17**	**8**	**4**	**5**	**47%**

Test Match-Series Record (As Captain)

	Series	Won	Lost	Drawn	Win%
Home	9	6	1	2	67%
Away	7	2	2	3	29%
Neutral	1	0	1	0	0%
Total	**17**	**8**	**4**	**5**	**47%**

Most Test-Match Runs Scored by Venue

Venue	Runs
Lord's, London	1937
Kennington Oval, London	1217
Edgbaston, Birmingham	869
Headingley, Leeds	718
Old Trafford, Manchester	685
Brisbane Cricket Ground, Brisbane	443
Melbourne Cricket Ground, Melbourne	435
Trent Bridge, Nottingham	397
Sheikh Zayed Stadium, Abu Dhabi	364
Kensington Oval, Bridgetown, Barbados	342

Highest Test-Match Scores

Score	v Country	Venue	Year
294	India	Edgbaston, Birmingham	2011
263	Pakistan	Sheikh Zayed Stadium, Abu Dhabi	2015
244	Australia	Melbourne Cricket Ground, Melbourne	2017
243	West Indies	Edgbaston, Birmingham	2017
235	Australia	Brisbane Cricket Ground, Brisbane	2010
190	India	Eden Gardens, Kolkata	2012
189	Australia	Sydney Cricket Ground, Sydney	2011
176	India	Sardar Patel Stadium, Motera, Ahmedabad	2012
173	Bangladesh	Zahur Ahmed Chowdhury Stadium, Chattogram	2010
162	New Zealand	Lord's, London	2015

Most Minutes at the Crease (Test Matches)

Minutes	v Country	Score	Ground	Year
836	Pakistan	263	Sheikh Zayed Stadium, Abu Dhabi	2015
773	India	294	Edgbaston, Birmingham	2011
634	Australia	244	Melbourne Cricket Ground, Melbourne	2017
625	Australia	235	Brisbane Cricket Ground, Brisbane	2010
588	West Indies	243	Edgbaston, Birmingham	2017
556	India	176	Sardar Patel Stadium, Motera, Ahmedabad	2012
540	New Zealand	162	Lord's, London	2015
492	India	190	Eden Gardens, Kolkata	2012
488	Australia	189	Sydney Cricket Ground, Sydney	2011
485	West Indies	160	Riverside Ground, Chester-le-Street	2009

Most Balls Faced (Test Matches)

Balls faced	v Country	Score	Ground	Year
545	India	294	Edgbaston, Birmingham	2011
528	Pakistan	263	Sheikh Zayed Stadium, Abu Dhabi	2015
428	Australia	235	Brisbane Cricket Ground, Brisbane	2010
409	Australia	244	Melbourne Cricket Ground, Melbourne	2017
407	West Indies	243	Edgbaston, Birmingham	2017
377	India	190	Eden Gardens, Kolkata	2012
374	India	176	Sardar Patel Stadium, Motera, Ahmedabad	2012
345	New Zealand	162	Lord's, London	2015
342	Australia	189	Sydney Cricket Ground, Sydney	2011
339	West Indies	160	Riverside Ground, Chester-le-Street	2009

How His Test Runs Were Scored

Balls faced	26562
Singles	3803
Twos	980
Threes	281
Fours	1442
All-run fours	3
Fives	4
Sixes	11
Dot balls	20038

Most Fours in a Test Innings

4s	v Country	Ground	Year
33	India	Edgbaston, Birmingham	2011
33	West Indies	Edgbaston, Birmingham	2017
27	Australia	Melbourne Cricket Ground, Melbourne	2017
26	Australia	Brisbane Cricket Ground, Brisbane	2010
23	India	Eden Gardens, Kolkata	2012

Bowler Most Dismissed by (Test Matches)

Bowler	Bowled	Caught	Stumped	LBW	Total
Morne Morkel (South Africa)	1	9	0	2	12
Ishant Sharma (India)	0	9	0	2	11
Mitchell Johnson (Australia)	1	5	0	3	9
Ravichandran Ashwin (India)	3	5	1	0	9
Trent Boult (New Zealand)	1	8	0	0	9
Nathan Lyon (Australia)	2	5	0	1	8
Ryan Harris (Australia)	1	4	3	0	8
Ravindra Jadeja (India)	0	3	1	3	7
Peter Siddle (Australia)	1	5	0	0	6
Mitchell Starc (Australia)	1	3	2	0	6
Mohammad Amir (Pakistan)	4	2	0	0	6
Umar Gul (Pakistan)	0	4	0	2	6
Stuart Clark (Australia)	1	4	0	0	5
Vernon Philander (South Africa)	0	3	0	2	5

Test Centuries

Year	Country	Venue	Runs
2006	India	Nagpur	104
2006	Pakistan	Lord's	105
2006	Pakistan	Old Trafford	127
2006	Australia	Perth	116
2007	West Indies	Lord's	105
2007	West Indies	Old Trafford	106
2007	Sri Lanka	Galle	118
2009	West Indies	Bridgetown	139
2009	West Indies	Chester-le-Street	160
2009	South Africa	Durban	118
2010	Bangladesh	Chattogram	173
2010	Bangladesh	Dhaka	109
2010	Pakistan	The Oval	110
2010	Australia	Brisbane	235
2010	Australia	Adelaide	148
2011	Australia	Sydney	189
2011	Sri Lanka	Cardiff	133
2011	Sri Lanka	Lord's	106
2011	India	Edgbaston	294
2012	South Africa	The Oval	115
2012	India	Ahmedabad	176
2012	India	Mumbai	122
2012	India	Kolkata	190
2013	New Zealand	Dunedin	116
2013	New Zealand	Headingley	130
2015	West Indies	Bridgetown	105
2015	New Zealand	Lord's	162
2015	Pakistan	Abu Dhabi	263
2016	Pakistan	Old Trafford	105
2016	India	Rajkot	130
2017	West Indies	Edgbaston	243
2017	Australia	Melbourne	244
2018	India	The Oval	147

Total 33

Centuries v Country

v Country	Centuries
India	7
West Indies	6
Australia	5
Pakistan	5
New Zealand	3
Sri Lanka	3
Bangladesh	2
South Africa	2

Centuries in Country

in Country	Centuries
England	15
Australia	5
India	5
Bangladesh	2
West Indies	2
New Zealand	1
South Africa	1
Sri Lanka	1
UAE	1

Top Five Run Scorers in Test History

Player	Country	Matches	Innings	Runs
Sachin Tendulkar	India	200	329	15921
Ricky Ponting	Australia	168	287	13378
Jacques Kallis	ICC/South Africa	166	280	13289
Rahul Dravid	ICC/India	164	286	13288
Alastair Cook	**England**	**161**	**291**	**12472**

Statistics correct at time of print

England's Top Five Run Scorers in Test History

Player	Matches	Innings	Runs
Alastair Cook	**161**	**291**	**12472**
Graham Gooch	118	215	8900
Alec Stewart	133	235	8463
David Gower	117	204	8231
Kevin Pietersen	104	181	8181

Statistics correct at time of print

Most Test Matches (England)

Player	Matches
Alastair Cook	**161**
Jimmy Anderson	148
Alec Stewart	133
Stuart Broad	126
Ian Bell	118
Graham Gooch	118

Statistics correct at time of print

Longest Individual Test Innings (Minutes)

Player	Country	v Country	Venue	Year	Minutes
Hanif Mohammad	Pakistan	West Indies	Bridgetown	1958	970
Gary Kirsten	South Africa	England	Durban	1999	878
Alastair Cook	**England**	**Pakistan**	**Abu Dhabi**	**2015**	**836**

Most England Catches in Test Matches (Non-Wicketkeeper)

Player	Matches	Catches
Alastair Cook	**161**	**175**
Andrew Strauss	100	121
Ian Botham	102	120
Colin Cowdrey	114	120
Wally Hammond	85	110

Statistics correct at time of print

Most Test Centuries (England)

Player	Matches	Centuries
Alastair Cook	**161**	**33**
Kevin Pietersen	104	23
Wally Hammond	85	22
Colin Cowdrey	114	22
Geoffrey Boycott	108	22
Ian Bell	118	22

Statistics correct at time of print

Most 50S and Over in Tests (England)

Player	Matches	50+
Alastair Cook	**161**	**90**
Ian Bell	118	68
Graham Gooch	118	66
Geoffrey Boycott	108	64
Michael Atherton	115	62

Statistics correct at time of print

Most Nineties in Test Matches (England)

Player	Matches	90's
Alastair Cook	**161**	**7**
Geoffrey Boycott	108	6
Ken Barrington	82	5

Statistics correct at time of print

Most Test Runs in a Series (England)

Player	Series	Runs
Wally Hammond	1928/9 v Australia (away)	905
Alastair Cook	**2010/11 v Australia (away)**	**766**
Denis Compton	1947 v South Africa (home)	753

Statistics correct at time of print

Most Test Runs on a Single Ground (England)

Player	Ground	Runs
Graham Gooch	Lord's	2015
Alastair Cook	**Lord's**	**1937**
Andrew Strauss	Lord's	1562

Statistics correct at time of print

Most Test Runs in an Innings by a Captain (England)

Player	Country	Venue	Year	Runs
Graham Gooch	India	Lord's	1990	333
Peter May	West Indies	Edgbaston	1957	285*
Alastair Cook	**Pakistan**	**Abu Dhabi**	**2015**	**263**

Statistics correct at time of print

Most Test Matches	Matches
Sachin Tendulkar (India)	200
Ricky Ponting (Australia)	168
Steve Waugh (Australia)	168
Jacques Kallis (ICC/South Africa)	166
Shivnarine Chanderpaul (West Indies)	164
Rahul Dravid (ICC/India)	164
Alastair Cook (England)	**161**

Statistics correct at time of print

Most Test Matches as Captain	Matches
Graeme Smith (ICC/South Africa)	109
Allan Border (Australia)	93
Stephen Fleming (New Zealand)	80
Ricky Ponting (Australia)	77
Clive Lloyd (West Indies)	74
MS Dhoni (India)	60
Alastair Cook (England)	**59**

Statistics correct at time of print

Most Consecutive Tests as Captain	Matches	From	To
Allan Border (Australia)	93	7 December 1984	25 March 1994
Ricky Ponting (Australia)	73	3 November 2004	26 December 2010
Stephen Fleming (New Zealand)	65	1 July 1999	15 December 2006
Alastair Cook (England)	**57**	**15 November 2012**	**16 December 2016**
Michael Atherton (England)	52	5 August 1993	20 March 1998

Statistics correct at time of print

Test-Match Bowling

Tests	Innings	Balls	Runs	Wickets	Best innings	Best match	Average	Economy	Strike rate
161	2	18	7	1	1/6	1/6	7.00	2.33	18.00

Test-Match Bowling – Breakdown of Matches

Country	Venue	Year	Balls	Runs	Wickets	Economy	Player dismissed
South Africa	Lord's, London	2008	6	1	0	1.00	
India	Trent Bridge, Nottingham	2014	12	6	1	3.00	Ishant Sharma (caught Prior)

Test-Match Catches

v Country	Matches	Innings	Catches
Australia	35	64	40
India	30	57	38
New Zealand	15	28	21
Pakistan	20	39	20
South Africa	19	35	20
West Indies	20	35	20
Sri Lanka	16	30	9
Bangladesh	6	12	7
Total	**161**	**300**	**175**

Most Catches in a Test Match

Catches	v Country	Year	Venue
6	New Zealand	2008	Hamilton
5	South Africa	2012	Leeds
5	Bangladesh	2016	Dhaka
5	India	2018	Southampton
4	West Indies	2007	Manchester
4	Australia	2009	The Oval
4	India	2018	Nottingham

Batsmen He Caught the Most in Tests

Batsman	Catches
Michael Clarke (Australia)	6
Virat Kohli (India)	5
Ajinkya Rahane (India)	5
Steve Smith (Australia)	4
Peter Siddle (Australia)	4
Morne Morkel (South Africa)	4
Azhar Ali (Pakistan)	4

Most Catches in Test Matches (England)

Player	Catches
Alastair Cook	**175**
Andrew Strauss	121
Ian Botham	120
Colin Cowdrey	120
Wally Hammond	110

Most Consecutive Test Matches

Player	Country	Years	Consecutive test matches
Alastair Cook	**England**	**2006–2018**	**159**
Allan Border	Australia	1979–1994	153
Mark Waugh	Australia	1993–2002	107
Sunil Gavaskar	India	1975–1987	106
Brendon McCullum	New Zealand	2004–2016	101

One-Day Internationals

All One-Day International Innings

Year	Country	Venue	Runs	Year	Country	Venue	Runs
2006	Sri Lanka	Manchester	39	2011	Sri Lanka	Manchester	31
2006	Sri Lanka	Leeds	41	2011	India	Chester-le-Street	4
2007	West Indies	Lord's	29	2011	India	Southampton	80
2007	West Indies	Birmingham	19	2011	India	The Oval	23
2007	West Indies	Nottingham	18	2011	India	Lord's	12
2007	India	Southampton	102	2011	India	Cardiff	50
2007	India	Bristol	36	2011	India	Hyderabad (Deccan)	60
2007	India	Birmingham	40				
2007	India	Manchester	0	2011	India	Delhi	0
2007	India	Leeds	4	2011	India	Mohali	3
2007	India	The Oval	0	2011	India	Mumbai	10
2007	Sri Lanka	Dambulla	46	2011	India	Kolkata	60
2007	Sri Lanka	Dambulla	1	2012	Pakistan	Abu Dhabi	137
2007	Sri Lanka	Dambulla	0	2012	Pakistan	Abu Dhabi	102
2007	Sri Lanka	Colombo (RPS)	80	2012	Pakistan	Dubai (DSC)	80
2007	Sri Lanka	Colombo (RPS)	28	2012	Pakistan	Dubai (DSC)	4
2008	New Zealand	Wellington	11	2012	West Indies	Southampton	0
2008	New Zealand	Hamilton	53	2012	West Indies	The Oval	112
2008	New Zealand	Auckland	9	2012	Australia	Lord's	40
2008	New Zealand	Napier	69	2012	Australia	The Oval	18
2008	New Zealand	Christchurch	42	2012	Australia	Chester-le-Street	29
2008	New Zealand	Lord's	24	2012	Australia	Manchester	58
2008	India	Cuttack	11	2012	South Africa	Cardiff	10
2010	Bangladesh	Dhaka	64	2012	South Africa	Southampton	0
2010	Bangladesh	Dhaka	60	2012	South Africa	The Oval	20
2010	Bangladesh	Chattogram	32	2012	South Africa	Lord's	2
2011	Sri Lanka	The Oval	5	2012	South Africa	Nottingham	51
2011	Sri Lanka	Leeds	48	2013	India	Rajkot	75
2011	Sri Lanka	Lord's	119	2013	India	Kochi	17
2011	Sri Lanka	Nottingham	95	2013	India	Ranchi	17

Continued

Year	Country	Venue	Runs
2013	India	Mohali	76
2013	India	Dharamsala	22
2013	New Zealand	Hamilton	4
2013	New Zealand	Napier	78
2013	New Zealand	Auckland	46
2013	New Zealand	Lord's	30
2013	New Zealand	Southampton	34
2013	New Zealand	Nottingham	0
2013	Australia	Birmingham	30
2013	Sri Lanka	The Oval	59
2013	New Zealand	Cardiff	64
2013	South Africa	The Oval	6
2013	India	Birmingham	2
2014	Australia	Melbourne	4
2014	Australia	Brisbane	22
2014	Australia	Sydney	35
2014	Australia	Perth	44

Year	Country	Venue	Runs
2014	Australia	Adelaide	39
2014	Scotland	Aberdeen	44
2014	Sri Lanka	The Oval	11
2014	Sri Lanka	Manchester	30
2014	Sri Lanka	Lord's	1
2014	Sri Lanka	Birmingham	56
2014	India	Cardiff	19
2014	India	Nottingham	44
2014	India	Birmingham	9
2014	India	Leeds	46
2014	Sri Lanka	Colombo (RPS)	10
2014	Sri Lanka	Colombo (RPS)	22
2014	Sri Lanka	Hambantota	34
2014	Sri Lanka	Pallekele	20
2014	Sri Lanka	Pallekele	1
2014	Sri Lanka	Colombo (RPS)	32

All One-Day International Results

Year	Country	Venue	Result
2006	Sri Lanka	Manchester	Lost
2006	Sri Lanka	Leeds	Lost
2007	West Indies	Lord's	Won
2007	West Indies	Birmingham	Lost
2007	West Indies	Nottingham	Lost
2007	India	Southampton	Won
2007	India	Bristol	Lost
2007	India	Birmingham	Won
2007	India	Manchester	Won
2007	India	Leeds	Lost
2007	India	The Oval	Lost

Year	Country	Venue	Result
2007	Sri Lanka	Dambulla	Lost
2007	Sri Lanka	Dambulla	Won
2007	Sri Lanka	Dambulla	Won
2007	Sri Lanka	Colombo (RPS)	Won
2007	Sri Lanka	Colombo (RPS)	Lost
2008	New Zealand	Wellington	Lost
2008	New Zealand	Hamilton	Lost
2008	New Zealand	Auckland	Won
2008	New Zealand	Napier	Tied
2008	New Zealand	Christchurch	Lost
2008	New Zealand	Lord's	Lost

Year	Country	Venue	Result
2008	India	Cuttack	Lost
2010	Bangladesh	Dhaka	Won
2010	Bangladesh	Dhaka	Won
2010	Bangladesh	Chattogram	Won
2011	Sri Lanka	The Oval	Won
2011	Sri Lanka	Leeds	Lost
2011	Sri Lanka	Lord's	Lost
2011	Sri Lanka	Nottingham	Won
2011	Sri Lanka	Manchester	Won
2011	India	Chester-le-Street	No result
2011	India	Southampton	Won
2011	India	The Oval	Won
2011	India	Lord's	Tied
2011	India	Cardiff	Won
2011	India	Hyderabad (Deccan)	Lost
2011	India	Delhi	Lost
2011	India	Mohali	Lost
2011	India	Mumbai	Lost
2011	India	Kolkata	Lost
2012	Pakistan	Abu Dhabi	Won
2012	Pakistan	Abu Dhabi	Won
2012	Pakistan	Dubai (DSC)	Won
2012	Pakistan	Dubai (DSC)	Won
2012	West Indies	Southampton	Won
2012	West Indies	The Oval	Won
2012	Australia	Lord's	Won
2012	Australia	The Oval	Won
2012	Australia	Chester-le-Street	Won
2012	Australia	Manchester	Won
2012	South Africa	Cardiff	No result

Year	Country	Venue	Result
2012	South Africa	Southampton	Lost
2012	South Africa	The Oval	Won
2012	South Africa	Lord's	Won
2012	South Africa	Nottingham	Lost
2013	India	Rajkot	Won
2013	India	Kochi	Lost
2013	India	Ranchi	Lost
2013	India	Mohali	Lost
2013	India	Dharamsala	Won
2013	New Zealand	Hamilton	Lost
2013	New Zealand	Napier	Won
2013	New Zealand	Auckland	Won
2013	New Zealand	Lord's	Lost
2013	New Zealand	Southampton	Lost
2013	New Zealand	Nottingham	Won
2013	Australia	Birmingham	Won
2013	Sri Lanka	The Oval	Lost
2013	New Zealand	Cardiff	Won
2013	South Africa	The Oval	Won
2013	India	Birmingham	Lost
2014	Australia	Melbourne	Lost
2014	Australia	Brisbane	Lost
2014	Australia	Sydney	Lost
2014	Australia	Perth	Won
2014	Australia	Adelaide	Lost
2014	Scotland	Aberdeen	Won
2014	Sri Lanka	The Oval	Won
2014	Sri Lanka	Manchester	Won
2014	Sri Lanka	Lord's	Lost
2014	Sri Lanka	Birmingham	Lost
2014	India	Cardiff	Lost
2014	India	Nottingham	Lost
2014	India	Birmingham	Lost

Continued

Year	Country	Venue	Result
2014	**India**	**Leeds**	**Won**
2014	**Sri Lanka**	**Colombo (RPS)**	**Lost**
2014	**Sri Lanka**	**Colombo (RPS)**	**Lost**
2014	**Sri Lanka**	**Hambantota**	**Won**
2014	**Sri Lanka**	**Pallekele**	**Won**
2014	**Sri Lanka**	**Pallekele**	**Lost**
2014	**Sri Lanka**	**Colombo (RPS)**	**Lost**

Bold (as captain)

One-Day International Record v Countries

Country	ODIs	Won	Lost	No result	Tied	Win%
AUSTRALIA						
Home	5	5	0	0	0	100%
Away	5	1	4	0	0	20%
Total	**10**	**6**	**4**	**0**	**0**	**60%**
BANGLADESH						
Away	3	3	0	0	0	100%
Total	**3**	**3**	**0**	**0**	**0**	**100%**
INDIA						
Home	16	7	7	1	1	44%
Away	11	2	9	0	0	18%
Total	**27**	**9**	**16**	**1**	**1**	**33%**
NEW ZEALAND						
Home	5	2	3	0	0	40%
Away	8	3	4	0	1	38%
Total	**13**	**5**	**7**	**0**	**1**	**38%**
PAKISTAN						
Neutral	4	4	0	0	0	100%
Total	**4**	**4**	**0**	**0**	**0**	**100%**
SCOTLAND						
Away	1	1	0	0	0	100%
Total	**1**	**1**	**0**	**0**	**0**	**100%**

Country	ODIs	Won	Lost	No result	Tied	Win%
SOUTH AFRICA						
Home	6	3	2	1	0	50%
Total	**6**	**3**	**2**	**1**	**0**	**50%**
SRI LANKA						
Home	12	5	7	0	0	42%
Away	11	5	6	0	0	45%
Total	**23**	**10**	**13**	**0**	**0**	**43%**
WEST INDIES						
Home	5	3	2	0	0	60%
Total	**5**	**3**	**2**	**0**	**0**	**60%**

TOTAL

	ODIs	Won	Lost	No result	Tied	Win%
Home	49	25	21	2	1	51%
Away	39	15	23	0	1	38%
Neutral	4	4	0	0	0	100%
TOTAL	**92**	**44**	**44**	**2**	**2**	**48%**

One-Day International Record V Countries (As Captain)

Country	ODIs	Won	Lost	No result	Tied	Win%
AUSTRALIA						
Home	5	5	0	0	0	100%
Away	5	1	4	0	0	20%
Total	**10**	**6**	**4**	**0**	**0**	**60%**
BANGLADESH						
Away	3	3	0	0	0	100%
Total	**3**	**3**	**0**	**0**	**0**	**100%**

Continued

Country	ODIs	Won	Lost	No result	Tied	Win%
INDIA						
Home	10	4	4	1	1	40%
Away	10	2	8	0	0	20%
Total	**20**	**6**	**12**	**1**	**1**	**30%**
NEW ZEALAND						
Home	4	2	2	0	0	50%
Away	3	2	1	0	0	67%
Total	**7**	**4**	**3**	**0**	**0**	**57%**
PAKISTAN						
Neutral	4	4	0	0	0	100%
Total	**4**	**4**	**0**	**0**	**0**	**100%**
SCOTLAND						
Away	1	1	0	0	0	100%
Total	**1**	**1**	**0**	**0**	**0**	**100%**
SOUTH AFRICA						
Home	6	3	2	1	0	50%
Total	**6**	**3**	**2**	**1**	**0**	**50%**
SRI LANKA						
Home	10	5	5	0	0	50%
Away	6	2	4	0	0	33%
Total	**16**	**7**	**9**	**0**	**0**	**44%**
WEST INDIES						
Home	2	2	0	0	0	100%
Total	**2**	**2**	**0**	**0**	**0**	**100%**

TOTAL

	ODIs	Won	Lost	No result	Tied	Win%
Home	37	21	13	2	1	**57%**
Away	28	11	17	0	0	**39%**
Neutral	4	4	0	0	0	**100%**
TOTAL	**69**	**36**	**30**	**2**	**1**	**52%**

One-Day Internationals v Country

Country	ODIs	Runs	Highest score	Strike rate	100s	50+	4s	6s	Ducks
Australia	10	319	58	76.31	0	1	39	1	0
Bangladesh	3	156	64	90.69	0	2	16	1	0
India	27	822	102	77.11	1	7	103	2	3
New Zealand	13	464	78	74.95	0	4	49	3	1
Pakistan	4	323	137	88.98	2	3	34	1	0
Scotland	1	44	44	93.61	0	0	4	0	0
South Africa	6	89	51	54.60	0	1	10	0	1
Sri Lanka	23	809	119	74.56	1	5	85	1	1
West Indies	5	178	112	80.54	1	1	23	1	1

One-Day Internationals in Country

Country	ODIs	Runs	Highest score	Strike rate	100s	50+	4s	6s	Ducks
Australia	5	144	44	82.28	0	0	19	1	0
Bangladesh	3	156	64	90.69	0	2	16	1	0
England	49	1600	119	78.20	3	11	179	4	5
India	11	351	76	76.97	0	4	53	1	1
New Zealand	8	312	78	69.48	0	3	32	1	0
Scotland	1	44	44	93.61	0	0	4	0	0
Sri Lanka	11	274	80	61.43	0	1	26	1	1
UAE	4	323	137	88.98	2	3	34	1	0

One-Day Internationals in Venue

Venue	ODIs	Runs	Highest score	Strike rate	100s	50+	4s	6s	Ducks
Home	49	1600	119	78.20	3	11	179	4	5
Away	39	1281	80	73.40	0	10	150	5	2
Neutral	4	323	137	88.98	2	3	34	1	0

One-Day Internationals by Year

Year	ODIs	Runs	Highest score	Strike rate	100s
2006	2	80	41	86.95	0
2007	14	403	102	66.28	1
2008	7	219	69	66.36	0
2010	3	156	64	90.69	0
2011	15	600	119	93.16	1
2012	15	663	137	79.97	3
2013	16	560	78	75.16	0
2014	20	523	56	71.25	0

Best One-Day International Partnerships

Runs	Player	v Country	Venue	Year
178	Ian Bell	India	The Rose Bowl, Southampton	2007
171	Craig Kieswetter	Sri Lanka	Trent Bridge, Nottingham	2011
170	Kevin Pietersen	Pakistan	Dubai International Cricket Stadium	2012
158	Phil Mustard	New Zealand	McLean Park, Napier	2008
158	Ian Bell	India	Saurashtra Cricket Association Stadium, Rajkot	2013

One-Day International Record

	Captain	%	Not Captain	%
Won	36	52%	8	35%
Lost	30	43%	14	61%
No result	2	3%	0	0%
Tied	1	2%	1	4%
Total	**69**	**52%**	**23**	**35%**

One-Day International Batting Record

	Innings	Runs	Highest score	Strike rate	100s
Captain	69	2502	137	80.08	4
Not captain	23	702	102	68.15	1

Highest One-Day International Scores

Year	Opposition	Venue	Runs
2012	Pakistan	Abu Dhabi	137
2011	Sri Lanka	Lord's	119
2012	West Indies	The Oval	112
2007	India	Southampton	102
2012	Pakistan	Abu Dhabi	102
2011	Sri Lanka	Nottingham	95
2011	India	Southampton	80
2007	Sri Lanka	Colombo (RPS)	80
2012	Pakistan	Dubai (DSC)	80
2013	New Zealand	Napier	78
2013	India	Mohali	76
2013	India	Rajkot	75
2008	New Zealand	Napier	69
2010	Bangladesh	Dhaka	64
2013	New Zealand	Cardiff	64
2010	Bangladesh	Dhaka	60
2011	India	Hyderabad (Deccan)	60
2011	India	Kolkata	60
2013	Sri Lanka	The Oval	59
2012	Australia	Manchester	58
2014	Sri Lanka	Birmingham	56
2008	New Zealand	Hamilton	53
2012	South Africa	Nottingham	51
2011	India	Cardiff	50

T20 Internationals

T20 International Results

Year	Country	Venue	Result
2007	West Indies	The Oval	Lost
2007	West Indies	The Oval	Won
2009	South Africa	Johannesburg	Won
2009	**South Africa**	**Centurion**	**Lost**

Bold (as captain)

Acknowledgements

In all the bars, in all the world, we were in Al Forsan, Abu Dhabi, unwinding after a three-session, nine-hour, series of interviews for this book. Alastair empathized with the unobtrusive pianist in the corner, playing to general indifference. 'You've got to be really good to do that,' he said.

My eye was taken by an aspiring county cricketer from another team, hovering on the edge of the group. He picked his moment, introduced himself with as much confidence as he could project, and asked if Alastair could spare some time to go over his game. It was readily given.

The notion of respect is exaggerated in professional sport, but here it was in its most pure form, as an interaction between generations. It is in Alastair's nature to play down such an exchange, but it struck me as being as significant as any trawl through *Wisden*, as a measure of stature.

Like many top sportsmen, he is a fiercely driven individual who has an instinctive understanding of the importance of a team. In that context, it is appropriate to thank those who have helped us put together this book.

It would not have been possible without the foresight of publishing director Dan Bunyard, head of non-fiction at Michael Joseph, and of Mike Martin, Alastair's representative at Paragon Sports Management. I'm grateful for the insight of my literary agent, Rory Scarfe, of the Blair Partnership.

Dan's team, headed editorially by Nick Lowndes, is

multi-talented. Thanks to Agatha Russell, Laura Nicol, Jennifer Porter, Lucy Beresford-Knox and Charlie Richardson. Trevor Horwood's copy-editing was forensic, but sympathetic. My life was made immeasurably easier by Caroline Flatley and Christine Preston, who transcribed hours of interviews.

Cookie is immersed in farm life. The work is constant, dictated by the seasons and a duty of care. He admits it doesn't fit easily with the discipline of writing a book, but I came to appreciate the bonds of friendship it allows him to form. He is rarely happier than when he spends a day in the fields with Henry Bright, his great countryside companion.

Though our respective schedules ensured that around half of our interviews were conducted over the course of a week in the United Arab Emirates, Alastair lives no more than a couple of miles from me. Sheep from his family farm graze in the village, and he is a familiar figure at local events. We might do different jobs, but we would not be able to do so without the support of our families.

Thank you, above all, to Alice and Lynn, our respective wives, for putting up with us.

Michael Calvin, July 2019

Picture Credits

Pictures 12, 20, 22, 23, 24, 25 courtesy of Alastair Cook

1. © Adam Davy/PA Archive/PA Images
2. © Adam Davy/PA Archive/PA Images
3. © Mike Hewitt/Getty Images
4. © Hamish Blair/Getty Images
5. © Jordan Mansfield/Getty Images
6. © Laurence Griffiths/Getty Images
7. © Scott Heavey/Getty Images
8. © Mike Egerton/EMPICS Sport/PA
9. © ADRIAN DENNIS/AFP/Getty Images
10. © Gareth Copley/Getty Images
11. © Tom Shaw/Getty Images
13. © Popperfoto/Getty Images
14. © Gareth Copley/Getty Images
15. © Gareth Copley/Getty Images
16. © Michael Steele/Getty Images

17. © Michael Dodge/Getty Images
18. © Gareth Copley/Getty Images
19. © Gareth Fuller/PA Wire/PA Images
21. © Dominic Lipinski/PA Wire/PA Images

Index